Fat Cats

&

Running Dogs

The Enron Stage
of Capitalism

Vijay Prashad

Common Courage Press   Monroe, Maine

Cover by Matt Wuerker.
Cover Design by Erica Bjerning.

ISBN: 1-56751-218-6 paper
ISBN 1-56751-219-4 cloth

**Library of Congress Cataloging-in-Publication Data is
available on request from the publisher**

First Printing

Common Courage Press
Box 702
Monroe, ME 04951

(207) 525-0900; FAX (207) 525-3068
orders-info@commoncouragepress.com

See our website for e versions of this book.
www.commoncouragepress.com

Dedication

For Vishnu Vardha Reddy,
who was killed with revolution on his lips.

"Our struggle will be everywhere,
And in our hearts, these flags
That witnessed your death,
That were bathed in your blood,
Will be multiplied like the leaves
Of the infinite springtime."
—Pablo Neruda, *Cantos General.*

Contents

Acknowledgments

In 1997, *People's Democracy* ran a piece by me on Frank Wisner and Enron, and since then I have watched Enron's machinations around the planet with deep interest and growing anger. Thanks to Prakash Karat for that assignment. Mike Albert at ZNET and N. Ram at *Frontline* allowed me space to write about the Enron Stage of Capitalism—much of the material in this book came from those articles. *Frontline* indulged me to write about the Americas and forced me to cultivate a deep and abiding interest in the entire length of the two continents; I have much to thank Ram for his trust in what I had to say. Greg Bates of Common Courage read one of those pieces and invited me to do this book: it was a pleasure to write about such sleaze. Robert Molteno (of Zed) and Sudhanva Deshpande (of Leftword) reacted so well to Greg's idea that it pushed me to write faster than I had anticipated. Greg read the early draft, and despite the war on Common Courage by Bank One, he took time out to do a thorough edit of the book. The logic and prose owes much to his precision.

I have benefited from the work of some very fine journalists from Argentina, India, the Philippines and the United States of America. Their work is represented in the endnotes. While too many journalists tend to write along the grain of power, I'm glad to live in a world where there are still many who distrust power. Among them is my friend P. Sainath who reminded me that when Enron hit the fan, most people around the world celebrated its demise.

Most of this short book was written in conversation with comrades and friends across the planet. Endless discussions with

Lisa Armstrong form the bedrock of what follows. Boses, Karats and Roys gave me courage, love and a critical ear at various steps of this journey. My siblings and mother eagerly followed the progress of this book and laughed at all the jokes as only family can. Rosy taught me the everyday value of labor and love. Mir Ali Raza, Amitava Kumar, Biju Mathew and Sangeeta Kamat kept me afloat. Comrades who make life difficult for the normal dynamic of corporations are an inspiration. My spur is your tomorrow, Zalia Maya: I hope we can struggle together to make it a better one.

Why Not the Worldcom Stage of Capitalism?

As this book went to press Worldcom blew up, unleashing the biggest bankruptcy in U.S. history. With nearly $4 billion (and perhaps more!) down the toilet, it makes Enron look like a pickpocket in comparison. Wall Street hath no fury like an investor bilked. So why not subtitle this book "The Worldcom Stage of Capitalism"?

Worldcom and Enron share something in common with Richard Nixon. All three parties made the fatal mistake of defrauding the powerful. And the powerful struck back. Congress and the media didn't like being lied to by Nixon and his administration; investors, banks, regulators, Congress, and the media didn't like being lied to by Enron and Worldcom. And so, their houses of deception were blown down.

But unlike Worldcom, Enron and Nixon share a further parallel. Both Nixon and Enron committed crimes on a huge scale against millions of people in other countries.

Nixon (with his predecessors Johnson and Kennedy), dropped a greater tonnage of bombs on Southeast Asia than was dropped in all of World War II. This killed well over 1 million people (possibly over 3 million people), mostly civilians, and set in motion a ferocity which would turn Cambodia and the region into a nightmare. But these were not crimes against those he lied to; they were not among the ones he tried hard to cover up. The spectrum of respectable debate ran a narrow gamut from what we did during the Vietnam War was right to what we did was the mistake of a benevolent state. Because the opinion of most Americans—that the war was "fundamentally wrong and immoral"—was excluded from this spectrum, Nixon never had to answer charges that he was a war criminal, only that he was a liar.

In both Nixon and Enron's cases the powerful who brought them down cared so little about those crimes that when the good regulators brought the offenders to heel, these particular charges never made the wrap sheets.

Enron, in its international escapades detailed in this book, represents a type of criminal capitalism far more devastating to most of the people in the world than its fraud was to investors and employees. But charges of this devastation are nowhere to be heard in the hand-ringing halls of the regulators. The Securities and Exchange Commission along with Congress define accountability strictly by numbers, while moral accountability remains outside their mandate. The regulators' harrumph is unmistakable: we must make the world safe—for investors.

Because of its international crimes—a pattern carried from one country to another that far outstrips the stupidity of Worldcom—the moniker for this stage of capitalism belongs to Enron.

—Greg Bates
Publisher
October 2002

The United States of Enron

An Introduction

I'm getting hustled
Only knowing half the game
> —The Coup, "Fat Cats, Bigga Fish"
> (*Genocide and Juice*, 1994).

Enron declared bankruptcy in the wake of the Fifth Afghan War, just as Argentina pulled up to the currency devaluation window. The model neoliberal state and the model neoliberal corporation went under in tandem. Consternation erupted from many quarters of the world. The wrath was intense from the Japanese government, Enron's Brazilian partners and those who had joined hands with the corporate behemoth to "reform" their systems: Enron's disappearance meant the interruption of their access to the calculated largess of Wall Street. Enron, the gas giant, had become for most of the world's power elites the pipeline to dollars, since Enron used its reputation on Wall Street and in Washington to funnel money for its projects in parts of the capital-starved regions of the world. But the sound from the victims of Enron's gangsterism was different: from protestors in India to the Mozambiquan government, we heard cries of jubilation.

Meanwhile, back at the ranch, the only story worth telling focused on a narrow set of questions. How could such a vast firm collapse? Did the domestic political ties between Enron and the Republicans create the problem? And what is to happen to those who lost their jobs and retirement funds? Given the global scale of Enron's operations and its close links to U.S. imperialism (regardless of party affiliation), the parochial view on the tale told within the U.S. borders is extraordinary.[1]

While mindful of the key role Enron played within U.S. energy markets and in governmental circles, *Fat Cats and Running Dogs* tells the much more important global story. Opening with the collapse of Enron, I take on the problem of the investment screens and Arthur Andersen's necessary fudges used to turn a profit. We'll stop and visit with the Gramms and with others who live beside the revolving door, all the while aware that those who acted did so in an environment of general consensus in favor of deregulation. The intangible element in all this is the further denigration of democracy.

Enron's fiscal games provide the immediate reason for its collapse. The United States of Enron, meanwhile, enabled firms of its ilk to be as fiscally irresponsible as possible within the letter of socially irresponsible laws. But this is not a new frontier. Lawmakers in the 1990s, like their counterparts in the previous century, opened up vast spaces to unregulated prospecting for dollars. If once the state gave cowboys and ranchers the rights to the West if only these "pioneers" killed the Amerindians, now the state opens vast areas of economic activity to firms like Enron.

And Enron has Company

Enron is a symptom of a general condition of neoliberalism—the new wave of imperialism that engendered poverty even as it spreads its impoverished platitudes about free markets as liberation from privation. In the mountains of southeastern Mexico, Subcomandante Insurgente Marcos of the Zapatista Army of National Liberation (EZLN) addressed the First

Intercontinental Encounter for Humanity and Against Neoliberalism on 3 August 1996, just two years after it rocked the world with its appearance in southern Mexico. In those days Enron was on a high, eager to set in motion numerous extortionist deals with governments across the world and to lay claim to a sizable chunk of what was starting to become known as the New Economy. Marcos, in the mountains, joined the multitudes who knew a rat when they saw one.

> Millions of women, millions of youth, millions of indigenous, millions of homosexuals, millions of human beings of all races and colors only participate in the financial markets as a devalued currency worth always less and less, the currency of their blood making profits. The globalization of markets is erasing borders for speculation and crime and multiplying them for human beings. Countries are obligated to erase their national borders when it comes to the circulation of money but to multiply their internal borders. Neoliberalism doesn't turn countries into one country. It turns one of them into many countries.[2]

That one country is actually a continent—the continent of sleaze where firms are incorporated, where money is sheltered and where the fat cats meet the running dogs for poolside meetings.

Furthermore, U.S. military aid or else U.S. military bases provide increasingly illegitimate regimes, such as the Saudi royal family, with a shield against their own people. U.S. imperialism provides cover for those who live on the continent of sleaze, and even as it is the principle problem for progressivism, it is not alone in the mire.

Enron, then, is a manifestation of U.S. imperialism, of the close nexus between U.S. corporate power on a global scale and the military-bureaucracy that backs it up with taxpayer dollars. The fat cats (those bureaucrats in suits) run with the dogs (the ones in fatigues), the dogs eager to act as the advance guard and as emergency back-up for the shenanigans of their feline friends. But there are also running dogs in regions of the world dominated by the exploited; that zone a French journalist once called the Third World (like the Third Estate in the French Revolution, the space of those who were once voiceless). A region we can more aptly hail as the two-thirds world to indicate its demographic plurality. These running dogs welcome imperialism as long as they can secrete at least ten percent of the transaction into their own vaults in great havens of free enterprise, Switzerland or the Cayman Islands.

The Fat Cats are the Running Dogs

With the sovereign power to be sleazy stand the running dogs of the two-thirds world and the fat cats of transnational corporations. Neoliberals, together.

We may date the birth of neoliberalism, the dominant ideology of our times, to 1974, when the Bank of Sweden gave its prize in Economic Sciences to two very different men. The Swedish Gunnar Myrdal and the Austrian Friedrich August von Hayek received the prize in Memory of Alfred Nobel for "their pioneering work in the theory of money and economic fluctuations and for their penetrating analysis of the interdependence of economic, social and institutional phenomena." Myrdal represented the dominance of Keynesianism, of some kind of Scandinavian liberalism. An age that was to lapse soon enough. A member of the Social Democratic Party in Sweden, Myrdal spent his career on the production of social justice against the socialized injustice of capitalism.

Hayek, meanwhile, represented the future. In 1944 came his classic, *The Road to Serfdom*, arguing against the attempt to create social justice. Any effort, he argued, would lead inevitably to the Gulag. Perhaps the most illiberal and conservative thinker of his time, Hayek became the visionary curmudgeon for those who became the agents of neoliberalism on the world stage. Agents like Margaret Thatcher (who made sure he earned a knighthood) and Ronald Reagan. On the heels of the 1973 oil crisis, in search of an increase in the productivity of its domestic economy and looking to stem the flow of commercial capital into the Third World, the managers of the European and U.S. states turned their attention to the destruction of the labor movements' gains, to the creation of strong currencies, and to technological innovation at the expense of jobs. If the state form from the 1930s to the mid-1970s took as its modus operandi the creation of social welfare, the state form of neoliberalism disavowed any role in that regard for itself. The neoliberal state-form was this: minimal regulatory capacity over capital; maximum repressive capacity over the working-class; cultural conservatism as the binding ideology to maintain legitimacy over the repressed people.[3] The fat cats enjoyed the end to regulation, but they did not ride roughshod over a state that tried to constrain their power. The neoliberal state is not weak at all; indeed, the running dogs continue to wield enormous power, but only in areas of law and order either domestically (police) or internationally (army). The running dogs are the allies of the fat cats.

To indict corporations like Enron alone for the chaos that befell the world after the rise of neoliberalism is to miss the crucial function of the running dogs in the tale. Politicians who managed the neoliberal state did not willy-nilly have to give in to rapacious corporations. But they connived with the corporate logic to wrest sovereignty from the people and turn it over to profit. What neoliberalism did in the last three decades for the nations of the overdeveloped world was to make democracy into a commodity and to turn the people's representatives into its employees. Outrage greeted the Bush administration when it became clear that Vice President Dick Cheney's task force on energy policy was made up of corporate executives, many of who contributed generously to the Bush-Cheney campaign. But the culprits did not feel any embarrassment or see any illegality in their actions.

Frederick Palmer of Peabody Energy (the world's largest coal mining firm owned by Lehman Brothers) spelled out why no embarrassment was needed—and exactly how far the process has extended. "We're all on the supply side—the electric utilities, the coal companies—and the energy plan is basically a supply side plan," he said, invoking one brand of economics. "But that's not the result of back room deals or lobbying the vice president of the United States. People running the United States government now are from the energy industry, and they understand it and believe in increasing the energy supply, and contribution money has nothing to do with it."[4] When the administration offered a positive assessment for pebble-bed nuclear reactors in its report, this offered a direct benefit to Exelon Corporation, a major campaign contributor to Bush-Cheney. But, as Exelon's spokesperson noted, "We didn't influence anybody. A good thing for the industry and the country was the fact that the administration came out with a recommendation for new forms of nuclear power, and our pebble-bed modular reactor is a byproduct of that. We just happened to have it. They took a look at what we gave them and they said this kind of makes sense."[5] The running dogs did not sell their votes; they are not opportunists and did not act on behalf of the fat cats only because they had been paid via campaign contributions. Rather, they acted for the fat cats because both live on the continent of sleaze and see the populace as a vast labor pool intended to fatten the hog upon which both feed.

The Enron Stage of Capitalism

The Enron Stage of Capitalism is represented by GATS.

GATS is the General Agreement on Trade in Services, an agreement of the powers launched in Geneva, Switzerland, just a few months after the smoke cleared from the Battle of Seattle (December 1999). The powers first broached GATS in 1994 and hoped to get it into place by the end of 2002—they are on track.

But what is GATS? Early in the deliberations, the U.S. specified, "The mandate of the negotiations is ambitious: to remove restrictions on trade in services and provide effective market access, subject to specific limitations. Our challenge is to accomplish significant removal of these restrictions across all service sectors." Or, in English, to open all those areas hitherto protected for the public good to the profit motive.

Enronistas worldwide salivate before the enormous market of services: $1 trillion in water services, $2 trillion in educational services and $3.5 trillion in health services. And then there is power generation and other utilities.

The story of Enron, then, is the tale of the Second Enclosure Movement, and follows from the earlier movement to enclose land with barbed wire and other fencing. Here is another push by capitalist forces to entrap areas of economic life that had once been outside the sway of the commodity form. During the era of social democracy from the 1930s to the mid-1970s, capitalist relations did not overwhelm the realm of water, air, energy, health and education. But for over three decades, especially since the 1990s, during neoliberal times, these protected zones have come under pressure from transnational corporations and international finance institutions arguing that unproductive zones need to be opened to the efficiency of the profit-driven marketplace. Governments, so the argument goes, cannot protect their right to deliver these services to their citizenry at a subsidized rate. To do so "discriminates" against the right of a transnational corporation to underbid the state and offer its own paltry services instead. Government effort and regulation crowds out private enterprise, and must therefore be minimized.

The Second Enclosure Movement draws much of its logic from the First Enclosure Movement that took place, most spectacularly in England and in North America during the 17th century. John Locke, the ideologue of the first movement, spelled it out in his Second Treatise of Government (1689). "For I aske whether in the wild woods and uncultivated waste of America left to Nature, without any improvement, tillage or husbandry, a thousand acres will yield the needy and wretched inhabitants as many conveniences of life as ten acres of equally fertile land doe in Devonshire where they are well cultivated."[6] In other words, Locke argued that the Amerindians do not have the right to the lands of Virginia because the Amerindians, in Locke's view, did not cultivate the land and make it productive. Drawing from the Biblical verse in Genesis (1.28), "be fruitful and multiply and replenish the earth and subdue it," Locke justified the expropriation of the resources from the people and putting them in the hands of the power elite. Locke's actions and advocacy serve as a stunningly prescient harbinger of today's predicament: while he was Secretary of the Lords Proprietors of Carolina and Secretary to the Council of Trade and Plantations, Locke owned land that benefited from his theory of right.

By moving people off the land, the First Enclosure Movement gave birth "to new kinds of workers in a new kind of slavery, enforced directly by terror."[7] From the 17th to the 19th Century, workers toiled as if enslaved, yoked to the notion of manual labor, of being unskilled. Then the labor movement in the past two hundred years regained the dignity of work.

But in the last three decades, the Second Enclosure Movement sought to again enclose the public's commons. This time it was not land that was the target of privatization—accomplished long ago—but to reduce our notion of social welfare and the social good. Writer Arundhati Roy visited the World Water Forum in March 2000 in Holland, where talk inevitably focused on turning one hot target of privatization into a basic human right: water. "How would this be implemented, you might ask. Simple," said Roy. "By putting a market value on water. By selling it at its 'true' price. (It's common knowledge that water is becoming a scarce resource. As we know, about a billion people in the world have no access to safe drinking water). The 'market' decrees that the scarcer something is, the more expensive it becomes. But there is a difference between valuing water and putting a market value on water. No one values water more than a village woman who has to walk miles to fetch it. No one values it less than urban folk who pay for it to flow endlessly at the turn of a tap."[8]

The Second Enclosure Movement sharply attacks the well-being of women, many of whom now bear the burden of the destruction of the commons—not only do they have to walk further and further for water and firewood, but women of the working-class and peasantry lose control over domains of economic activity hitherto their province. In addition, the destruction of public care (health, retirement, childcare) has meant, in most parts of the world, that for women those aspects of unpaid, "domestic" work absorbed by the state for several decades is now once again the task of their third shift.[9] The new kind of worker in the Second Enclosure Movement is one that has lost the hard-won freedoms of an earlier era and gained the freedom to be thankful for degraded work (because they, at least, have jobs). What we as human beings took to being a natural right, understood as ours freely given by the earth, becomes now a privilege of the corporations to be sold to us like any other commodity. Even labor, once the right of a human being to sell for recompense, now becomes the gift of the corporation who doles it out through hiring at demeaned wages. The dignity of our relationship to the earth and to each other is now changed further, as money begins to determine all aspects of life, even those that had been held in trust by the social democratic state for the people's good.

Scientist Vandana Shiva calls this exertion of the votaries of profit, "corporate terrorism." "Greed and appropriation of other people's share of the resources are at the root of conflicts, and the root of terrorism," and therefore, "terrorists are not just those hiding in the caves of Afghanistan," but "some are hiding in corporate boardrooms and behind the free trade rules of the WTO, NAFTA and Free Trade Area of the Americas (FTAA)."[10] In these times as power uses the idea of terror to build legitimacy for its acts of war against the planet, let us keep in focus those forces that perpetuate the oppression of the earth's peoples, stealing from us our right to the planet.[11]

Enron has collapsed. But the Enron stage of capitalism, that Second Enclosure Movement, moves onward at full throttle.

CHAPTER ONE

Blowout on the Continent of Sleaze

Prophet of Profit

The eighth continent is the Continent of Sleaze. You and I have never been there, only heard rumors about it. Intrepid travelers make their way to that continent, into the heart of the *real* darkness. But they are belittled, called conspiracy theorists or else paranoid leftists, or else they are simply ignored. In mischievous places, like on obscure websites or in poorly produced newsletters, their adventurous journey is documented and we hear a little about that continent of maximal xenophobia. The screech of the travelers' wisdom is infectious if only you decide to take the plunge. Few do: it is far easier to live innocently without that dangerous knowledge, that outrageous Promethean fire.

But sometimes there is a blowout on the Continent of Sleaze and the rest of us perforce find ourselves with information about its mysteries. The medium of that information, the media, is prone to minimize the sludge and slime as it pretends that the residents of that far continent are actually just like us: ordinary people, but for one or two individuals who have all too ordinary traits that drive them to do bad, bad things. The Continent of Sleaze, this media convinces us (and it doesn't take much because we are so invested in these narratives), does not really exist. There is no El Dorado, there is no Atlantis, there is no Shangri-La inhabited by the Fat Cats and the Running Dogs.

So it goes.

Emblazoned on the banners of our travelers is the word

Enron. Like other residents on the continent, Enron has a name that defeats our lexicon, a name for a future that it will not meet, a name that tries to evoke something that we cannot understand, like the names of so many car brands or of pharmaceuticals—Elantra or Allegra. Founded in 1986 in the wild west of the late 20th century known as Houston, Texas, it became the eighteenth largest firm by 1999 with revenues upwards of $40 billion. By 2001, when its Wall Street value was more than $80 billion and it claimed $100.8 billion in revenues for 2000, Enron moved to seventh place. What did Enron do to more than double its girth so fast? Did it invent something crucial for the everyday people of the planet, or did it control some critical aspect of the economy? Nothing of the sort. Its business was natural gas, both its removal from the earth and then its transmission and sale to retail businesses who shipped it to our homes. But the 1990s saw a dramatic decline in the global price of natural gas—a sign Enron should have deflated. Instead, how did it become such a giant? Because the leadership was "visionary."

Kenneth Lay, 57 years old as the company slid into bankruptcy in 2002, is the founder and, as of this writing, head of Enron. A fairly ordinary man, Lay started his economist career at the poorly named Humble Oil (soon to be merged into Esso and renamed as Exxon) in Houston before he moved to the Navy in 1968. Rather than go to the front, Lay worked at the Pentagon for over a decade, then moved fortuitously in the 1980s to the Federal Power Commission. Friend of then Vice President George H. Bush (GHB), Lay left his government job to first work at Florida Gas and Continental Resources Company, then Houston Natural Gas. Finally, he created Enron (formed by the merger of Houston Natural Gas and InterNorth, two financially mediocre firms) to take advantage of his strategic contacts in the power field.

Lay calls himself a "visionary," and says that he saw the big picture of profit, that he became the prophet of profit. The big picture came in one word: deregulation. Lay created an apparatus to eek profits not so much in natural gas any longer, but in the creation of energy monopolies, the use of political clout to produce and maintain these monopolies, and finally, an exuberance that fakes regulators into the belief that you actually have a product to sell, that there is production in the Old Economy for the siphoned cash from the New Economy. Enron represents the entry of e-commerce into the terrain of economic infrastructure, as Enron traded all manner of items like natural gas, electricity, steel, pollution credits and even weather through the Internet. In June 2000, Ken Lay told a reporter, "We were a New Economy company before it became cool." Donato Eassey (Merrill Lynch) felt then, "Enron is uniquely positioned to be the General Electric of the new economy." And Lay, with his boast to expand Enron nine-fold again, said, "Enron's strongest growth is still ahead of us."[1]

Visionary can mean two things: a person who is remarkably sagacious with a capacity for imaginative insights; or conversely one who indulges in visions and fanciful theories, lives in an impractical imagination. There is a fine line between imaginative and imaginary. Lay was not delusional: he imaginatively lined his pockets, just as his minions—and the country—imagined that this was the American Dream.

Another one bites the dust.

Lay walked away with a fair amount of cash. According to Enron filings with the Securities and Exchange Commission, in 2000 Lay earned a base salary of $1.3 million, a bonus of $7 million, and he exercised stock options worth $123.4 million. In a year when inflation was in the rock bottom single digits, this was a 184% increase from his 1999 take. In the past three years, Lay earned more than $200 million from stock options, and, his lawyer Earl Silbert told the press, he had a revolving credit line of $7 million from Enron that he drew from each year. In

January 2001, Enron gave Lay a $3.6 million bonus for a few weeks of excellent work.[2] By the end of 2000, Lay held 6.5 million options of Enron stock (total worth $357.5 million), but in 2001, Lay unloaded a fair amount of these holdings (at least $100 million): from February to October, he sold at least $70 million, and in August, the month that he heard news of Enron's bad situation and when he told his employees to sit tight, he sold $16.3 million of his options.[3] So far there is nothing imaginary here. As Enron went bust on 2 December 2001, Kenny Boy's wife, Linda, appeared on television for a Hilary Clinton-style "Stand By Your Man" interview. Ken, she said, "is a moral human being who would do absolutely nothing wrong." And besides, she moaned, "We've lost everything. It's gone. There is nothing left." Of course, the reporter who interviewed her did not ask about the $7 million mansion that they sat in. What the reporter referred to was that the family had to dispose of three of their four Aspen vacation homes, two of them priced at $6 million. For a family that earned hundreds of millions of dollars over the years, much of that money probably went along with the Enron cash to several offshore accounts, this was small change. A third of Enron's 2,832 subsidiaries are located in tax havens like the Cayman Islands, so it is possible that Mr. Lay's nest egg is also conveniently beyond the reach of the weak law. Lay envisioned his future. He's set.

Not so the low-level and mid-level employees. They also envisioned their future, but they couldn't control it. Eleven thousand of them lost a total of $1.3 billion in the collapse. Most of them did not have any choice about their investments, their 401(k)-retirement money was locked into Enron stock. When Enron did well, no one complained. Now they are furious.

These low-level employees do not suffer alone. With much more freedom than the employees, pension fund managers were seduced by the impressive share price and the dynamism of Lay, investing vast amounts of their holdings in Enron. The scale is breathtaking: almost two-thirds of Enron's 744 million shares sat in the hands of pension and mutual funds, run by the nation's top financial "experts" who are entrusted with the savings of millions of everyday Americans. The funds' total loss approached $50 billion.

This is the new safety net. The employees and the fund managers did just as President George W. Bush (GWB) wants us all to do—forget mandatory social security, but take your money, get seduced by the latest South Sea Bubble and pray that the odds are better than the lottery or the casino. Where's that lock-box when you need it? What was criminal at Enron was that the safety net applied differently to different classes. As the share price started to drop, the management refused to allow the low-level employees to sell their shares, to walk away with anything before the Emperor stepped out for his parade in the clothes of the New Economy. But the high-level employees grabbed overcoats: as the share price dropped precipitously from $80 to one or two pennies, they cashed in their shares for over $1 billion. Between 1 January and 31 August 2001, just before the slide, the following Enron top-level executives sold their shares to walk away with a mint:

- Lou Pai (Chairman and CEO, Enron Xcelerator): $33.6 million.

- Jeffrey K. Skilling (Former President and CEO, Enron): $15.5 million.

- Kenneth D. Rice (Divisional Officer, Enron): $14.7 million.

- John C. Baxter (Director, Vice Chairman, Enron): $9.2 million.

- Steven J. Kean (Executive Vice President, Chief of Staff, Enron): $5.4 million.

A certain visionary was concerned about their welfare; they're all set.

In an interesting footnote to this financial fable, one class of employees escaped the wiles of a corrupt system tempting most to gamble their future for fool's gold. As journalist William Greider notes:

> The employees who were not wiped out were sheet-metal workers at subsidiaries acquired by Enron, whose union locals insisted on keeping their own separately managed pension funds. Labor-managed pension funds, with holdings of about $400 billion, are dwarfed by corporate-controlled funds, in which the future beneficiaries are frequently manipulated to enhance the company's bottom line. Yet pension funds supervised jointly by unions and management give better average benefits and broader coverage (despite a few scandals of their own).[4]

The American Federation of Labor-Coalition of Industrial Organization (AFL-CIO) could be having a field day. But no one seems to be making much of the fact that, despite the clarion call of the New Economy that unions are anachronisms, they continue to have an indispensable role in the protection of the workers' future.

Enron is not alone. Fiber optics giant Global Crossing collapsed as its share price dived from $60 to nothing. But leader Gary Winnick saw the light, selling his cache for $600 million. Lucent, another telecom darling, also went down. Yet its executives walked away with $12 million from sales of their shares just as their leader Richard McGinn took an $11.3 million severance package. When the collapse comes in the New Economy, executives still throw themselves out of windows— with golden parachutes, leaving everyday Americans to suffer the loss of retirement security. We've come a long way, baby, from the days when Real Men took risks, put on their cowboy hats and boots, went West with a six-gun, tried their luck, massacred Amerindians, made their fortunes or drank themselves silly if they went bust. Now the Real Men wear the hats and boots, and make sure that they have enough cash tucked away in the saddle-bags of their limos as they drive off into the sunshine of the Caribbean tax-havens. The first time as tragedy, the second as farce.

Where were the checks and balances to prevent Enron's implosion? Was it just a matter of a shell game played by top executives in an aberrant grab for dough? These questions provoked the numerous Congressional inquiries, and the answers to them will probably be somewhat clearer in the years to come. But the writing of impending collapse had been on the wall for almost a decade, suggesting more structural fault lines rather than the individual greed of executives like Andrew Fastow who allegedly created the famous partnerships to hide debt and made a mint doing it. In November 1992, Enron and eight other energy firms asked the U.S. Commodity Futures Trading Commission to exempt energy derivative contracts from federal government oversight as well as from laws that prosecute against fraud. The three Republicans on the five-member commission found a worthy leader in Wendy Gramm, a well-known proponent of deregulation of all markets and previously a senior staff member at the Reagan White House. (She is currently director of the Regulatory Studies Program at George Mason University.) Gramm advised her staff to begin to formulate the rules for the change, a tedious process that indicated that Enron and others had won their case. As the Clinton administration took power, Gramm (a Republican appointee) resigned her post on 21 January 1993. But before Clinton put his people on the Commission, it voted 2-1 to approve Enron's request.

The exemptions requested by Enron and others became

retroactive to 1974, when the Commission was created, which meant that this section of the energy market was to be without regulation across time. Despite an attempt by Wendy Gramm's husband, Senator Phil Gramm of Texas to back these shenanigans, Congressional objection overturned the exemption from fraud provisions. But everything else was given to Enron. Just weeks after her resignation from the government, Gramm joined the Enron board.

The Gramms' help didn't end there. On December 15 2000, Phil Gramm pushed the passage of the Commodity Futures Modernization Act, a piece of legislation tacked onto an appropriations bill as the Clinton administration gave way to GWB. The law, passed without discussion, reduced the regulation of energy trading and allowed unregulated subsidiaries, such as Enron OnLine to trade energy futures without federal scrutiny. Watchdog groups such as Public Citizen argue that the law produced the power crisis in California.[5] Overwhelmed by the scandal, Wendy Gramm went underground and Phil Gramm decided not to seek reelection.[6]

Enron happened *because* of Congressional policy. The checks and balances were there to begin with, until they were yanked away by the guardians of the Constitution.

The deregulation of these energy markets enabled Enron to earn a tenth of its profits by adventures on financial markets, and it emboldened the firm to pay more attention to these aspects of its business than to the tedious natural gas provision work. The New Economy beckoned and Enron lunged headfirst. Initially, Enron's entry came through the use of the web to trade in energy resources. In May 2001, Enron announced that its subsidiary, Enron Online completed its millionth transaction. By then, Enron Online was the planet's largest e-commerce platform for commodities.

Building on that success, Enron moved into the world of derivatives to try to make massive profits off risky trades.

Derivatives, according to journalist Doug Henwood, emerged in the public consciousness in 1994 when the Federal Reserve raised interest rates and sent money toward these creative instruments.[7] A suspect in the making of the Great Depression of 1929, futures and options form the heart of derivatives, a contract that *derives* the price of one set of securities from another. By 1999, when Enron's trades seemed to be doing quite well, the derivatives market totaled $90 trillion. Keep in mind that the annual global trade in merchandise and services totals $6.5 trillion, itself only equal to less than four and a half days of trades on foreign exchange or forex markets.[8]

Like the Municipality of Orange County and the hedge fund Long Term Capital Management (LTCM), Enron was not immune to the wiles of the derivatives industry. One bad trade followed another. Orange County's treasurer Robert Citron put a section of the municipal money into risky transactions from 1991 onwards, but by 1994 it turned out that his bets were wrong and that the municipality had to sue for bankruptcy having lost $1.6 billion. (A $1.2 billion debt incurred by Orange County will be retired in 2027, and it is only then that the municipality will leave the condition of bankruptcy.) LTCM, backed by two Nobel laureates in Economics (so much for that prize!), leveraged its capital of $5 billion to control $125 billion in assets and $1.4 trillion in derivates (mostly in interest rate swaps). As credit tightened, LTCM found itself overextended by $200 billion. It went to Clinton's Treasury Secretary Robert Rubin who was eager to protect his banker friends. At a meeting organized by Federal Reserve Bank Chairman Alan Greenspan, banks, fearing LTCM's collapse might spread panic, bailed it out for a spectacular $3.5 billion.

The trials of LTCM did not deter Enron, now poised in its mind to become the leading e-commerce firm in the world. But, as is inevitable, bad trades did occur. To hide them, Enron raised capital from banks invested in its success, and it hid its risky transactions by setting up fraudulently independent companies (Raptor I-IV, Southampton Place, Chewco: named after golf courses where Enron executives plotted the dirty tricks) that it owned and ran. Enron reported the cost of setting up these firms and of bailing out their bad trades as a profit, another way to bulk up its balance sheets behind a web of phony screens. The cover-up worked: even in 2001 things didn't look bad for Enron on the books. Enron reported that in the first three quarters of 2001, the firm's revenue totaled $140 billion, ninety percent of which came from its energy trading business. These numbers looked so good thanks to Arthur Andersen.

The most boring profession, accountancy, suddenly became a swashbuckling adventure from where vast profits could be pirated. But this news was only sudden for the uninitiated. At once the watchdog as accountant and the ally as consultant, Arthur Andersen papered over the fake transactions that let Enron boost its stock to the detriment of the public. None of this is new terrain for Andersen or for the accounting profession. Andersen has been on the frontlines of scandals as the accountant for Lincoln Savings and Loan (run by Mother Teresa's dear friend, Charles Keating)[9], a firm that was bailed out at a cost to taxpayers of more than $2 billion. More recently, it helped Sunbeam (run by "Chainsaw" Al Dunlap).[10]

Two of the big five accounting firms are not without their own scandals: Ernst & Young had to pay $335 million to New York and California's public employee pension funds for its misrepresentation of Cendant Corporation's health; PriceWaterhouseCoopers helped Lucent inflate their books by $679 million and came under a Securities and Exchange Commission investigation in 2000.

On January 15 2002, Andersen fired its partner in charge of the Enron audit, David Duncan, because it appeared that Duncan told auditors to shred many Enron-related documents on October 23 2001, just a day after the Securities and

Exchange Commission (SEC) had begun an inquiry of Enron. According to a report in the *Wall Street Journal*, Andersen's firing of Duncan "was seen as an effort by Andersen to isolate the Enron affair to its Houston office and shield itself from more serious charges. New evidence emerged that [Andersen's Chicago headquarters] knew details about controversial Enron financial arrangements that contributed to the energy company's downfall."[11] Duncan refused to take the fall alone, and in April 2002, he entered a guilty plea and fingered Andersen and Enron executives as parties to the obstruction of justice.[12] The agent refused to take the fall for the structure.

The federal government's indictment of Andersen on the grounds of obstruction of justice is revealing. It focuses on the firm's destruction of documents, more than on Arthur Andersen's shady practices to hide bad trades. For instance, there is little concern with what is called "top-level adjustments," when the corporate core receives reports from its subsidiaries, then reworks the financial assumptions behind the report without informing the subsidiaries. These routine forms of deceit (the increase in value of assets, avoidance of depreciation by an increase in salvage value) have transformed the accountant from a keeper of books to a generator of additional profit. As the General Agreement on Trade in Service (GATS) tries to sell the routine deceit of U.S. accountancy around the world, groans rise from unexpected corners. In South Africa, for instance, the government held a hearing into the collapse of Leisurenet, a fitness and health firm. Deloitte Touche Tohmatsu (DTT) had signed off on its boosted numbers, so Leisurenet used these figures in its financial reports to garner more investment for a loss-making outfit. When it validated the Leisurenet's returns, DTT had not even looked at all the documents.[13]

Andersen certainly connived with Enron to boost profits and then to hide its shady deeds. But Enron and Andersen bought protection all round, not only in Congress but at the watchdog that was founded after the Great Crash of 1929, the Securities and Exchange Commission. Now heading this guardian of accounting regulations is Harvey Pitt, a lawyer who once represented Andersen and fought vigorously against tougher regulations for accountants.[14] It is unlikely that Pitt will follow the dictum of William Douglas, an early chairman of the SEC, "We are the investor's advocate."

Meanwhile, in Congress, there is Senator Joe Lieberman, among others, that fixture of tired theocratic morality, whose white horse in this context was not Clinton's sex life, but the Financial Accounting Standards Board. When the Board attempted to put stringent regulations against the alchemy of accountancy, Lieberman blocked them. Firms, such as Enron, give stock options to their employees as a bonus and then add those "gifts" as a charge against their profits. The Board found this practice to be unsound finance, but Lieberman did not concur.[15] Anyone misled by Enron's performance should blame Lieberman because his action made its unethical conduct legal.

Even as Andersen's hastily hired oversight committee (headed by former fed head Paul Volcker) recommended that Andersen split its audit and consulting department, Andersen's managers tried to liquidate themselves and offer their assets to one of the five big accounts firms, DTT. If Andersen declares bankruptcy, then DTT will not inherit its liabilities, and perhaps it can disregard the only decent thing that has happened in the profession for a while: the admittance by the Volcker committee that the rot in the system is deep. But Volcker's committee did not get any support from either Andersen or DTT, even as he himself did not favor governmental action against the firms. "Are we going to have an indictment, are we going to have a merger or are we going to have reform?" asked Volcker at a press conference on 11 March 2002. A DTT spokesman cagily reported, "Every good idea deserves a good hearing, particularly ideas from someone as highly regarded as Paul Volcker. While we are still reviewing his document, at this point it is not clear to us how under the proposal audit teams would gain access to all the skills and capabilities necessary for world-class audits."[16] In other words, a calculated comment designed to block Volcker and forge the merger. In response, Volcker noted, "I had hoped that Andersen would become a model for reforming the profession. It was a dream, like Don Quixote. Still, trying to bring change does make the blood run."[17] Or boil...

The U.S. government was forced to indict Andersen because of a deal it cut with the firm over the criminal inflation by \$1.7 billion of Waste Management's books from 1992 to 1997. In 1998, the SEC began to investigate Waste Management and Andersen, and by June 2001, the SEC agreed to drop the case if Andersen changed its ways and promised not to do anything illegal again. When Andersen broke the agreement, the indictment had to follow. Deputy Attorney General Michael Chertoff told Andersen's lawyers, "The obstruction here demonstrates that several prior attempts to deal with improper activity at Andersen, short of criminal prosecution, have not been successful in accomplishing the reforms that would remold Andersen into a good corporate citizen." Furthermore, "The conduct here was not the isolated act of a few low-level employees acting out of panic or engaging in misjudgment."[18]

The problem, in other words, is endemic and systemic. The seeds of Andersen's addiction to illegality and of its relapse appear on two registers. First, there is its long and progressively worse history of illegal and inappropriate acts:

- It paid the State of Ohio \$5.5 million to cover losses to taxpayers for their bad oversight of Home State Savings Bank (1988);

- It paid \$22 million to settle a lawsuit over its falsification

of the books for American Continental Corporation
(1992);

- It paid $75 million to shareholders of Waste Management
(1998);

- It paid $90 million to investors of Colonial Realty (1998);

- It paid $110 million for misstated accounts (2001),

- And finally Enron.

Second, right after the 1998 agreement with the SEC,
Andersen continued to play fast and loose with the rules.
Andersen, like other accounting firms, has procedures to
destroy "useless" documents. So on 10 October, five days before
Enron hit the fan in public, Andersen's practice director
Michael C. Odom told the troops in Houston, "If documents
are destroyed and litigation is filed the next day, that's great.
We've followed our own policy, and whatever there was that
might have been of interest to somebody is gone and irretriev-
able."[19] The troops went on a mammoth operation to shred
documents.

The firms of the New Economy and their accountants are
certainly culpable. But so too are the investment banks that
pumped up these firms with capital, boosted them in the networks of investment gossip, and then drew vast profits for themselves from the capital they provided. In 1997, Enron took a
$500 million hit in a transaction over British natural gas and
over fuel additives, so that its stock fell by a third. Desperate to
right the ship, the Enron managers (according to a complaint
filed by Enron shareholders in early April 2002), made a deal
with several banks and investment houses to finance one of
Enron's fraudulent partnerships, LJM2. J. P. Morgan Chase,
Citigroup, Credit Suisse First Boston, Canadian Imperial Bank
of Commerce, Merrill Lynch, Bank of America, Deutsche Bank,

Lehman Brothers and Barclays Bank "chose to become partners in deceit," said William S. Lerach, one of the lawyers in the suit. "They were not only willing participants, but profiteers."[20] In other trades, Goldman Sachs gained $69 million from among the $323 million Enron paid Wall Street firms for their efforts— all the while Goldman Sachs' people pushed Enron stocks on gullible investors. "We're finding what may clearly be securities fraud," said Representative Billy Tauzin (Republican-LA), Chairman of the House Energy and Commerce Committee, to NBC's Meet the Press. As the phoenix collapses among the ashes, Citigroup and J.P. Morgan Chase expect to lose upwards of $500 million each in unsecured loans for derivative trades and other such things.[21]

Enron went down on the false valuation of assets, bogus deals between related parties and millions of dollars pocketed by executives. But if this is all that it takes to go down, then there are many to follow. The truth is that Enron exceeded the bounds of greed, and that it generally boosted it earnings to bilk its shareholders and lift its stock price. But when it was forced to post an enormous 2001 third quarter loss of $618 million, its value dropped by $1.2 billion and things spiraled down from there. In 1997, editor of *Left Business Observer* Doug Henwood wrote, "All these [derivative] strategies, simple purchases or sales or complex combinations of both, can be motivated either by gut instinct or complex mathematical models, by the desire to limit exposure or to bet the house, by routine business decisions of interested parties or speculative interests of players who couldn't tell soybeans from seed corn. But whatever the motivation or strategy, it's usually estimated that 80-90% of nonprofessional futures and options traders lose money."[22] If Henwood is unsure about the ability of amateurs in the derivatives market, one should pause before we put too much stock in the ability of professionals. Robert Citron, of Orange County, reportedly took advice from an astrologer and a mail-order psychic to help him make the trades that collapsed, and LTCM visited Nobel Prize winners to set up their tsunami.[23] When Enron collapsed, Henwood noted, "As is standard with complex financial instruments, the selling point is management of risk...It looks like Enron itself ended up holding some [risk], though you'd never have known it from reading Enron's inscrutable and devious accounts."[24] Sometimes the truth does leak out, even as the big boys try to cover it all up and suck more of our money to cover their margins.

Enron's Global Crossings

As Enron went out to conquer the planet in the 1990s, it created a force of firms to manage the assault. Enron's operations came under five main divisions: Enron Broadband Services, Enron Energy Services, Enron Transportation Services (until September 2000 it was called the Gas Pipeline Group), Enron Wholesale Services, and Online Marketplace Services (Enron Online which includes Water2Water.com, Waterdesk.com, EnronCredit.com and ClickPaper.com). This shell owned various businesses such as Azurix Water, Enron Global Exploration and Production, Enron Investment Partners, Enron Oil and Natural Gas, Enron Wind, Houston Pipeline, Northern Natural Gas, Portland General Electric, Transwestern Pipeline.... Enron International manages deals for Enron's global crossings and it limits the liability of the behemoth by the creation of joint-ventures with local firms as well as by cut-out companies that it sets up to run the concern elsewhere (such as the Dabhol Power Corporation in India and Enron Japan).

In April 2001, Enron's 10(k) form detailed some of its ventures outside the U.S. Enron entered the cash-starved utilities industry in the UK when the regime was forced, after a decade of Thatcherism, to "liberalize" its energy markets in 1992. The UK was Enron's beachhead into Europe, as it moved into Norway, Germany, Turkey, Poland and Italy. Enron acquired at least three power plants in Europe's version of "emerging markets": in Poland (a 116MW natural gas power plant), in Italy (a 551MW oil-natural gas plant in Sardinia), and in Turkey (a 478MW power plant in Trakya). Enron informed the SEC that it "is also pursuing opportunities in continental Europe where there is a need for customized, flexible energy supply contracts to benefit from liberalizing gas and power markets." In other words, Enron sought to expand into zones that came under financial pressure in the 1980s to seek funds from the buyer of last resort, the homeland of the Dollar-Wall Street complex. The Wall Street boom in the 1990s, matched with the drive for structural adjustment across the world (that is, open markets for corporations), enabled firms like Enron to garner vast amounts of cash to invest in these cash mired zones of the world. This extended even into Europe, and soon into Australia. The practice was to be extended to Japan, but is now blocked. Enron's CEO Jeffrey Skilling was prosaic about Enron's world historical role: "we are on the side of the angels. People want to have open, competitive markets."

But firms like Enron do not take U.S. savings and invest them, in an act of good grace, in places that *need the money*. The money raised on Wall Street is not from U.S. savings: personal savings as a percentage of disposable income dropped from 1.2% in 1997 to a miniscule 0.5% in 1998, then fell to a negative figure in 1999, all this just as private consumption expenditure began to rise sharply. Given the lack of domestic savings, where have the funds for overseas ventures originated? A considerable amount comes from the U.S. pension funds, now invested heavily in the stock market. Ecstatic commentators saw the stock market boom as a great social equalizer: anyone can get rich, that is, anyone with the dynamic spirit of the age. What these mouthpieces of wealth did not mention was that during this entire bull market, the top five percent of stockowners (by household wealth) owned almost ninety-five percent of all stocks held by individuals. In other words, the stock market boom produced the illusion of equality when in fact it was another avenue for the maintenance (or even motor) of inequality.[25]

To keep up with the Joneses, the U.S. public went into massive consumer debt. Like the countries of the global South, U.S. households in 1995 spent a total of almost seventeen percent of their after tax incomes on debt service ($903 billion), an enormous upward redistribution of income (because the lenders who get that interest are the wealthy).[26] Analysis of the data in the Survey of Consumer Finances shows that for the poorest forty percent, the borrowed money was not expended on new indulgences but instead to compensate for stagnant or battered incomes. Only the richest twenty percent borrowed money to invest in the stock market, to suffer the occult movements of the Big Board as part of the small, but influential investor class.[27] The U.S. public may want to keep up with the Dow Joneses, but their negative savings were not what financed Enron and other forays into "developing" the Third World.

There is another source of funds used for financing investment in the Third World, one that often goes by without comment except when provoked by exceptional circumstances. One such event was the so-called Yen Carry Trades in the mid to late 1990s. Currency speculators borrowed funds in yen from the Japanese credit and finance firms, moved the funds to offshore locations like the Cayman Islands, converted them into dollars and then bought U.S. Treasury bonds. In 1996, for example, U.S. bonds had been bought by $19 billion of borrowed Japanese funds that may have been put to productive use there, but which moved to the U.S. to take advantage of better interest rates and investment opportunities on Wall Street. The scale of these trades gave the IMF cause to finger them as one reason for the weakness of the Japanese economy.[28]

A second event is the recycling of petro-profits from Saudi

Arabia into the U.S. In 1971, under U.S. Treasury Secretary and Texas oilman John Connally's watch, President Nixon delinked the dollar from the gold standard, and put pressure on the Saudis (as the closest oil ally) and OPEC to raise the price of oil. Far from weakening the U.S. economy, these twin drives, the administration felt, would secure U.S. domination over the world's economy and ensure that the dollar become the premier currency on the planet. Here's how that paradoxical move worked. In October 1973, OPEC did raise the price of oil that, as expected, had two results beneficial to the U.S. and to Wall Street. First, it put an immense squeeze on the US's two main economic competitors, Western Europe and Japan. Second, it earned profits for the Gulf States in the form of a kind of regressive taxation against car drivers and consumers who paid for the gas hike. Because the Gulf States did not have adequate productive capacity to absorb the petro-dollars, these profits were then recycled into U.S. financial institutions. The elimination of capital controls in the U.S. economy by 1974 eased this recycling, in turn facilitating the global status of the dollar as the instrument of "hard currency."[29] This money, from the world over, entered Wall Street and then returned to the world as foreign direct investment now not in the service of development, but to make firms like Enron vast profits. The world's currencies suffered the hegemony of the dollar, but as Connally put it in 1971 with characteristic Texan bluntness, "our currency, your problem."

If the Third World was unable to fund projects on its own soil, built by Enron-type firms who then make enormous profits for years on end, funds from the U.S. government and international development banks came to their aid. Since 1992, Enron alone appropriated more than $7 billion in public funds to finance thirty-eight of its projects in twenty-nine countries.[30] In the mid-1990s, Ken Lay sat before various Congressional committees and laid out Enron's position with regard to public finance. In 1995, he told the people's representatives, "We prefer to use all U.S. sourcing as much as possible, as we have well-established working relationships with our fellow U.S. firms, we share the same approach and experience base, and we believe U.S. firms are world class in these areas. However, we can only source in the U.S. to the extent sufficient financing is available here." The next year, he warned Congress if the agencies that enabled Enron to go global did not receive adequate funds, Enron would buy its hardware from Germany, Japan or Korea, "whose governments understand the benefits of expropriation insurance, financing and other things that make companies competitive." In other words, Enron went to agencies such as U.S. Overseas Private Investment Corporation (OPIC) and the U.S. Export-Import (Ex-Im) Bank to win funds for projects in the Third World. These funds are used to buy merchandise and services from other U.S. firms. The U.S. government, then, subsidizes not only Enron's endeavors overseas, but also those of the firms whose goods are now bought by Enron using government funds.

OPIC, Ex-Im Bank and other allied U.S. government agencies gave Enron $3.68 billion for twenty-five projects from 1992 to 2001. So much for Skilling's "open, competitive markets." Meanwhile, the World Bank gave Enron $3.54 billion in this period, just as a host of Export Credit Agencies in other countries paid billions of dollars for Enron's entrepreneurship: Andean Development Bank ($165 million), Asian Development Bank ($26.4 million), Canadian International Development Agency ($12.3 million), COFACE of France ($90 million), Commonwealth Development Corporation ($104 million), European Investment Bank ($631 million), Inter-American Development Bank ($751 million), Japanese credit agencies ($433.4 million), Kreditanstalt für Wiederaufbau ($150 million), Mediocredito Centrale (along with ABN-Amro and CIS, of $1.2 billion), Office National du

Ducroire ($90.8 million), and Sezione Speciale Per l'Assicurazione Del Credito All-Esportazione (almost $386 million).

In 1995, Lay plainly told Congress, "Public finance agencies are the only reliable source of the financing that is essential for private infrastructure projects in developing countries." When Enron hit the fan, Representative Nina Lowey (Democrat-NY) told her Congressional colleagues on 7 March 2002, "I cannot fathom frankly how both the Ex-Im and OPIC could have been so misled over such an extended period with respect to the Enron Corporation." Note the limits of respectable debate as defined by Lowey, on the liberal wing. The bad trades made by the banks in this case were egregious. But the question of using public funds for private business was off limits. Even as Enron disappears the Enron stage of capitalism continues.

Enron had a vast and growing stake in the "emerging markets" during the 1990s, now financed by recycled Third World funds or US-European governmental subsidies. The 2001 SEC filing offers Enron a place to reflect on the challenges faced by white firms in the world of color:

> In many markets outside of North America and Europe, a shortage of energy infrastructure exists, which has provided Enron with opportunities to develop, construct, promote and operate natural gas pipelines, power plants and other energy infrastructure. In these markets, Enron's strategy is to facilitate completion of vital energy networks to connect areas of energy supply to areas where energy is consumed. By creating energy networks, Enron provides reliable delivery of physical energy commodities and develops risk management and financing services to wholesale customers in key international regions. Enron's energy infrastructure projects are, to varying degrees, subject to all the risks associated with project development, construction and financing in foreign countries, including without limitation, the receipt of permits and consents,

the availability of project financing on acceptable terms, expropriation of assets, renegotiation of contracts with foreign governments and political instability, as well as changes in laws and policies governing operations of foreign-based businesses generally.

Reading this, one is led to believe that Enron is really on the side of the angels, providing the much-needed infrastructure for the development of the misbegotten world. Where colonialism and nationalism failed, U.S. corporatism will certainly succeed at last. And it is Enron who has to bear all these terrible risks in dangerous places. Where once the white man braved the weather and disease to bear his burden, now we hear about those horrid tropical hindrances like "permits and consents" and "acceptable terms" for finance, as well as that ultimate alarm for the corporate entity, "political instability." Dear Enron braves the waters, sets ashore and, despite the dangers from irrational regimes, it goes it alone...for the people!

The list of Enron's adventures on the following pages is a vast and revealing snapshot of today's corporate dominance.

Even as U.S. revenues dwarfs overseas profits (in 2000, Enron earned $77.8 billion in the US, and $22.8 billion from the rest of the world), the gradual increase in revenue from the latter since 1998 is startling: $6 billion in 1998, $9.9 billion in 1999 and $22.8 billion in 2000. Between 1998 and 2001, furthermore, Enron's foreign revenues increased from seven percent of the total take to 23 percent. Enron went after the "emerging markets," one might argue, to subsidize its e-commerce ventures in Wall Street, just as its position in New York enabled it to garner commercial funds to further penetrate what Enron calls "developing markets." In other words, as Enron stretched its financial resources within North America, it used its overseas business to cover its margins, then used that good position to leverage more finance with which to continue its

Country	Company	Project	Interest
Argentina	Transportadora de Gas del Sur	4104 mile pipeline, 1.9 Bcf/day	35%
Bolivia	Transredes Transporte de Hidrocarburos S. A.	3570 mile system.	25%
Brazil	• • Elektro Electricidade e Servicos S. A.	• Cuiaba 480MW power plant • 358 mile, 18in natural gas pipeline • 51,000 mile electricity transmission system for 1.5 million consumers.	• minority • minority • majority
China		• Chengdu 359MW coal-fired power plant. • Hainan Island 160MW Diesel power plant.	• 51% • 100%
Colombia		357 mile natural gas pipeline	50% (Ecopetrol is the sole customer in a 15 year contract)
Dominican Republic		Puerto Plata 185MW power plant	80%
Guam		Piti 80MW Diesel power plant	50%
Guatemala		Puerto Quetzal 234MW fuel oil power plant	37.5%.
India	Dabhol Power Co.	Dhabol 2450MW natural gas power plant	50% voting interest
Nicaragua		Port of Corinto 70MW power plant	35%
Panama		Bahia Las Minas 355MW power plant	51%. *continued*

Country	Company	Project	Interest
Philippines		• Batangas 110MW fuel oil power plant • Subic Bay 116MW fuel oil power plant.	• 100%. • 50%
Puerto Rico		Penuelas 522MW natural gas power plant.	47.5%
South Korea		14 firms that distribute natural gas liquids	50%
Venezuela	• Vengas	• distribution of natural gas liquids. • natural gas liquid extraction in northeastern Venezuela.	• 97% • 49.5%

overseas operations.[31] The screw turned over and over again.

The data above masks how Enron financed much of its global work. Rather than use its own assets to raise the money, Enron used its position as a U.S. firm to force the two-thirds world to accept its high offers and reduce statutory oversight. Then, frequently (and this is the stunner for a firm committed to the small state) it forced the state to invest in the project as a down payment against all that trouble of being in the tropics in the first place. If the states in the two-thirds world didn't have the cash flow necessary for the project, Enron turned to the U.S. government for funds. A few examples of this Enron form of "free market capitalism" show that what is "free" for the corporation comes off the backs of others:

The Invisible Hand: Ex-Im Bank

In 1994-95, Commerce Secretary Ron Brown took a host of U.S. executives on a world tour, first to Russia, then Indonesia, China and India. On board with Brown came almost three dozen corporate executives from firms such as Westinghouse, AT&T, Dresser Industries, Litton Industries, General Electric, Rockwell International, Bristol-Myers Squibb and, of course, Enron. In a signal to the world of President

Clinton's commitment to "the economy, stupid," the gala tour allowed these U.S. firms to sign onto hundreds of millions of dollars of business ventures.

Just as Brown planned the trip in 1993, the Export-Import Bank (a U.S. government agency) changed its rules to allow it to finance projects on the basis of projected cash flow, not assets in hand. This policy shift enabled firms to take much greater risks and to extend themselves beyond their ability to cover their debts. In November 1993, before the Brown trip, the Export-Import Bank financed $285 million of a $1 billion Enron deal to develop two power plants in Turkey. On board with Brown, Lay got $100 million from the Ex-Im Bank for the Dabhol (India) deal in August 1994 and then, in November of that year, $130 million for the Chinese plant. Enron's Dabhol deal was awarded an additional $300 million from the Overseas Private Investment Corporation, at the time headed by Ruth Harkin (wife of the liberal Iowa Senator Tom Harkin).

The most egregious use of the Ex-Im Bank comes in the US-driven catastrophe in Russia, where what we call crony capitalism is only an offshoot of what we exported there in the 1990s.[32] Dresser Industries, backed by the Bank, closed a $2 billion agreement to sell Russia gas and petrochemical equipment. The torrents of the East being what they are, the Ex-Im Bank organized a sweet deal: the Russian firms serviced this large debt by borrowing against their oil and gas revenues and, as a surety, putting these in an off-shore escrow account. The Ex-Im Bank became the broker of the shakedown. The Ex-Im/Dresser deal is only a fraction of the $150 billion that fled Russia in the 1990s, leaving 70 percent of the population below the poverty line. In the 1990s, Itera Holding, a small gas trader based in Jacksonville, Florida, entered the Russian market and, in ten years, became the second largest gas firm next to Gazprom. How did this mysterious Florida firm reach these heights? Because of the largess of the U.S. government, whose U.S. Trade and

Development Agency as recently as February 2002, gave Itera a grant of $868,000 for a feasibility study (to be conducted by a U.S. engineering firm). When Gazprom complained that Itera bought plant and equipment and then sold them for scrap ("asset stripping"), a U.S. official told the press that the grant "made sense because of U.S. exports—we want to give U.S. firms a leg up in the development of this field—and because Itera has become a major player in Eurasian gas."[33] In other words, the U.S. government flagrantly came out on behalf of the right of a U.S. corporation to destroy the physical plant of another country for profit despite the needs of the people of that part of the world. Such grants subsidize U.S. firms because they contractually obligate the firm to use the aid for the purchase of U.S.-made equipment, thereby helping those firms "get a leg up." The U.S. government is the invisible hand in the global economy.

The Shakedown: USAID and Mozambique

In 1995, Mozambique sought investment to develop the Pande natural gas fields in its southern region (with an estimated 2 trillion cubic feet of reserves) as well as to build a 900km pipeline to carry the gas to a direct reduced iron steel plant in South Africa. When the government of Mozambique saw the bids, PlusPetrol of Argentina was second on the list, and Sasol, the South African petrochemical agency, seemed to be in the lead.

This was surprising. From 1975 to 1994 Mozambique, a nation of only about 18 million lost over 200,000 people in a bloody civil war between Frelimo,the national-liberation movement, and Renamo, the South African apartheid state and U.S. right backed force. Eager to break free of this history, the government in Mozambique attempted to do justice to its people. But with a per capita average annual income of under $100 and with legal minimum wages of under $14/month, things looked bleak. In the mid-1990s, Mozambique considered a 37.5% increase in the minimum wage, about half the rate of inflation. But the International Monetary Fund's local official Sergio Leite said that this was "excessive."[34] As the apartheid regime ended in South Africa in 1994, the relations between the two countries improved and the former racist state now appeared as a major economic anchor for Mozambique's economy (as it did for the regional economy).

Given this context, Enron's power play to displace the South Africans in Mozambique is scandalous. They had leverage and they used it. Consider Mozambique's financial dilemma. A year after its civil war ended, $1.1 billion of its $1.5 billion budget was financed by foreign aid, with at least $40 million from USAID itself. USAID held such a crucial hand in this game, that it is sophistry to consider Mozambique a sovereign nation-state. John Kachamila, Minister of Mineral Resources, told the following story to the *Houston Chronicle*:

> There were outright threats to withhold develop-
> ment funds if we didn't sign [the deal with Enron], and
> sign soon. Their diplomats, especially Mike McKinley
> [deputy chief of the U.S. Embassy], pressured me to sign
> a deal that was not good for Mozambique. He was not a
> neutral diplomat. It was as if he was working for Enron.
> We got calls from American senators threatening us
> with this and that if we didn't sign. Anthony Lake [U.S.
> national security adviser] even called to tell us to sign...
> They put together a smear campaign against us... Enron
> was forever playing games with us and the embassy for-
> ever threatening to withdraw aid. Everyone was saying
> that we would not sign the deal because I wanted a per-
> centage, when all I wanted was a better deal for the
> state... So Enron caved in to our demands, especially
> after the World Bank commissioned a study that found
> many of our concerns were warranted. Now let me ask
> you: Who is corrupt here? To me it is Enron for trying

to shove this rotten deal down our throats.

The view of an unnamed State Department official quoted in the same article indicates that Kachamila's assessment of Enron's tactics is correct: "This project represents tax revenue, hard currency earnings in a big way for the Mozambican state... If the Mozambicans think they can kill this deal and we will keep dumping money into this place, they should think again."[35] In 1995, when the deal was in trouble, National Security Advisor Anthony Lake wrote to President Joaquim Chiassano that the U.S. would not release $13.5 million in aid funds unless Mozambique accepted the Enron bid. Lake's efforts reveal the real meaning of "free trade": government bullying to force weaker countries to favor global corporations.

The shakedown in Mozambique is commonplace across the planet. We heard from Kachamila mainly because of the type of values preached by Frelimo from the mid-1970s onward. In February 1980, Mozambique's President Samora Machel (also the leader of Frelimo, the left political formation) told his ministers:

> We have not broken with the colonial methods of work. We live in our offices, inundated with piles of paper, do not know our own secretaries, do not visit hospitals, schools, farms, etc., do not listen to popular opinion, knowing reality only through memorandums and dispatches. We lose direction and focus only on small, daily routine problems. We don't punish saboteurs; we coexist with them and even pay them salaries. Courtesy, serving the public with delicacy, with good presentation are not integrated into the behavior of the workers of the state apparatus.[36]

Would that all leaders gave their officials this advice!

If Mozambique provides details of how Enron and the U.S. government operated, from India we get confirmation that Mozambique is not an isolated example. Rumor mills in New

Delhi buzzed in the mid-1990s with the tale that Ron Brown told the government, then chary about the terms of the Enron deal, that the deal had to go down because it was the flagship of U.S. entry into the Indian market. If it didn't work, the U.S. would reconsider several goodies wanted by the Indian state: entry into the UN Security Council, financial investments, arms shipments. In 1995, the *New York Times* reported:

> The negotiators for the Enron Corporation, the lead bidder in an American consortium, have been shadowed and assisted by a startling array of Government agencies. In a carefully planned assault, the State and Energy Departments pressed the firms' case on behalf of Enron, General Electric, and Bechtel. The American ambassador to India, Frank G. Wisner, constantly cajoled Indian officials. The Secretary of Energy, Hazel O'Leary, brought in delegations of other executives...to make the point that more American investment is in the wings if the conditions are right.[37]

If not, no money.

With economic and political muscle such as this, no wonder Enron earned a reputation for being the bad boy on the global corporate block. All this despite the secret Enron Code of Ethics (2000) in which Lay wrote, "we are responsible for conducting the business affairs of the Company in accordance with all applicable laws and in a moral and honest manner."[38]

In 1997, Rebecca Mark, then Chairperson of Enron Development Corporation, the overseas arm of the operations, told the Indian press that "Enron's reputation is being attacked, and we do not do business under the table." That she needed to say this tells us that the fat cats and their running dogs smelt a rat somewhere, a parasite somewhat different to those who gave in to the USAID-type threats and sold out their countries. Around this time, Enron International, which oversaw the Enron Development Corporation, held a gala event for over a thousand employees at the Del Lago Resort outside Houston. The event reveals much about the culture and aims of global corporations. Rebecca Mark and Joseph Sutton, another executive, entered one of the morning sessions on a Harley-Davidson motorcycle (a "Fat Boy" perhaps?), dressed in leather jackets and chaps, as the sound system blasted "Eye of the Tiger": Mark told the troops that "the international unit was unstoppable." The divisions then did a skit on their regions. The people responsible for Enron in India entered their section on a horse and an elephant—throwbacks to the British Raj, perhaps?[39]

In the late 1990s, New York-based Human Rights Watch went to India to cover the Enron debacle and they produced a report on human rights violations that took place around the time of this Houston event and of Mark's comment about Enron's reputation. Many people around the world began to use the word Enron to refer to all that was despicable about corporations, in much the same way Union Carbide was spoken of in the 1980s following the Bhopal disaster. Ruthless firms that entered insecure economies to make a profit. But in terms of image there were two Enrons, and the U.S. media did not care much about this one with the reputation of international bad boy. Instead, they concentrated on the Enron of the stock market, and of the prophet of profit, Ken Lay. All this would change at the end of 2001, when Enron's stock fell, and when the ruthlessness came back home when a different kind of rat began to talk to the feds.

Houston, We Have a Problem...

The forty-story Enron tower was rocked late last year as news filtered through the ranks that a senior employee turned into a rat. But the rat, it turns out, did not go to the federal regulators at that time, but to the prophet of profit himself. This was the rebellion of the minions against the managers in the name of the infallible big boss, as unlikely as a rebellion of the peasants of India against the colonial officials in the name of Victoria, a rebellion of the serfs of Russia against the barons in the name of the Tsar. Vice President Sherron S. Watkins, now called a hero, told her boss, Ken Lay, in August 2001 that Enron may "implode in a wave of accountancy scandals." And if anyone, she would know. Watkins came to Enron from Arthur Andersen, one of the five mighty accounting firms that also sent Enron its treasurer and general counsel.

Rule by fear applies not only to relationships between corporations and governments, but apparently with employees as well. Ms. Watkins stood before the House Energy and Commerce Committee on 14 February 2002 and had the following revealing interchange with Greg Ganske (Republican-Iowa):

> **Ganske:** Were you worried about your own personal safety?
>
> **Watkins:** At times, I mean, just because the company was a little bit radio-silent back to me, so I didn't know how they were taking my memos or the investigation.
>
> **Ganske:** Why would you be worried about your personal safety?
>
> **Watkins:** Because it was the seventh-largest company in America.
>
> **Ganske:** And you were dealing with a really powerful person...
>
> **Watkins:** Yes.
>
> **Ganske:** ...and a really powerful company.

When she stood before Congressman Ganske, Watkins must have had Enron Vice Chairman Clifford Baxter on her mind. Baxter died on 25 January 2002 in the wake of the Enron scandal. His death has been called a suicide, but this verdict does not seem conclusive, perhaps giving ample reason for Watkins' fear of her own safety. Baxter had resigned from his post in May 2001 after he expressed his anger to Jeffery Skilling at the accountancy practices of Chief Financial Officer Andrew Fastow and at Skilling's complicity in these matters. In a press interview on 9 February, Baxter's lawyer, J. C. Nickens, said that just before Baxter's death he told Nickens that he believed "people were going through his mail, that they were going through his garbage, that people were showing up at his home late at night, and making phone calls that were unwelcome." When Baxter was found slumped over in his car, Nickens was in the process of creating the ground rules for his client's testimony to Congress. Constable Hal Werlein claimed that Baxter was alive when the police found him, but the official report says that he was already dead. The police in Sugarland, home of the Republican Majority Whip, Congressman Tom DeLay, neglected to send Baxter's body for an autopsy, and it was only the intercession of Baxter's family that forced an official autopsy. While the mainstream media accepted the coroner's suicide verdict, many continue to raise questions, including Police Chief Ernest Taylor (who noted, "We are not in any way saying we disagree with the medical examiner's findings. We are simply saying we want to make sure we cross all the Ts and dot all the Is in order to be absolutely sure that nothing is overlooked in this investigation"[40]).

Two important points emerged from the scrutiny of this death. First, CBS News (on 10 April 2002) interviewed Bill Wagner, a former homicide detective, who showed that while Baxter may have committed suicide, a fair amount of evidence points to murder. "Murder can be made to look like a suicide," he said. "Someone who is knowledgeable about forensics can very well have the ability to stage a murder, commit a murder and stage it to look as if it was a suicide, understanding what the police are going to be looking for." Coroner Cyril Wecht, on the same program, said that the ammunition that killed Baxter, known as "rat shot," "cannot be easily or readily traced back to the gun from which it was fired." "It's not as frequently used by people for any reason. It's not the type of ammunition one finds in guns. It has a specific purpose: shooting at snakes and rodents in order to get a distribution pattern of the small pellets contained within the nose portion of the bullet. It's not something that a person is likely to have and to use if they intended to kill themselves." Second, the coroner, Dr. Joyce M. Carter ruled *within a day* that Baxter killed himself, but it took her almost a month to rule that Andrea Yates drowned her five children in their bathtub. Right after the Yates' drowning, Carter told the *Houston Chronicle*, "It appears to have been drowning of all five victims. We're going to continue doing a thorough workup. We've x-rayed all the bodies as is customary with children. We will still be awaiting the results of the toxicology texts to make sure that nothing was given to the children."[51] These lingering doubts raise questions about the lucky break for some Enron executives that this insider decided to sleep with the fishes.[42]

Baxter is not the only Enron "suicide." James Daniel Watkins from Arthur Andersen is said to have committed suicide in November 2001. Mr. Watkins' body was discovered on 1 December, two weeks after he had been reported missing. He was found in the back seat of his locked car, shot by a .38 handgun that lay near his right hand. The authorities first announced that they felt that suspicious circumstances surrounded the death, but later changed their verdict to suicide. Wes Riber, Chief Deputy Coroner for Douglas County, Colorado, said that the body had been in the car for a long time. The coroner conducted a delayed autopsy and switched the verdict from foul play to suicide. The police, by Riber's hesitancy, appeared to be unhappy with the switch.[43] Watkins, no relation to the Enron Vice President of the same name, worked in the Denver office of Andersen as a telecommunications consultant, and had, reportedly, been working on the file of Anderson's client, Enron.

Then, as matters got sticky for the oil powers in Houston,

Charles Dana Rice shot himself in the head on 2 June 2002. Rice was the treasurer for El Paso Corp., a natural gas supplier that moved to energy trading on Enron's heels. While there is no SEC investigation of El Paso, the state of California charged the company with collusion to fix prices in 2000-2001, a case pending before a Federal Energy Regulatory Commission judge. The Houston police announced that Rice "died of a self-inflicted gunshot wound" and coroner Dr. Joye Carter told the press that he had "an apparent gunshot wound to the head." But, unlike her urgency to get the Baxter case settled, Dr. Carter noted, "We cannot confirm suicide at this time until a full examination is completed." The media reported and adopted El Paso's own position, which was that Rice's suicide led from his own kidney problems and not from anything at work. The Associated Press repeated this assertion twice in its widely run story: "Wall Street executives who dealt with El Paso said it was widely known that Rice had suffered from heart and kidney problems."[44]

To be an executive in an energy firm is a public health hazard.

Enron is not alone in the power industry to have executives die under mysterious circumstances. Journalist Greg Palast recounts the April 1989 death of Jake Horton, senior vice president of Gulf Power (a subsidiary of Southern Company, and a competitor with Enron). Present in the region during an investigation of Southern's finances, Palast offers us the following insight:

> Horton apparently knew about some of his company's less-than-kosher accounting practices; and he had no doubts about its illegal campaign contributions to Florida politicians—he'd made the payments himself. But unlike Baxter, who took the money and ran, in April 1989, Horton decided to blow the whistle, confront his bosses and go to state officials. He demanded

and received use of the company's jet to go and con-
front Southern's board of directors. Ten minutes after
take-off, the jet exploded. While the investigation into
the plane crash was inconclusive, the company's CEO
believed his death was suicide. He told the BBC: 'I
guess poor Jake saw no other way out.' Ultimately,
Southern pleaded guilty to the charges related to the
illegal payments.[45]

Most of what we have on the Horton case is innuendo,
mainly because press coverage of it was insufficient and the official report is threadbare. While I hate the invocation of culture,
the U.S. Centers for Disease Control does not report an overwhelming rate of suicide among U.S. executives, whereas in
contemporary Japan, there is a suicide crisis to match the economic one. During the 1990s, the suicide rate of Japanese executives increased dramatically, with a jump of over sixteen percent between 1996 and 1997 (during the Asian financial crisis).
In 1999, over thirty-three thousand people committed suicide
in Japan, twice the U.S. rate, and the government proposed to
set up a ministry to deal with the problem at hand.[46] If the suicides took place in Japan, one might be less skeptical, even as
the customs of life without honor (*ome-ome-to*) are now not as
they once were. That the Enron suicides came at such oppor-
tune moments should, at least, give us pause. It is reasonable
that a vice president of a firm may commit suicide to hide from
the shame of the collapse, but it is too convenient that it was
the whistle-blowers who went down. Meanwhile those who
made their killings went on in all arrogance with their lives.

These events in the world of oil invite comparisons with
John Grisham's *The Firm* (1991) about the world of law. Then a
member of the Mississippi House of Representatives, Grisham
wrote this novel about the Faustian bargain of young Mitchell
McDeere (played by Tom Cruise in Sydney Pollack's film version) who sold his soul to a law firm for the enormous annual

salary of $120,000, the perks and a BMW. Mitch discovers that his income came to him because his Memphis law partnership (Bendi, Lambert and Locke) does business with such firms as .the Morolto family, a mafia operation. Mitch also finds that any dissent with the corrupt practices leads to murder. So he goes to the FBI with care and preparation. That Grisham, a distant cousin of Bill Clinton, needs the bad guys to be the mafia is perhaps a bit unnecessary, because there are so many blue-blood firms, such as Enron and Southern, that bear within their crypts at least one or two tales that would chill those of us who live our innocent lives on the outskirts of power. Mitch, our hero, makes it out alive in the book and film, but we can only imagine how many suicides and accidents take place on the road to the local regulatory agency.[47]

Baxter-Watkins-Horton don't fit the profile of the suicide victim: they are generally under 24 or over 65, with one-fifth of high school students having considered suicide and one in thirteen having tried it. Older adults account for a fifth of all suicides that take place. Since 1933, those over 65 have the highest rate of all ages. While more women attempt suicide than men, the latter are eighty percent more successful at putting an end to their lives. But most importantly, those who commit suicide tend to be from the farm states, people who have lost their livelihood and moved from the edge of subsistence into the gloom of poverty. The rate of suicides among executives is low, even though there is a tendency toward the convenient "suicide" during the outbreak of scandals (Whitewater had its Vince Foster). You do the math.

That Watkins told Congress that she feared for her safety gives some credibility to this analysis. Was her fear realistic? It is hard to say, because she just might be a paranoid person. Nevertheless, the tales of Baxter-Watkins-Horton and the fiction of Grisham indicate that *perhaps* Sherron Watkins was not delusional, that *perhaps* such things happen on the continent of sleaze. Regardless of whether these were actual murders, it is a telling statement about corporate culture that a high-ranking executive with access to the pinnacle of power feared for her safety.

The rats sleep with the fishes, as the cats and dogs run unimpeded.

We Bring Evil Things to Light

On 20 February 2002, U.S. President GWB joined by National Security Advisor Condeleeza Rice stood at the front-line of one of the three legs of his "Axis of Evil" (North Korea, but further afield Iran and Iraq). He carried with him a satellite picture of the peninsula taken at night. In the picture, South Korea is suffused with light, while in the North there are only a few bright spots near the capital, Pyongyang. GWB drew an important lesson from this picture as he stood beside an uncomfortable South Korean President Kim Dae-Jung (the architect of the Sunshine Policy to bring the two sides of Korea closer together): "Kim Dae-Jung has put forward a vision that can illuminate the whole peninsula. We want all the Koreans to live in the light."

Light and darkness, evil and good—these are the parameters of GWB ethics. On the night of 11 September 2001, after the commercial airliners became horrendous cruise missiles, GWB spoke then too about Good and Evil, about how the United States embodied the Good and the terrorists (in the person of bin Laden) embodied Evil. And now the same tone with North Korea, Iran and Iraq. The GWB ethics is hardly Christian. Instead, it resembles an early 4th century Manichean belief in old Persia that held its ground against a Catholicism that had only just vanquished Mithraism, the ancient faith of the Iranians. Mani, from whom the faith is named, disregarded the complexity of human life and of its concomitant ethical dilemmas. His interest was to preserve the Good against the

Evil, and he literally believed that the dark was evil and that the light was good. Standing on the edge of the Demilitarized Zone or else in the Oval Office, GWB is Mani redux, drawing from an ancient Iranian philosopher king to take an anti-Iranian stance.

And when Bush says that the North is in darkness, who better than U.S. power companies to come and straighten things out, to literally bring lights and make the Good flourish.

Regardless of what improprieties the Bush Presidency may have committed on Enron's behalf once the Supreme Court installed it, we do know that the DNA of the Bush clan is all over the crime scene at the House of Enron.

The story begins with the patriarch, the senior George Bush, whose Tanglewood home in Houston is just down the road from Lay's River Oaks home. Just before he left office, GHB signed the 1992 Energy Policy Act, a law that weakened the power of regional utility firms and local government to the benefit of energy traders like Enron. An aspect of the 1992 law that has not been given much attention is that it resulted in a spate of mergers among what are known as investor-owned utilities (IOUs): twenty-six mergers in the 1990s, with sixteen also in the works.[48] More mergers have meant that mega-firms like Enron have dominated parts of the market that, despite unbundling, give them power over the entire industry—areas such as wholesale distribution. The 1992 law was the first salvo against regulation of the energy sector on behalf of Enron. Of course, GHB helped secure Enron deals in Kuwait (via James Baker and the sons of Bush, Neil and Marvin) and in Argentina (via Neil, after GHB's friend Carlos Menem came to power in 1990). The patriarch is not outside this relationship, even as it was left to the sons to make the most of it.

Could all this presidential help with regulations on mergers, Kuwait and Argentina, have any bearing on what Enron did for son George W. Bush? By most counts, Enron gave close to $2

million for GWB's political career, as he moved from governor
to president. His Texas campaigns in 1994 and 1998 won him
$312,500, while his presidential run got him $113,800. Investor
Warren Buffet may have made the practice of fractional ownership of jets famous. But who needs fractional ownership when
you have Enron? The company let GWB use its corporate jets
at least eight times. Proving that Enron was a company you can
count on, it helped Bush swing the election through $10,500 to
the Bush-Cheney Recount Fund. Enron then followed that
with $300,000 for the gala celebration of democracy embodied
in presidential inauguration festivities. About $1.2-$1.8 million
entered the coffers of the Republican Party from Enron, a sum
that dwarfs the amount taken by the Democrats from the energy firm. Nevertheless, 259 members of Congress, more than half
the elected representatives of the people, are beholden to
Enron's brand of generosity.

It would be tempting but misleading to argue that GWB
and Cheney changed their views because of the money. Rather,
that money went toward propelling proponents of the free market to seize power. Once that was accomplished, GWB-Cheney
hired the best "free market" proponents they could find—from
Enron. Among them: Lawrence Lindsey, a former Enron consultant, is the White House's economics advisor (he took a policy proposal from Enron and imbedded it into the campaign
platform); Robert Zoellick, who served on Enron's advisory
council, is the U.S. Trade Representative; Lewis Libby, a major
Enron stockholder, is Cheney's Chief of Staff; Thomas White,
an Enron executive for a decade, is Secretary of Army (and disposed to deregulation of the power sector owned by the Army);
Marc Racicot, Enron's Washington lobbyist, is Republican
Party National Chairman; Karl Rove, Senior Adviser to the
President, who owned up to $250,000 in Enron stock, met fre-
quently with Ken Lay to talk about regulation issues. Only the
White case became an embarrassment. The "General" (as he

was known while an Enron executive) continued as Secretary of the Army to be in touch with Enron officials and to hold options on Enron stock, just at the point when he was in a position of power to offer Enron prestigious Pentagon contracts.[49]

These positions of authority do not exhaust the power wielded by Enron in the administration. Ken Lay was GWB's chief energy advisor during the California power crisis, and Lay turns out to be one of the eighteen energy executives who formed GWB's National Energy Task Force in 2001. These meetings helped the ultra-secretive Cheney fashion the energy policy of the White House. When challenged about the impropriety of these meetings (especially given that the eighteen firms are part of the top twenty-five contributors to the Republican Party), Frederick Palmer of Peabody Energy (the world's largest coal mining firm owned by Lehman Brothers) moved to defuse the bad publicity. He told the media, "We're all on the supply side—the electric utilities, the coal companies—and the energy plan is basically a supply side plan, but that's not the result of back room deals or lobbying the vice president of the United States. People running the United States government now are from the energy industry, and they understand it and believe in increasing the energy supply, and contribution money has nothing to do with it."[50] You couldn't wish for a more naked display of power and privilege.

One of the recommendations of the Task Force was that the government dismantle the monopoly control of electricity transmission networks, a feint that would at the time give Enron virtual monopoly control over power at the middleman juncture. GWB considered Lay for Commerce Secretary and Energy Secretary, but he bowed to political pressure on two scores. First, since Spencer Abraham lost his re-election bid in Michigan, he was a perfect candidate for the Energy post in the multi-racist Bush cabinet—being of Arab ancestry, Abraham enabled the oily Texan to strengthen his already deep ties with the oil sheikhs. Besides, Abraham is part of the Enron family. In his failed 2000 Senate race, Enron plied $10,500 into his campaign coffers. Second, though Lay did not join the cabinet, he was part of the shadow government. Kenny Boy and others in Enron interviewed several candidates to fill empty spots on the Federal Energy Regulation Commission (FERC), the main regulatory body that oversees most of Enron's business interests.[51] Forget guarding: the fox became owner of the henhouse. GWB took his backwards position on the Kyoto greenhouse gas treaty (seeking to water it down until it became meaningless and then backing out when that failed) under pressure from Enron and five of its friends (Royal Dutch/Shell, BP, Cinergy, AEP and Entergy). And, if this is not enough, Enron received an outright tax break from the government. Even though Enron has not paid taxes from 1996 to 2000, it received a net tax rebate of $381 million—$278 million in 2000 alone thanks to GWB's tax cut. If the loopholes had not existed, Enron's place in the thirty five percent bracket would have earned the treasury $625 million in this period.[52] The media has played up the amount of campaign contributions. But stacked up against the hundreds of millions in tax breaks and hundreds of millions more in regulatory advantages these mere millions in contributions, or what might be more appropriately called users fees, are very, very low. U.S. democracy is a great value at these prices.

GWB's most enormous service to Enron came during California's power crisis. In 1996, the California legislature removed all regulation over the purchase and sale of electricity in the state's wholesale market. Enron moved in and began to manipulate the wholesale price now that it did not have to trade electricity in a regulated commodities exchange. Public Citizen notes that, "Despite the fact that Enron did not own a single power plant in the state, its control of the venue in which electricity was bought and sold placed Enron in almost total control of California's energy supply."[53] With Enron came two other Houston firms (Dynegy and Reliant Energy), one from North Carolina (Duke Energy), and the four of them quickly earned the name "the Confederate Cartel" from Daniel Berman, co-founder of the Coalition for Local Power, based in Davis, California.[54] While Enron led the cartel, Dynergy and Reliant did not innocently go along with the fraud even as Enron's mid-2002 "jailhouse confession" has led most politicians after it and not its confederates.[55] California Public Utilities Commission's president, Loretta Lynch, told Congress in mid-April 2002 that Enron should be prepared for legal action because its trades in late 2000 "were sham transactions."[56] Certainly from Enron's internal documents we hear only of its shenanigans through its memorable nicknames for its slimy trades: Fat Boy, Death Star, and Get Shorty. Anyone with a passing familiarity with popular culture will know that "Fat Boy" is the name of the 1990 silver Harley-Davidson motorcycle (named, one might argue, after Fat Man and Little Boy, the two nuclear devices the U.S. used over Japan; and here, combined to signal Harley's attempt to thwart the boom in the sale of Japan-based transnational's motorcycles), "Death Star" is Darth Vader's flag-ship from Star Wars, and "Get Shorty" is perhaps named for the 1995 movie about mobsters and loan sharks in the film industry. Each name intimates a macho hustle, something in which Enron and its confederates specialized.

During the height of the imbroglio between the cartel and the government in 2001, Reliant's head, Joe Bob Perkins, came down hard on the administration. "Reliant hopes the Governor and others will stop these baseless accusations and focus on true solutions to California's energy shortage. We are now being singled out because we believe in an open market." In April 2001, Duke Energy offered to reduce premiums on its price for electricity if the state dropped its investigations of the cartel and if it did not reintroduce regulation of the energy sector. Its confidential proposal noted, "Governor will continue to indicate that the California crisis is an aberration due to tion of Gov. Wilson, not a necessary consequenc tion, and will not advocate scrapping deregulation in wholesale power markets."[57] Governor Davis' administration did not proceed with the negotiation, but on 2 May 2001, California's Lt. Governor Cruz M. Bustamante filed a civil lawsuit against the cartel. He claimed that the cartel systematically manipulated the energy market and set California toward bankruptcy. "A cartel of out of state generators has been holding us hostage through a practice of illegal and unfair price-fixing," he said.[58] In 2001 lawmakers recognized the systematic nature of the cartel, and even as California's regulators and law-makers kept up the pressure on the other companies, Washington DC and the media focused on Enron as the scapegoat to preserve the system intact.

At the Congressional hearings in mid-April, David Freeman, chairman of the California Power Authority, said, "We must recognize that the so-called invisible hand of Adam Smith was Enron and their fellow gougers picking the pockets of Californians to the tune of billions of dollars. Prices were skyrocketing in California in late 2000 and early 2001 as a direct result of Enron's influence and participation." Loretta Lynch of the Public Utilities Commission explained, "Enron was selling the same megawatts back and forth to itself, causing the price to rise with each sale, all under the rules it had helped to create. The selling back and forth also created the illusion of an active, volatile market."[59] The practice Enron followed in this instance is called "megawatt laundering." In late 2000, as energy prices rose, California imposed price caps at $250 per megawatt-hour. The companies beat the regulation through a loophole that said if there is a shortage of power, then the utility can buy power out of state at a higher price. Enron bought electricity in California, *exported* it, sold it to another of its cutout firms, bought it back at a higher price and then sold it to the utility.

To prove that shortages exist, Enron and its cartel (along with the utilities) produced blackouts, mainly to blackmail the legislature. Credit Suisse First Boston sent a memo to its clients in 2001 reassuring them that the blackouts did not mean a catastrophe in the energy markets, but they were "intended to soften up the legislature and the voters to the need for rate increases." When the memo entered the business press, Morgan Stanley Dean Witter upgraded Pacific Gas & Electric's rating to "outperform."[60]

There should be no doubt about Enron's leadership in the crisis, but others joined Enron to bilk California's ratepayers. Pacific Gas & Electric (PG&E) as well as Southern California Edison had to buy electricity from the cartel and then resell it to consumers. Even as the two firms went into massive debt, they transferred the costs onto the public, first with high rates and second with governmental bailouts. While both PG&E and Southern California painted themselves as victims of the cartel, neither suffered on the Big Board. PG&E created a barricade between the loss-making utility in California and PG&E National Energy Group, this to protect the latter's thirty power plants in ten states. The National Energy Group's energy is sold to PG&E's utility company at inflated rates, a pattern that Enron did not invent and that has not died with its demise. Edison International, who reported to the Securities and Exchange Commission in the early days of 2001 that it had $1.9 billion of liquid cash, owns Edison. The managers of PG&E and Edison did not get hoodwinked. They participated in the fleecing of California.

The blackouts were notable after December 2000 when the federal law (pushed by Senator Gramm) allowed Enron to trade electricity without any disclosure of its practices. Enron's wholesale services posted an enormous increase in profits, from $12 billion the first quarter of 2000 to $48.4 billion in the first quarter of 2001, this entirely thanks to the Gramm law.

Meanwhile, with each day that went by, Enron took California for $12 billion in excess charges, and in mid-2002, Governor Gray Davis noted, "About $30 billion was extorted from this state. Those who claimed that there was no price manipulation here were just plain wrong."[61] Enron and the Confederate Cartel indulged in "direct access contracts" that allowed them to charge California's utilities for all the highly-priced power that it could muster; the excess power that California did not use had to be sold back to the cartel at a low rate; this power was then sold to big businesses at a cut price. The ratepayer, then, subsidizes big business.

Setting a new standard for the word "audacity," the protector of Enron, Phil Gramm told the press, "As [Californians] suffer the consequences of their own feckless policies, political leaders in California blame power companies, deregulation and everyone but themselves, and the inevitable call is now being heard for a federal bail-out. I intend to do everything in my power to require those who valued environmental extremism and interstate protectionism more than common sense and market freedom to solve their electricity crisis without short-circuiting taxpayers in other states."[62] Gramm evoked the specter of "environmental extremism," to explain the blackouts. But the problem was not supply. California had already built ample power plants during the 1990s to generate 1200MW of electricity. The problem was the distribution crisis created by Enron so that it might scalp California for the maximum profit.

These events reveal precisely the nature of "free markets." Big players get help from politicians to design a system where they can win. When the system is implemented, the big guys quickly monopolize supply. This is the logical outcome of completely unfettered competition. Eventually, only a small handful of competitors survive, making it possible for them to reduce or eliminate the "free market" so that profits for the few can sky-rocket.

This dynamic did not pass unnoticed. When federal regulator (and a fan of the market himself) Curtis Hebert began to make noises about the crisis, the Bush White House, with input from Lay, reassigned him. Bush replaced Hebert with a Texan, the notorious de-regulator Pat Wood III.[63] In February 2001, GWB, following energy guru Ken Lay, refused to cap the electricity prices in California, preferring to let Enron feast. On 29 May 2001, Bush noted that price controls would lead to "more serious shortages and even higher prices," a position backed by Enron but not even by neoclassical economists.

The level of arrogance matched the level of greed. On 14 June 2001, CEO Skilling was in a playful mood at the Strategic Directions 2001 Conference held by the Reuters Group and Tibco Software. "You know what the difference is between the State of California and the Titanic?" he asked. "This is being webcast, and I know I'm going to regret this, but at least the lights were on when the Titanic went down." During a lecture just seven days later, as if in response to his heartless comment, the Biotic Baking Brigade tossed a pie in Skilling's face. Protests rocked California, as unions and consumers, leftists and centrists, and all manner of everyday Americans came out onto the street to call Bush and Cheney "Fossil Fools" and demand, "We Want Our Money Back." These "rolling demonstrations" in response to the rolling blackouts had an impact, as did the reasonably strong pressure from Governor Gray Davis. Eventually, FERC regulators prevailed and capped the prices on 19 June 2001. The market, finally, calmed down and California's energy crisis ended (spot prices dropped by eighty percent), even as the rates charged to the customers continued at an all-time high. Some say that Enron's troubles began with the action of the FERC, because from here Enron lost its vast profits in dollars, went into a tailspin, lost its CEO (Skilling quit in August) and then moved to the subsequent collapse.

If we think that the powers learnt anything from the scandal, pay attention to the fact that one of California's main utility firms, PG&E, paid its senior executives bonuses totalling $64 million for their services during 2001, the year of the rolling blackouts and the subsequent declaration of bankruptcy by the utility. The board increased the rewards by $14 million from 2000, an indication that, however bad the performance of a firm, the fat cats must be well fed.

California is only GWB's most recent service for Enron. His relationship goes back to the old days. In 1988, with daddy in the White House, GWB phoned the Argentinean Minister of Public Works and Services, Rodolfo Terragno, to "exert some influence" on behalf of Enron. GWB failed at that bid, mainly because Terragno belonged to a regime not yet sold-out to the neoliberal ideology that set Argentina on the path to bankruptcy along with Enron. More on that later.

GWB is not the only sleazy brother in the picture. There is Marvin, Neil and Jeb to contend with. In 1993, Marvin and Neil accompanied their father, the ex-President, to Kuwait where he received honors for saving that country of 2.2 million (with the citizenry only twenty-eight percent of this number) from the wrath of Saddam Hussein. (Bear in mind the irony here. It was GHB's ambassador, April Glaspie, who gave Saddam Hussein the green light to invade Kuwait in the first place.) With them was former Secretary of State, James Baker, who was on the Enron payroll. After the father left with his award, the sons and Baker went to work with the Kuwaiti powers to lobby on behalf of an Enron contract. In alliance with Britain's Midland Electricity—they formed the Wing Group and sought to rebuild the Shuiaba North power plant, destroyed during the 1991 Gulf War (or as Tariq Ali puts it, the Third Oil War).[64] With an installed capacity of 400MW, the Shuiaba North plant in the mid-1990s would have added to Kuwait's electricity capacity (9,280MW), but its peak electricity demand at the time was only half of that in the summer of 1995 (4550MW). Perhaps this was Kuwait's way to payback the U.S. for its military assistance. Enron offered 11 cents per kw/hour as its price, whereas Deutsche Babcock asked for 6 cents per kw/hour (this in the context of the Kuwaiti rate which was half a cent per kw/hour). The Bush Boys and Baker won Enron the contract.[65]

Follow this chain of logic for a moment and see how deeply implicated the United States is in the rot of our world: the U.S. taxpayers fund the military; the Pentagon authorizes contractors to sell Iraq weapons during the 1980s and Bush's ambassador, backed by the Pentagon, leads Saddam Hussein to believe he has the green light to invade Kuwait; Bush attacks Iraq and a state of continuous war exists in our own time. The hapless taxpayer once more funds the Gulf War and the enormous deployment of troops that continues to create congestion in Arabia and its environs;[66] Kuwait now responds to this by its award of an energy contract not to the U.S. taxpayer, but to a private, transnational corporation. Taxpayers front the costs of warfare, but private corporations reap the benefits.

By Kuwait, Neil was a veteran player. Neil is familiar with the world of scandals, being one of the poster children of the Savings and Loan collapse and bailout during the 1980s. As boss of Silverado S&L, Neil Bush loaned money to Ken Good of Good International ($32 million), some of which ($100,000) he used in a joint venture with JNB Explorations, a considerable number of shares of which was owned by Good. Neil Bush also loaned $106 million to Bill Walters, another JNB shareholder. Walters defaulted on the entire amount. The NB in JNB is Neil Bush—meaning that the CEO of Silverado was lending huge sums (about $100 million) to his own corporation. The "Explorations" in the company's moniker referred to the thirty oil wells that the firm successfully drilled *without striking oil*. When Silverado inevitably collapsed, taxpayers shelled out $1 billion to clean up that corporate toxic spill. In keeping with the free market spirit of his kin, Neil Bush remarked after the scandal broke, "I'm not going to be bullied by an overzealous agency of the United States government."[67]

So much for Enron's agent Neil Bush, first working in Kuwait (with his brother Marvin and James Baker) and then later in Argentina. In the latter case, Neil flew down the day after Carlos Menem took power to play golf with the neoliberal leader, bringing him regards from GHB and to make sure Menem's people signed on with Enron. Not only did Neil help Enron swing the deal in Argentina, but in the spirit of "never give in," he also tried to funnel $900,000 of loans from Silverado to drill oil there—never give in… But, again, more on that later.

Which brings us to Jeb Bush, the current governor of the Sunshine state. Jeb is also no stranger to scandal. In 1986, Jeb worked as the leasing agent for a Cuban con man named Camilo Padreda who had just built a commercial building with $1.4 million in Department of Housing and Urban Development (HUD) loans. Like Bush's brother, Padreda had gutted an S&L, this one in McAllen, Texas. But unlike Neil, he faced a federal indictment of embezzlement and his partner was charged with the unholy trinity of drug smuggling, money laundering and gun-running. When caught for his HUD fraud, Padreda pled guilty and disappeared from history. Jeb Bush was undeterred by this encounter with corruption. In the late 1980s, Jeb Bush hooked up with Miguel Recarey, another con man. Jeb's job was to lobby the Department of Health and Human Services (HHS) to exempt Recarey's HMO from regulatory oversight. When Recarey won the waiver, thanks in no part to Jeb's work in the legislature, the HMO took in a vast amount of Medicare patients. In 1986, the HMO collected in excess of $30 million/month from Medicare. In total, Medicare paid Recarey's HMO $1 billion. When HHS found that Recarey's HMO was in the midst of widespread fraud (false invoices, embezzlement, excess charges), Recarey took the first flight to Venezuela.[68] Unscathed, Jeb moved on with tens of thousands of dollars. In light of this history, one can only recall with a sense of irony Jeb's later consternation over his wife, Columba's failed attempt to smuggle $19,000 worth of goods past customs.[69] Hers was a mere infraction addressed by the payment of fines. But she got caught.

When Jeb put out feelers expressing interest in the governorship of Florida, Enron opened its campaign coffers. Jeb had made money from Enron just a few years before he entered politics. In 1995 he invested $92,000 in Enron Liquid Pipeline and ten months later he sold his shares for a $7,100 profit. A modest amount to sweeten the Bush-Enron connection. Meanwhile, the real money began to move between Enron and the Florida Bushes at a new level. Between 1995 and 2001, Enron donated $420,000 to Florida's election campaigns with eighty percent to Republican candidates. In 1998, Enron donated $765,000 to the Florida Republican Party to elect Bush, with an additional $200,000 to the Bush campaign directly (and with $6500 from Enron executives). These vast funds pushed Bush into the governorship. Enron was not to be disappointed. First, Jeb appointed Ken Lay's old time friend Walter Revell to chair the Florida 2020 Energy Study Commission. The real favor, and scandal, came in 2001, when Enron shares began to slide. Perhaps to boost the share price as a favor to the prophet of profit, Jeb Bush authorized the pension fund for Florida's state employees to put its money into Enron. Yet another means for working Americans to help the rich: following Jeb's move, the fund lost $334 million.[70]

But before we leave the Bush clan, let's return to GWB, a man whose dirty business deals have faded away even as Kenny Boy's firm collapses all around us. In 1986, Harken Energy merged with an almost defunct firm called Spectrum 7. The only asset that Spectrum 7 held was GWB on the payroll. He had already earned Spectrum 7 a good deal from Enron—on 16 September 1986, Enron announced a new well north of Midland, Texas, that began to produce 24,000 cubic feet of natural gas and 411 barrels of oil per day. Spectrum 7 held a percentage of this Enron-owned well and it benefited from Enron's success. Enron, in other words, was in cahoots with GWB long before the 1990s, and certainly the arrangement helped GWB in the oil business.[71] Things don't stop there. When the Harken-Spectrum 7 deal went through, GWB joined the board of Harken, received 1.5 million shares and a large salary as consultant to the firm. GWB, at this time, was at GHB's side, helping him run for President. In 1990, tiny Harken won a large contract over the giant Amoco to do some offshore drilling in Bahrain. Even as much of the media continues to deny any wrongdoing from GWB,[72] the facts are this: that a Harken insider told *Mother Jones*, "Hell that's why [GWB's] on the damn board. You say, 'By the way, the president's son sits on our board.' You use that. There's nothing wrong with that." The Bahrain contract raised the value of Harken's stock.

In June 1990, GWB sold sixty percent of his holdings (212,140 shares) and earned a tidy $848,500. A week later Harken's quarterly report showed a loss of $23 million. Good timing! A month later, on 20 August 1990, Saddam Hussein and the U.S. decided to part company and go to war. Harken's stock collapsed from $4 (when GWB sold) to $2.37 on 20 of August and then downwards. But GWB walked away a rich man. The sale enabled GWB to become a multimillionaire and enter the high-stakes game of gas and oil. In 1991, the SEC prepared a document that showed that GWB had violated security laws that govern insider stock sales. By not reporting the sale to the SEC, Bush had violated federal law.[73] GWB moved on.

It is an interesting comment on our culture to see what constitutes a crime worthy of note. At the close of GWB's campaign for president, a drunk driving violation in Maine that had occurred many years back was exposed, causing a major stir. The media discussed at length whether this indicated poor judgment. That was, justifiably, major news. But there was virtually no media discussion of his clearly good judgment in violating SEC laws to enrich himself. Such behavior from our rulers merits little mention.

So it goes.

And Then There is His Sidekick, Caveman Dick

After 9/11, Vice President Dick Cheney went underground. This has been a convenient ploy: and it helped when the General Accounting Office (GAO) started to hound Cheney about the energy briefing he had held earlier in the year. Mr. Secret Vice President Man, underground and untouchable.

Cheney is the corporate connection, as if GWB isn't intertwined enough, the CEO of a cabinet filled with CEOs. He comes to the cabinet from Halliburton, a firm that deals in global oil services. Cheney converted both his role as Secretary of Defense during GHB's tenure and his connections created during the Gulf War in that position into profits for Halliburton. Once Cheney left the control room for the cartel room he used his Pentagon links to move Halliburton on the list of corporations doing businesses with the Defense Department from seventy-third to eighteenth. As head of Halliburton, he saw to it that $3.8 billion per year transferred from the taxpayers to Halliburton via the Pentagon. His links to the emirates enabled Cheney as Halliburton CEO to win the contract to quell the oil fires in Kuwait. Making the charitable connection, his links to the UN enabled Halliburton to refurbish Iraq's oil refineries through the oil-for-food program. Even as Cheney remains on the team of the hawks eager to bomb Iraq as the irreconcilable enemy, Cheney responded to those who criticized this deal with, "The good Lord didn't see fit to put oil and gas only where there are democratic regimes friendly to the United States."[74]

Jordan Green of the Institute for Southern Studies and Dana Milbank of the *Washington Post* make a still more serious charge against Cheney, Halliburton and the Pentagon.[75] In the fall of 2001, both Halliburton and Enron lost value on the stock market, both availed themselves of Arthur Andersen's special skills, and both seemed poised for trouble. Andersen, it turns out, helped Halliburton boost its books by postponing losses and counting uncollected money as revenue. So-called "unbilled receivables" allowed Halliburton to carry $234 million in disputed claims in 2001 (in 2000, the firm carried $113 million by the same strategy). Halliburton and Andersen changed the rules on "unbilled receivables" while Cheney was its CEO. When Cheney moved to Bush's side, his second-in-command, David Lesar took over the firm. Before Lesar joined Halliburton, he was a senior partner at Andersen.[76]

Additionally, Halliburton was in the midst of potentially lethal lawsuits over its use of asbestos.

Then, miraculously, two things happened. First, rumors began to float in January of 2002 that GWB's tort reform would put a cap on asbestos lawsuits, a tale that was sufficient to send Halliburton stock up by 43% in mid-January. As the Dow Jones News Service noted, "Companies under the cloud of potential asbestos liability saw their bonds gain Friday on speculation that President Bush may address the question of mounting asbestos litigation." Second, Halliburton, following up on its lucrative post-Gulf War game, did the same thing again by scoring crucial contracts from the Pentagon to build forward operating bases in the region of the Fifth Afghan War and elsewhere. The Pentagon has not reported the value of these contracts. In the 1990s, Halliburton earned $2.5 billion for similar work and the Pentagon spokesperson indicated that these contracts were substantially more. It also got a contract from the UK Ministry of

Defense to supply large tank transporters ($418 million).

Halliburton CEO David Lesar, who bagged a compensation package of $11.3 million in 2001, boasted, "Augmenting our military troops with contractor-provided support has proven to be an invaluable force multiplier." What he said, in essence, was that the Pentagon and the UK Ministry of Defense provided the bailout to prevent an Enron-like burnout. Cheney, who walked away with $20.6 million from his sale of Halliburton stock, must surely have been aware of the events with his former firm. Angry at the GAO request for information, Mr. Secrecy told his friends at Fox News, "Can you imagine an FDR or Teddy Roosevelt, in the midst of a grave national crisis, dealing with the problems we're having to deal with now, over here on the side of a matter of political expediency, trading away a very important fundamental principle of the presidency?" The principle is secrecy, not for the national interest, but for the interest of the plutocratic chamber of commerce.

The General Accounting Office went after Cheney for his secret meetings to fashion the White House's energy policy. Rumor has it that Ken Lay was a major part of the proceedings within the National Energy Policy Development Group or NEPDG (with his penchant for such acronyms and secrecy, perhaps Cheney still believes he is at work in the Pentagon, the hive of concealment). In an unusual move, the GAO sued the White House. Eleanor Clift, writing in *Newsweek*, noted of this standoff, "What started out for Cheney as a matter of principle has now taken a very different turn. Whatever his contacts were with the titans of the energy industry, those associations will be judged in the light of what has happened to Enron. Keeping those relationships secret was never smart policy; now it threatens the very credibility of the Bush administration."[77]

"Corruption" derives its meaning from "rupture," and means "to break entirely" or "to break up morally." To many, corruption seems endemic to places of the two-thirds world, where it appears everyday (in the form of bribes) and as periodic spectacle (in the form of scandals). Certainly, we, in the U.S. do not experience corruption in its everyday form on a regular basis.[78] Corruption does not come to us so crudely, so honestly. Ours is a more dishonest, codified type of theft: you can't see an elected representative unless you fork over cash (campaign contributions), government bureaucrats don't take you seriously unless you hire a lobbyist. Corruption is structural, visible, and yet underground. A bit like Cheney.

The extraordinary thing about the pay-to-play system is that, as hinted at earlier, it is so very cheap. Ken Silverstein tracked lobbyists for his 1998 book, *Washington on $10 Million a Day: How Lobbyists Plunder the Nation.* As he reported, "When you consider the enormous benefits bestowed on Corporate America by the White House and Congress, the big sums companies spend to win favors are revealed as chump change." He offers as an example the behemoth Lockheed Martin who paid a measly $5 million to lobby Congress in 1996, but "won approval for the creation of a new $15 billion government fund that will underwrite foreign weapons sales."[79]

Much froth and blather has been made over the passage of the Shays-Meehan/McCain-Feingold bill in the aftermath of Enron. But they do not address the problem of money in DC. As far as the U.S. Public Interest Group analysis is concerned, the bill does not address the Enron issue. Almost two-thirds of Enron and Arthur Andersen's $11.2 million contributions since 1990 came as "hard money" and not the newly banned "soft money"; the Lays gave $882,580 in both types of money since 1990, and the new bills will allow them to increase this contribution to $975,000. Enron employees gave $508,000 since the 1990 elections, $1,000 per head, whereas now they can double their bids. The bill does not address lobbying, the main arena by which Enron ($7.5 million since 1997) and Andersen ($9.6 million) gave money to the parties. These amounts were far more than what Enron and Andersen gave via election contributions, $3.8 million and $2.8 million, respectively.[80] Despite Shays-Meehan, Washington continues to be a cheap city: the lawmakers offer vast amounts of corporate welfare for a very small bribe.

The real corporate control over the government, however, is not in the campaign finance scandal. The real scandal is that the culture of corporations is the culture of politics, and the corporate fat cats have now become the running dogs. Cheney went from Secretary of Defense to CEO of Halliburton and now to the Vice Presidency; GWB went from scion of the Bush legacy to oil money to the Presidency; and the story of the rest of the cabinet is too well known to repeat here. Whereas the Clinton team courted corporations, the Bush team is the corporation. Certainly Clinton had the Robert Rubins beside him, but his cabinet was mainly comprised of the civil servant and professional politician type figure that had to go out of their way to please corporations. Ron Brown's world tours in the mid-1990s are an illustration of this attempt to stabilize the bridge between the White House and the Penthouse.

Even as there is something specifically oily about the Bush Men, it would be unfair to them not to point out that much of Enron's dirty deals took place during the Clinton years. Both Clinton's Secretaries of the Treasury, first the Texan Lloyd Bentsen and Goldman Sachs' Robert Rubin had Enron connections, with Bentsen taking $14,000 for his first Senate campaign and Rubin being linked by the deals he did as an investment banker. When Rubin joined the Treasury in 1994, he wrote to Enron to say that he "looked forward to continuing to work with you in my new capacity."[81] Startled by the collapse of LTCM in 1998, Rubin engineered the deal to save the integrity of the stock market. Years later, when Enron started to go under, it was Rubin who called the Bush administration to see if anything could be done to save it. The story that we get in the next chapter, then, is clearly a tale of the alliance between the two parties in the execution of U.S. imperialist strategy in the 1990s. There is no partisanship here, because both parties (with different inflections) worked to benefit Enron and other U.S. business interests at the expense of the planet.

CHAPTER TWO

A Manual for Corporate Terrestrial Conquest

Powers' Revelations

In 1995, Enron's Senior Vice President for Global Finance, Linda Powers took a seat before the U.S. House Appropriations Committee. Ms. Powers was no stranger to Washington, DC. A law professor at Georgetown University, Ms. Powers joined the administration of GHB as Deputy Assistant Secretary of Commerce for Service Industries and Finance (1989-1993). The long title is no reflection on her lack of importance: Ms. Powers spent her time in government as the lead negotiator for the financial services part of NAFTA and as U.S. negotiator for the GATT round, the treaties now shaping the world economy. A seasoned bureaucrat for U.S. imperialism, Ms. Powers now represented Enron before the elected representatives. Her testimony reveals the global game plan, worth quoting at length:

> Thanks to certain changes in the developing countries which I will describe in a minute, a new way of achieving the same development goals has become possible. Private parties like our company and others, are now able to develop, construct, own and operate private infrastructure projects in these countries. In the process of doing so, private parties are able to achieve the things which U.S. foreign assistance efforts have long been trying (without much success) to achieve: the projects are serv-

ing as action forcing events that are getting the host countries to finally implement the legal and policy changes long urged upon them…

Under this new approach, the private parties are bearing the costs, both for bringing the policy reform process to fruition, with the host country governments, and for the facilities to alleviate current problems…

This private sector driven approach I am describing applies not only to the energy sector, which is my company's area of activity, but also in other infrastructure sectors—toll roads and other transport facilities; water and sewage; telecom—and potentially in industrial sectors…

When a firm like Enron, Mission or AES goes into a foreign country to undertake a project, just what do we do? We make money by selling an important commodity—electricity—to the local people at a reasonable price. If we are successful, the results are not only the addition of valuable assets to the country, but equally important, the creation of 'commercial infrastructure.' These projects must be put together and financed using standard private sector tools. This process, which for the first round of projects is invariably painful and time consuming, forces government officials of the country in question to deal with the reforms needed in these key areas:

1. Property Rights, including the enforceability of contracts…

2. Market Pricing…One of the biggest problems in these countries is that they have all had hugely subsidized infrastructure services…Projects like ours aren't financeable as long as you have artificially depressed prices. So they have to bring the prices in alignment with market pricing.

3. Regulatory Reform. One of the most important regulatory reforms—privatization—is by definition, the necessary starting point for any of these private infrastructure projects….

4.   Sound Lending...

These are the kinds of important changes in laws, policies and practices that the private sector led infrastructure projects are causing to finally be implemented. By working closely with private developers, engineers, financial advisors, lawyers and lenders throughout the several year process of project development and financing, the host country authorities come to realize that the project can only go forward to fruition if these changes are made. Importantly the project also provides these authorities with some 'cover' against domestic criticism and resistance to these changes.

Let me give you a real world example to illustrate these points. Just yesterday Enron reached closing on a $920 million power plant project in Dabhol...This is the first privately developed independent power plant in India...Working through this process has given the Indian authorities a real and concrete understanding of the kinds of legal and policy changes needed in India, and has given the Indian banks a real and concrete understanding of sound project lending practices. Moreover, our company spent an enormous amount of its own money—approximately $20 million—on this education and project development process alone, not including any project costs...

Furthermore, the education provided by our project has had a greater impact than would further general technical assistance, and has finally achieved some key changes that have long been urged by development institutions such as the World Bank and AID. Just two of a number of examples:

• The State of Maharashtra, where our project is located in India, is now revamping its electricity rate structure to end electricity price subsidies.

• Five leading Indian banks are playing a major role in the total financing package for our power plant project....

The success of these private projects in achieving the

third key—benefiting U.S. interests—should already be obvious from my description of the projects, and I will touch on it only briefly. One of the main (though no the only) benefits to U.S. interests lies in the economic value of these infrastructure projects. They are very large, usually ranging from about $200-700 million per project. They include correspondingly large amounts of capital equipment, and engineering and other high value-added services. Since much of these goods and services can be sourced in the US, these infrastructure projects are the most important area of growth in export value to the U.S. In fact, they are already catching up to aircraft in export importance, and should surpass aircraft during this decade."[1]

Powers' revelations carried within them the germ of the framework for U.S. corporate terrestrial conquest.

The Indian press picked up on one paragraph of Ms. Powers' testimony: that Enron spent upwards of $20 million to "educate" the Indian public.[2] Indeed, as the government balked at the project, Enron published full-page advertisements in the leading English-language press (thereby buying their editorial acquiescence on the issue). But the real money went toward increasing the purchasing power of the elected representatives and their political organizations. In the early days after this revelation about the ads to buy editorial help, the press reported that a foreign firm was trying to buy the Indian house of the people, paying little heed to the fact that for the past fifty years, the representatives of the people had largely become beholden to corporate interests of one kind or another. Money from the coffers of Indian industrialists and financiers moved through the *Hawala* (correspondent banking) channels to make their way into suitcases found in the living rooms of the politicians—this to fund elections and to make life palatable for the hard-working *netas* (leaders). But $20 million from one firm far out-classed even the more affluent bribers, and indeed it set a new standard for corruption in India. It is a cherished view among what we might call the one-third world that the two-thirds world is "primitive" by comparison. Leaving aside discussion of such racist views, it is clear that bribery in India may have exceeded its American equivalent in sophistication: now a bribe can be called a fund for voter education!

Perhaps this is how Ken Lay explains his $24,000 support for the Congressional candidacy of Sheila Jackson-Lee in the 18th District in Texas. In 1994, Democratic Representative Craig Washington held the seat for Houston, home of Enron. But of all embarrassing things, he opposed capitalist globalization and, therefore, NAFTA. Washington stood with five others from the Texas delegation of thirty to oppose NAFTA (of the six, Washington, Charlie Wilson, Jack Brooks and Henry Gonzalez earned one-way tickets back home, while Gene Green and Ralph Hall held onto their seats). Strong labor and anti-racist ties moved Washington to buck the state's trend and he felt the wrath of Lay thereafter. Lay's support for Jackson-Lee enabled her to raise $600,000, thrice Washington's funds. She trounced him. The 18th District, with Lay's funds for "education," voted in favor of NAFTA. So far Jackson-Lee earned $38,000 from Enron, a full ten thousand more than Tom DeLay, the Republican attack-dog, and more senior Texas representative. This was the sort of political "education" that Enron hoped to export in its global crossings.[3]

But Ms. Powers revelation that U.S. campaign finance techniques had now arrived in India paled in significance compared to her announcement of Enron's overall economic and political strategy. Its three components follow the lines of the economic and political agenda of the International Monetary Fund (IMF)-World Bank-U.S. Treasury-U.S. Transnational Corporate nexus.

First, Enron-type firms do not enter "emerging markets" only to make a profit. (They do, after all, offer energy for a "reasonable price.") But they are there principally to create "action forcing events," to take International Monetary Fund ideas and make them vital through their projects. This includes:

- Wide-scale privatization.

- The curtailment of state regulation.

- The end to state subsidies geared toward the creation of a social good, such as the social safety net or of medical care.

Because Enron-type projects bring a vast amount of capital (often garnered from the "host" country itself through subsidies and contracts) it is able to conduct its neoliberal pedagogy (cousin of bribery and now labeled "education") in practice.

Second, since the intrepid Enron-type firm initiates the process, local politicians are protected (get "cover") for their attempt to sell the public's property and to undermine its well-being. Only a generation after colonialism, it is not easy for a politician to sell the assets of a state to a foreign-based transnational corporation without being compromised as a foreign agent. If the firm, call it Enron, makes it clear that it won't do business unless the government accedes, then the politician can go to the people and say, "I did my best, but we are forced to accept their terms or else we will go without electricity." The firm, meanwhile, cares little about its PR in the tropics, mainly because it does not have an investor base among the politician's constituency. Its investors, across the U.S. and Europe, may in fact be pleased with its hardball tactics and reward it for its tough love.

Third, since the projects are capital-intensive and because of the technological advantages secured by the U.S. (and preserved by the intellectual property decree from GATT), U.S. manufacturers can look forward to the generation of sales of spare parts and services to the "host" country for a lifetime, a net gain for "U.S. interests."

The experience of Argentina, India and the Philippines helps us to follow the story of Enron and its prehistory across the planet. Like the porcupine scurrying from the wolf, all three states once self-consciously tried to resist Enronization, only to be flipped over, their underbellies ripped open and served up for feasting. The history of this triad applies to vast sections of the planet.

Memories of Hope
(When "Development" Meant Freedom)

Before Enron, we had Bandung.

It was the destruction of the Bandung dynamic that facilitated the rapacious growth of Enron. If we disregard the history of Bandung, Enron's arrival looks like it was indeed the genius of Lay, that U.S. capital has a natural advantage over the benighted peoples of the planet. If we look at Bandung and why it failed, we might be more disposed to see Enron as a part of the IMF's assault on the planet during the 1990s, as part of global capital's attempt to cash-in on the demise of the Soviet Union and the engineered poverty of the Third World. Bear with me as we travel from an obscure Indonesian town on a journey that culminates in another obscure town, Houston, Texas.

At Bandung, Indonesia, in 1955, leaders from twenty-nine Asian and African states gathered to celebrate the victory of the national-liberation and anti-colonial dynamic, at the same time as they tried to find ways to deal with the devastation they inherited. Behind every monument of colonial power, stood a simple truth: it was purchased with the blood of a racist brutality that stripped away centuries of dignity and left devastation. The best example is Kolkata's Victoria Memorial, a monument to Queen Victoria. It was erected by her Viceroy to India, Lord Curzon in 1897, the same year that tens of millions of Indians perished in a preventable famine. As Curzon put it during the famine: "Any Government which imperiled the financial position of India in the interests of prodigal philanthropy would be open to serious criticism; but any Government which by indiscriminate alms-giving weakened the fibre and demoralized the self-reliance of the population, would be guilty of a public crime"[4] In other words, if the British opened the warehouses of foodstocks to the starved population, it might destroy their desire to work in the future. One can draw a straight line from the callousness of Curzon's imperialism to the workfare projects in Tommy Thompson's Wisconsin. For a host of reasons, the colonialists boarded their jets in the late 1940s and left for home. But colonialism's legacy persisted. Indonesia's President Sukarno welcomed the anti-colonial leaders with the following warning: "Colonialism has also its modern dress, in the form of economic control, intellectual control, actual physical control by a small but alien community within a nation. It is a skillful and determined enemy, and it appears in many guises. It does not give up its loot easily. Wherever, whenever, and however it appears, colonialism is an evil thing, and one which must be eradicated from the earth."[5] Despite Sukarno's own crackdown on the communists in the late 1940s, from the 1950s to the CIA-backed coup against him in 1965, Sukarno represented the Bandung dynamic.

To counter the post-war drive by U.S. and other corporations, the countries of the newly liberated Third World attempted to form a bloc both in the United Nations but also in the abstract channels of economic activity. The economic model to protect the Third World from the predators was "import-substitution," a theory well developed by the Argentinean economist Raul Prebisch in his 1949 paper *The Economic Development of Latin America and Its Principal Problems.*[6] The notion of comparative advantage, Prebisch argued, is internally contradictory: it claimed that because one region of the world produces meat well and another electronics, that if the two regions do what they do best the entire world community will see an improvement of the products and a low-ering of prices. The country that produces raw materials need not industrialize because it should continue to do what it does best and retain its conventional advantage in raw material pro-duction. "The flaw in this assumption," wrote Prebisch, "is that of generalizing from the particular. If by 'the community' only the great industrial countries are meant, it is indeed true that the benefits of technical progress are gradually distributed among all social groups and classes. If, however, the concept of the community is extended to include the periphery of the world economy, a serious error is implicit in the generalization. The enormous benefits that derive from increased productivity have not reached the periphery in a measure comparable to that obtained by the peoples of the great industrial countries. Hence, the outstanding differences between the standards of living of the masses of the former and the latter and the manifest dis-crepancies between their respective abilities to accumulate cap-ital, since the margin of savings depends primarily on increased productivity."

You don't have to be an economist to understand what Prebisch is saying: you can't compare unequal economies; the benefits of colonialism went to Europe and the U.S. Therefore, industrialized economies bear a great advantage in their rela-tionship with the raw material producers of the world. The cycle of what will later be called dependency leaves the two-thirds world in poverty while the overdeveloped world gallops forward to the moon. "The fundamental significance of the industrialization of the new countries," Prebisch wrote, "is not an end in itself, but the principal means at the disposal of those countries of obtaining a share of the benefits of technical progress and of progressively raising the standard of living of the masses."

To get out of this cycle of dependency, Prebisch and oth-ers fashioned a policy known as "import-substitution." If

Indonesia imported a relatively easy product like toothpaste, it would need to find money to pay for this. Since it did not have industrial capacity, it had to pay for this with its cheap agricultural raw materials. The comparative advantage of the industrial states would keep the cycle in motion to the disadvantage of the agrarian states. So, Indonesia should charge very high tariffs for the import of toothpaste and the government should invest in the creation of a domestic toothpaste industry (and therefore, a domestic chemical industry and so on). The import of toothpaste is substituted by the creation of domestic manufacturing. Prebisch's theory is not entirely novel: its precursor is in Alexander Hamilton's 1791 *Report on Manufacturers*, a text that should be read by all proponents of the "free market."

Import-substitution failed for principally three reasons: (1) capital didn't create industrialization mainly because of the strategy of lending followed by the former colonial powers; (2) a lack of urgency about, or disregard for, land reforms; (3) social life in the two-thirds world was not democratized in any meaningful way.

(1) Development Diplomacy (How to keep 'em down while promising prosperity)

Representatives from forty-five countries attended the UN's Monetary and Financial Conference in 1944 and set up the World Bank. Under U.S. tutelage, the powers called the Bank the International Bank for Reconstruction (aimed mainly at Europe). The Latin American delegates to the meeting insisted on appending *and Development*. The soon to be new nations looked forward to an international Marshall Plan to not only reconstruct the world devastated by the war, but also that part of humanity robbed of its riches by colonial plunder. But the United States, the new power, worried about the maintenance of economy hegemony as the basis for political power. Lest there be any doubt, Eugene Black, President of the World

Bank (1949-1963), spelled it out in 1960. The role of his institution was to conduct "development diplomacy" in the ex-colonies, and "economic aid should be the principle means by which the West maintains its political and economic dynamic in the underdeveloped world."[7]

In India, Argentina and the Philippines, aid did enter the state's coffers in uneven ways. But the one thing that each of these countries had in common is that the money did not come for the creation of economic independence and self-reliance. Blessed by vast agricultural exports, Argentina postponed the creation of technological expertise and allowed the terms of trade to squelch its hopes of being fiscally free. In the 1950s, the powerful Sociedad Rural argued, "It is easier, as a well-known military man has said, to put grass in a horse's stomach than gas in the tank of a heavy truck." Based on the agrarian elite's reticence to increase productivity, by the early 1970s Argentina faced stiff competition in the world market from the advanced industrial states—regions of the world that once bought food grains and meat products from the Southern Cone.[8] If Argentina lagged because of a lack of political will, the Philippines is a tale of flagrant colonial domination by the U.S. The Philippine Trade or Bell Act of 1946 from the U.S. Congress set the terms for the archipelagoes' economic relations from then through the late 1970s. While the U.S. had total control over Filipino economic plans, Section 341 of the Bell Act gave U.S. citizens the right to act with impunity in economic matters. "The disposition, exploitation, development and utilization of all agricultural, timber and mineral lands of the public domain, waters, minerals, coal, petroleum and other mineral oil, all forces and sources of potential energy, and other natural resources of the Philippines, and the operation of public utilities, shall, if open to any person, be open to citizens of the United States and to all forms of business enterprise owned or controlled, directly or indirectly, by United States citizens."[9]

The miniscule investment to the Philippines notwithstanding, the general path taken by the dependent governments did not forge the base for fiscal independence. India offers something of a contrast, because its rate of growth from 1950 to 1980 was three and a half percent (as opposed to under two percent during the entire colonial epoch) and, between 1951 and 1969, the index of industrial production rose by three hundred percent (seventy percent in consumer goods, four hundred percent in intermediate goods [such as those goods used to make a final product that don't get re-used, like wood in a chair or else nails in a ship] and a thousand percent in capital goods [such as those goods that are re-usable, like machines]).[10] India attempted fiscal freedom, but it was trapped by the failure to conduct land reforms and smash the unequal power structure erected during colonialism. Growth was important, but as it turned out, not as important as the creation of equity. In 1979, when the failure of this line became apparent, Prebisch speaking of the model, noted, "We thought that an acceleration of the rate of growth would solve all problems. This was our great mistake." What was needed alongside growth were "changes in the social structure," indeed "a complete social transformation."[11] The arena of land reforms should have, therefore, been the central focus of import-substitution development.

(2) Terra Firma

But political reform was not to be.

And the World Bank was gleeful for that, or at least those sections within the Bank who subscribed to the views of the U.S. Department of Commerce. In a 1943 document from that department, at the dawn of the bank's founding, Assistant Secretary of State W. L. Clayton developed the logic for industrialization of the soon to be freed colonies. The World Bank loan to these ex-colonies would "certainly be a good one for agricultural exports [from the US], because as you help develop these countries, help develop their resources, and help develop them industrially, you will shift their economy somewhat from an agricultural economy to an industrial economy, so that I think in the end you would create more markets for your agricultural products rather than otherwise." Since this was such a crucial point, Clayton argued again, "if you have a country that today is devoting all of its labor and nearly all of its economic activity to the production of agricultural products for export, if you help develop them industrially, and use their labor and other things for industrial development, I think it will take something from their agricultural activities, and to some extent reduce the competition which we have in this country."[12] Read: their "development" must be organized to help us.

The World Bank did provide loans for the development of the new nations, but mainly in the sector of industry and not for the restructuring of various exploitative and unproductive agricultural regimes. Argentina's latifundistas did not want to see land reforms erode their power base, even as their reticence foreshadowed their own eventual economic irrelevancy on the world scale. The Sociedad Rural, the organization of the land oligarchy, opposed an agrarian minimum wage, a basis for reforms. In 1944, it declared, "In fixing wages, it is essential to determine the standard of living of the ordinary peon. His material needs are sometimes so limited that the use to which any surplus will be put is of little social interest." In other words, the peons can be paid rock-bottom wages (since for some convenient reason they really aren't interested in money anyway!), they must remain serfs of their latifundias and the oligarchy must absorb the surplus not for technological innovation but for feudal consumption. When Juan Perón spoke against agrarian reform in June 1952, the Sociedad Rural noted that, "It was a masterly dissertation."[13] In 1975 the World Bank studied productivity based on farm sizes in Latin America and found that the productivity of small farms was three to four times greater than the bloated latifundias.[14] As Argentina's land became less productive, it lost even its comparative advantage and sunk into indebted despondency.

Recognizing the importance of agricultural issues, the Philippines enacted a Land Reform Act in 1955. But, as the veteran nationalist Claro M. Recto said at the time, it was written by representatives of the U.S. Foreign Operations Administration in the U.S. Embassy in Manila. "It is the declared policy of the state [by the Land Reform Act of 1955]." Recto argued, "to perpetually chain itself to an agricultural economy, making us, Filipinos, mere suppliers and providers of raw materials and consumers of foreign manufactured goods. No more conclusive evidence is needed to prove the determined purpose of their own country. It was bad enough that they hatched this idea of making our economy subserve theirs but they wanted to add insult to injury, attempting to press us into legislating it as our declared national policy to make it appear that it was our own doing."[15] Rather than provide land to those that worked it, the Land Reform Act froze land relations in plantation-like conditions.

In India, land reform was a fundamental part of the agenda of the national movement. But the development that followed in the republic avoided that legacy and followed instead the Bombay Plan of 1944, a growth-based, industrialization-based import-substitution model proposed by capitalists close to the ruling Congress Party. Since the Congress relied upon rural power brokers to deliver the vote, it did not want to alienate the landowners who financed these agents of the party. "During the mid-1950s," writes political scientist Sunil Khilnani, "it became evident that the legislative approach to alerting the property order had reached an impasse. There were hopeful attempts by the national leadership to pass the burden of reform down to the lowest village levels, through 'community development' projects and local democracy, *Panchayati Raj*, or rule by village councils. But the measures were rather half-hearted and ineffective, and the district and village councils were sequestered by the already powerful through a blend of cajolery, terror and usury."[16]

In sum, agricultural reform fell off the table in Argentina, India and the Philippines.

(3) Inequality Enshrined

The import-substitution model promised two things: in the short term, the formerly colonized state would build up a domestic industrial capacity and produce local wealth; in the long term, that wealth would be spread across the class divide and create equity among the population. The model fulfilled its short-term agenda, as growth rates in the Third World rose and as various industries sprang up under the shadow of tariff walls. But, the elite's fascination with growth, with the Gross Domestic Product (GDP), and with their grasp over wealth, the goal of equity fell off the agenda.

Latin America, as a whole, held the honor of being the zone with the highest rate of income inequality during the latter half of the twentieth century. But India was just behind Latin America in inequality, and tells the tale effectively: only a fifth of the population worked in the service sector since 1947; this part of the economy accounted for two-fifths of the GDP. The richest ten percent of the Indian population by the mid-1950s came from this section, and they benefited largely because of the increased concentration of capital in the sectors of industry, metals, finance and insurance.[17] In 1964, the Indian Planning Commission admitted, "The working of the planned economy has encouraged the process of concentration by facilitating and aiding the growth of big business." Even as the general well-being of the population increased, "the available data pointed to no significant change in inequalities in consumption."[18]

High levels of inequality turn the elites of a society away from any relations with the working-class in their society. They make common cause with elites elsewhere to fashion a global class of the moneyed. Alienation from one's own population breeds callousness among the elite. It also means that the working-class and dispossessed can see through the platitudes of this form of bourgeois nationalism, perhaps to seek something other than this, to fight for a state in which they have power. Instead, the elite turned their backs on the system that made them wealth (the Bandung dynamic) and adopted the IMF's dynamic to further plunder whatever was held in trust as the public good. We'll return to this in the next Chapter.

The possibility of an equal society, in India at least, was further constrained by the tendency of the Central government to control the realm of finance at the expense of the states and local administrations. The states can only raise funds through three methods: the beneficence of the center (based on reports of the Finance Committee); allocations from the Planning Commission; and its own meager ability to tax its population. These last taxes are principally in areas (such as land revenue, agricultural income tax) that are either unable to produce more funds in the era of structural adjustment, notably from the late 1960s onward, or are deeply regressive and therefore unpopular (sales and local excise taxes). Of the sixty-six items on the states' list of duties that it must fund, almost half entail law and order. Only a fifth concern development. Even on development, the state governments generally have to "consult" with central ministries, whose heavy hand is felt on the projects. For the fat cats, this means less bribes, a more efficient corruption: since the people are prevented from taking charge of their localities, in order for elite power to reign, it need only constrain the central government. Not that efforts haven't been made to control the local scene. The state of Kerala's Communist government in the 1950s is perhaps the best example.

The central government in India holds the abhorrent power to dismiss state governments, and it used that power in 1957 to overthrow the Communists in Kerala.[19] Every democracy has its "checks and balances." But this ability of the national government to use the threat of dismissal to keep the state governments in line turns such a concept on its head: the weak are kept in check by the powerful.

Vast technical and financial resources had been devoted to energy and transportation rather than to the expenditure of political capital for the reconstruction of the countryside. Even though land reform did not take place, the state did expend large amounts of the regressively taxed income of its citizens to create the infrastructure for public services (such as irrigation and education). Money paid into the common fund for the creation of these services represented decades of investment by working people. It was this investment that, by the 1990s, became fair game for corporations who bid for them in the epoch of privatization, paying incommensurately small amounts for the years of capital that created the services.

If the elite's addiction to inequality and the failure of social democratic states to constrain elite power destroyed the import-substitution model, then the rise of oil prices in the 1970s crushed it. At the middle of that decade each of our three states moved toward political authoritarianism and economic neoliberalism. Again, each of our examples opens the door to the IMF by a clever nationalist device: it couches its political authoritarianism in the guise of national self-determination and attempts to sell assets under the cloak of nationalism. In the Philippines the tale begins when Ferdinand Marcos declared martial law. Then, in 1973, he ordained a new Constitution that reneged on the open-door policy for U.S. corporations, thereby securing Marcos' partial reputation as a nationalist. But it also allowed for "service contracts" (where Filipino capital could go into "joint venture" with transnational capital).

Marcos also went forward with IMF reform conditions and loans.[20]

In 1975, Indira Gandhi suspended the Constitution and declared an Emergency, this just on the heels of her nationalization of the banks (1969) and the Indo-Soviet Defense Treaty (1971). As she spoke of the need to abolish poverty and rid the country of corruption, her Minister of State in the Ministry of Planning, I. K. Gujral, told the nominal parliament that the state will conduct the "liberalization of investment procedures," to allow industrial capitalists unfettered ability for growth and to pursue capital from all quarters.[21] In 1976, the Argentinean Minister of the Economy adopted IMF austerity measures to service external debts and to manage the collapse of the currency, but a general strike ended the ploy. Three weeks later, the military took power in the "coup of foreign credit," wrapped itself in the garb of military-nationalism and proceeded, not a week later, to sign on to the same conditions for the money used to service that debt.[22]

In the 1970s, commercial banks and transnational firms started lending money to what the United Nations calls the Least Developed Countries (LDCs) because they had accumulated so much wealth they had to find new avenues for investment. The institutionalization of savings and the increase in the investor base (through mutual and pension funds) in the overdeveloped world, as well as the arrival of petrodollars and of "black money" smuggled out of the two-thirds world by its elites, created a large fund of money that needed to be lent out somewhere to turn a profit.

The overdeveloped world was becoming an unattractive avenue for investment: low interest rates, dropping productivity rates, and high union pressure, among other factors, made the two-third world's cheap labor and vast resources enormously attractive. This coupled with the desperation of regimes that seemed cash starved was an additional incentive to try out colo-

gh financial means, without the administrative
ing to finance a police and military force, get the
maii delivered on time or take care of the infirm. Under pressure from the IMF (through the Structural Adjustment Policies
and corrupt local elites), the LDCs "liberalized" their financial
markets and became a haven for the speculator.

But if investment can provide needed capital for businesses and others to prosper (think, for example, how liberating it is
to have a mortgage that enables you to eventually own a house
instead of renting in perpetuity), what was so bad about this
investment in the two-thirds world? The speculation that began
in the 1970s wrought a vicious harvest. Foreign Direct
Investment (FDI—both private and government funds from
overseas) did create major social transformation: it widened
inequality in most LDCs with the creation of a dollar elite and
an impoverished mass.[23] Consider that forty-eight of the LDCs
hold ten percent of the world's population, but only one percent
of the world's wealth. Consider too a natural dynamic: offspring
of subsequent generations should generally stand on the shoulders of the wealth generated by their ancestors, having inherited the fruits of their labor. Prosperity should roll forward and
increase with time. But in forty-three of these countries, the
average income today is less than it was in 1970. In his fine
novel *Moth Smoke*, Mohsin Hamid offers a memorable parody of
this condition. Hamid's character Judge Julius Superb, in his
paper for a seminar on Social Class in Pakistan tell us:

> There are two social classes in Pakistan. The first
> group, large and sweaty, contains those referred to as the
> masses. The second group is much smaller, but its members
> exercise vastly greater control over their immediate envi-
> ronment and are collectively termed the elite. The dis-
> tinction between members of these two groups is made on
> the basis of control of an important resource: air-condi-
> tioning. You see, the elite have managed to re-create for

themselves the living standards of say, Sweden, without leaving the dusty plains of the subcontinent... They wake up in air-conditioned houses, drive air-conditioned cars to air-conditioned offices, grab lunch in air-conditioned restaurants (rights of admission reserved), and at the end of the day go home to their air-conditioned lounges to relax in front of their wide-screen TVs. And if they should think about the rest of the people, the great uncooled, and become uneasy as they lie under their blankets in the middle of the summer, there is always prayer, five times a day, which they hope will gain them admittance to an air-conditioned heaven, or, at the very least, a long, cool drink during a fiery day in hell.[24]

Argentina's Prebisch, who by the 1970s was the Secretary General of the UN Commission on Trade and Development, was well aware that growth itself led to inequities in places like Pakistan, where a section of the society lived lavishly, while the masses sweated and starved. Of course, the two-thirds world is not alone in this, because at this time inequality within the overdeveloped world also exploded as a result of a growth-oriented economic strategy that did not care for equity.

It was not as though the ruling class failed to grasp what they were doing to the rest of the U.S. and to the world. On 20 June 1997, Stephen Roach of Morgan Stanley gave a concise summary to the Group of 7 (with the inclusion of Russia, now G-8) economic forum held in Denver, USA. Roach noted in the context of the increase in wealth, "There has been no free lunch. The cost of these successes has been billed to the American worker in the form of downsizing, real wage compression, mounting inequalities of the income distribution, and a profound sense of economic insecurity." Echoing this dynamic about the state of U.S. wealth, the Children's Defense Fund reported that same year that "an American child was two times more likely to be poor than a British child, three times more likely to be poor than a French or German child, and at least six re likely to be poor than a Belgian, Danish or Swiss child." Furthermore, "the typical annual paycheck of young married fathers dropped by 30% between 1973 and 1994. These losses were partially obscured in the family income statistics, however, by the growing earnings of young married mothers, who increased their average paid work time from 18 weeks per year in 1975 to 29 weeks per year in 1994." Many families compensate for some of the loss of their income by working longer hours. Of these young families, while a bit more than six percent lived in poverty in 1973, almost sixteen percent do so now.[25] With rising costs of healthcare, daycare and education in the richest country in the world, it is unlikely that income will do more than keep people within their class fractions rather than be the lever for social mobility. If you're not already a billion-heir or else a dot.con artist who jumped ship in time, it is unlikely that you will ever be on the *Forbes* annual list of our civilization's heroes.

In 1964, Prebisch and others created the Group of 77, an organization of the two-thirds world to hold the line against the depredations of transnational corporations. By the 1970s and early 1980s, the Group of 77 and the Non-Aligned Movement were not up to the task as their member states turned themselves in for inoculation by the fiscal doctors at the IMF. The hope of Bandung was squandered for the moment.

In the wings of this economic train wreck sat Enron, waiting with its role already written into history even as it was not yet formed.

But before we jump to Enron, a further sketch of one particularly nasty institution is relevant to understanding the context in which it operated: the IMF.

The Smug Assassins of the IMF

The IMF appears as a beacon of hope in the sky, hovers around taking measurements, then swoops down and scuttles all

hope of deliverance, all hope of liberty. If this is w|
shouldn't be surprised that a third of the Thai childr
by Bangkok's Rafabhat Institute's Suan Dusit thought that the
IMF was a UFO. The body snatchers commenced their invasion. A host of acronyms (IMF, WTO, GATT, MAI, FDI), each
one more alien than the other, a brood of anonymous bureaucrats and technocrats, a tribe called the Chicago Boys, a specter
called the Sachs Effect, a UFO personnel school called
Wharton: all these aliens converge to create an index of reason,
a rationality, that resembles the double entry account book.
IMF Reason tells us that credits must exceed debits, outputs
must be greater than inputs, and Profit is king above all else. A
childhood friend of mine who failed geography in school and is
terrible at languages becomes the IMF's expert on a Central
Asian country. But he is good, all things remaining equal, in
economics.

In South Korea, during the trauma of 1997, the IMF
entered the lexicon not as a UFO, but in public interest activist
Kavaljit Singh's words, "as a synonym for gloom, doom and
despair."[26] The "IMF era" refers to a "period of national humil-
iation." The "IMF Sale" is a bargain for buyers, "IMF Fashion"
is used clothing, and "IMF Syndrome" is fear of future unemployment.

The IMF arrives with one prescription to fit all ailments:

- Tighten up the money supply

- Devalue the currency.

- Remove all tariffs.

- Encourage interest rates to rise.

- Reduce government expenditure.

- Cut wages.

The medication produces a patient who looks like this:

- A contraction of economic activity.

- The destruction of long-term economic growth.

- The cannibalization of resources ("asset stripping" and a consequent return to being an exporter of raw materials).

- Rising inequality in terms of class and gender.

- Environmental devastation.

If there is any lingering doubt about the IMF's ability to produce this result, consider this *Wall Street Journal* editorial: the IMF, it said, "has not been fighting financial fires, but dousing them with gasoline."[27]

When Americans exhibit stress as a result of an inhuman world, our doctors prescribe Ritalin for kids and Prozac for adults. We must learn to cope, not to be healed. The IMF has its own brand of fundamentalist medicine to teach the Third World to get on with its task of hard labor while a few of its kind join the global elite in the winner's circle. This is IMFundamentalism.

If you think about it, those Thai children are perhaps the only ones with their finger on the button of history. By 1997, Thailand was, to put it mildly, at the tail end of an unsustainable financial boom: ninety percent of Thailand's wealth resides in Bangkok alone, whilst farmers comprise sixty percent of the working population and hold only eleven percent of the wealth. During the "boom," the automobile industry grew astronomically in Thailand, as the country became the third largest consumer of Mercedes Benzes in the world. As Thailand's merchandise exports began to plummet (from 22.4% in 1994 to 0.1% in 1996), its economy entered a crisis.[28] Enter the IMF with a draconian set of rules. The austerity program put into place led to massive protests, including the erection of a protest "village" outside Parliament House in early 1997.

The Asian crisis of 1997 intensified the critique of IMFundamentalism from within its own ranks. After the government of Thailand abandoned any attempt to shore up the Bhat, and therefore set in motion an economic collapse among the "tigers" that was certainly in the making for other production reasons, the World Bank's chief economist, Joseph E. Stiglitz "notoriously clashed" with IMF deputy director Stanley Fisher. Stiglitz was angry that IMFundamentalism preyed on the state-guided growth that the Bank championed for the U.S. allies on the Pacific Rim.[29] In two issues of the U.S. Council of Foreign Relations' journal, Martin Feldstein (a Harvard University economist who headed the National Bureau of Economic Research and was President Ronald Reagan's Chief Economic Advisor) and Jagdish Bhagwati (a Columbia University economist and free trade theorist) berated the IMF interventions in the region. Feldstein noted, "A nation's desperate need for short-term financial help does not give the IMF the moral right to substitute its technical judgments for the outcomes of the nation's political process."[30] Bhagwati, in the next issue, assailed the "Wall St.-Treasury Complex" (a new version of Eisenhower's Military-Industrial Complex) because it pushed the rights of the dollar above the sovereignty and well being of nations.[31] Conservatives like Feldstein and Bhagwati don't always agree, and they don't generally sound critical alarms against the institutions that maintain the hegemony of global capital. But Feldstein is an old-school free market man who argued that the IMF could offer short-term credit assistance, but it should not get involved in the management of institutional and structural change in national economies. That is, for

Feldstein and Bhagwati, a job of the market. "The IMF would be more effective in its actions and more legitimate in the eyes of emerging-market countries," Feldstein argued, "if it pursued the less ambitious goal of maintaining countries' access to global capital markets and international bank lending." So whereas they wanted more free markets, they recognized that IMFundamentalism itself was a flawed strategy because its blatant disregard for national sovereignty uncovered the entire silent system of domination and put *that* at risk.

There was nothing new in these criticisms. Internal critiques of the IMF policy came in its own journals as early as 1991, the year after Argentina contracted IMFundamentalism and the year India got a dose of it. A senior economist within the IMF, Mohsin Khan, had already published an important paper that assessed the economic record of IMF-enforced stabilization measures from 1973 to 1988 and found that "the growth rate is significantly reduced in program countries relative to the change in non-program countries."[32] The United Nations Development Program (UNDP)'s annual report of 1992 noted, "The IMF has exerted a strong influence over developing countries by setting stiff conditions on the loans it offers. This conditionality has generally been monetarist and deflationary, obliging governments to reduce their demand for imports by curtailing overall demand—cutting back on both private and public spending. These cutbacks have often reduced consumption, investment and employment—and stifled economic growth."[33]

The list of critics is indeed long. In a set of papers indirectly critical of IMF-type policies, Douglass North, who won a Nobel Prize for economics in 1993, published his important work in 1990 explaining why institutions like the state government are central for development.[34] It is the cutback of these very institutions that time and again is a prerequisite to getting "help" from the IMF. The World Bank, too, weighed in with an important document on the need for state institutions to promote development.[35]

Enron Enters From Stage Right

The political authoritarian and economic neoliberal regimes in our three examples collapsed due to popular struggles in 1980 (Indira Gandhi), 1983 (Argentina's Junta), and 1986 (Marcos). In their place, emerged transition regimes that for a few years tried to recover the germ of economic nationalism before giving way to neoliberalism in toto. It was during Argentina's transition under the Presidency of Raul Alfonsin that Enron made its first attempt into the Southern Cone. In 1988, GWB telephoned Rodolfo Terragno, a former journalist who had been in exile for ten years and returned to serve in Alfonsin's cabinet as minister of public works and service. Alfonsin at the time had spent a year looking at two proposals for a $300 million deal to build a gas pipeline: one from the Italian firm, Ente Nazionale Idrocarbuni and the other from an Argentinean firm in collaboration with Dow, Perez Companc. GWB called Terragno to ask that he consider Enron's bid, in collaboration with Westfield. (On investigation, Terragno found that Westfield was a *prestanombre* firm, a borrowed name, a front for Enron itself, since its only assets were the $20 corporate filing fee.) Terragno complained to David Corn of *The Nation*, "[GWB] tried to exert some influence to get that project for Enron. He assumed that the fact he was the son of the [future] President would exert influence. I felt pressured. It was not proper for him to make that kind of call."[36] Enron sent Terragno's office a one-page outline with a "laughable price," and even as U.S. Ambassador Theodore Gildred tried to "exert influence," Terragno, the minister of this nationalist transition regime, refused to allow Enron its deal.

Note that Terragno says the call from the president's son was "not proper." That depends on one's understanding of democracy. If the elected president is an advocate for the electorate, then perhaps having a relative advocate for a private company is indeed improper, since citizens rarely get that kind of help unless they make big campaign contributions. But if the function of the president is to serve as an advocate for private power, then such pressure, even if carried out by a relative, would be seen as exemplary.

The tide soon changed.

The rise in oil prices from 1967 onward, but mainly after 1973, put pressure on the fragile balance of payments accounts for most Third World states. Only a few countries in the world are oil-sufficient, but the rest are forced to pay vast sums of money to keep their countries on the road. With high oil prices comes high transport costs and then comes inflation because everything will cost more. Desperate for money, the states of the two-thirds world dismantled capital controls that had been set up to prevent overseas investors to bring their money in, make a profit on an enterprise and then flee without seeing the project to completion. But now bowing to the inevitability of currency speculation, the Third World ended capital controls. Commercial cash came into these zones in the 1980s and 1990s to offset high oil prices, to conduct infrastructural development and to make short-term gains off the differences in the rates of exchange between the world's currencies. In 1996, net inflow of private capital into the two-thirds world was six times greater than in 1990. Of total FDI, forty percent went to the two-thirds world (it used to be fifteen percent in 1990), with the two-thirds world taking receipt of thirty percent of the global portfolio equity (two percent in 1990). This is no redistribution of global wealth (ten countries received over ninety percent of the inflows) nor is it a productive use of capital (since it mainly traffics in speculation, so-called "hot money").[37]

The turmoil of South-east Asia is sufficient illustration of this "ersatz capitalism."[38] The financial crisis was exacerbated by the debt crisis: those forty-eight countries of the two-thirds world owed $55 billion in 1980, but now they owe upwards of $215 billion. The net transfer of capital moved from the overdeveloped world to the two-thirds world, but in 1983 the direction of flow was reversed, as $242 billion moved from the impoverished world to the advanced industrial states from then till 1989. Profits generated in the overdeveloped world came due in large part to the inadequate terms of trade (a feature noted two decades earlier as a problem by Prebisch), routinely fixed against the agricultural and mineral markets. Since the prices of "raw materials" (already worked on by human labor in mines or else in the fields) is less than that of "finished products" (manufactured goods), "virtual products" (computer software) and "services" (financial and other such), those states that depend on "raw materials" will never be able to attain parity with those states that, by dint of a colonial history, dominate the service/virtual sectors. The unjust terms of trade is one reason that for every $100 earned in the markets, $73 moved to the overdeveloped world as interest and repayment of principal. At the same time the ability of people in the Third World to buy goods fell dramatically: from 1980 to 1991, their power of consumption fell by half![39]

In 1987 the Aquino regime in the Philippines (installed by a popular uprising aimed at curing the injustices of the Marcos regime) passed the Omnibus Investment Code that essentially opened the doors to foreign firms. The terms were stunning: no income tax for eight years, no need for the local partnerships, tax credits on domestic capital inputs, no export tax.... This regime perfected the Janus-faced nationalism-neoliberalism experiment. Even as the government opened the doors wider to foreign capital, the regime forbade the U.S. to use the Subic Bay Naval Base and the Clark Air Base in 1991. The military set-back for the U.S. was a feint, because the next year at the November US-Philippine Mutual Defense Board, the heads of the two navies signed a pact that gave the U.S. access to all Filipino bases. (Now, with the US-Filipino joint actions on Basilan all signs point to the renewal of the U.S. navy's presence in the archipelago).[40] In late 1989, the Aquino government signed a "Memorandum of the Philippine Stabilization Plan for 1991-1992" with the IMF and World Bank that called for the same list of goods as in all its IMFundamentalist prescriptions, among other things, devaluation, import liberalization (meaning allowing imports to wipe out local businesses), and debt servicing. Crucially for our story, it also included unrestricted repatriation of the profits reaped by foreign firms.

One of the sectors hardest hit by the fiscal crunch of the Filipino state was electrical power generation. By 1991, the state estimated that it required $18 billion to retool the power capacity of the country and double the output to 21,000MW—the money needed was twice the current foreign currency reserves. With the government bankrupt, the only alternative was to go overseas for the capital. But who would invest in the Philippines? To make the deal worthwhile, in 1992, President Fidel Ramos (elected in 1992) devised a build-operate-transfer concept. With this plan, a private sector firm would build a utility, run it for a stated number of years for a profit, and then turn it over to the state agency in charge of power.[41] When this policy was announced, Enron was on hand, assisted at every turn by the U.S. Ambassador to the Philippines Frank Wisner Jr. Enron took over control of two plants in 1992. One was the old Pentagon plant in the Subic Bay base, an 116MW generation unit that would be in Enron's hands until 2009. Wisner-Enron also won the contract for the 110MW Batangas plant which Enron would hold till 2003. Funds for buying the two plants from the government came from an obliging U.S. government's Overseas Private Investment Corporation (OPIC)—over $100 million for Batangas and over $16 million for Subic Bay (with over $26 million from the Asian Development Bank for

Batangas). Enron agreed to sell power to the National Power Corporation (NAPCOR), the state body, at a fee of 8 cents per kwh. That was about twenty percent more than NAPCOR charged its customers before Enron came on the scene. In 1993, the media assaulted NAPCOR for the high prices, seven members of its board resigned, but the cost of power to customers remained the same.[42]

Once Argentina's Alfonsin lost to GHB's old friend Carlos Saul Menem in May 1989, and that troublesome minister of public works, Terragno, was history, Enron moved in. Just days after the election results, Neil Bush arrived in Buenos Aires, played tennis with Menem and talked about Enron's bid to enter Argentina's power market. The next year, GHB made the first of his eight trips during Menem's tenure in Argentina. But even with the new regime, not all went smoothly. A few days after the first trip, U.S. Ambassador Terence Todman sternly, but privately, rebuked Menem's economics minister for not closing Enron's "extremely urgent" deal. If the Argentinean government did not stop favoring domestic firms, he said, eight of the largest U.S. corporations in Argentina would walk. The first firm for good treatment was Enron, which the Ambassador said was "poised to invest $250 million." Todman won, as Enron earned the right to invest in Argentina without tariffs and Value-Added Tax. An Argentinean Congressional inquiry said that this deal smacked of neocolonialism and that the people could not be betrayed after only a few years of freedom from military rule. Seeing the light, Menem took the inquiry seriously— by firing its special prosecutor. Enron was safe.

In 1996, Enron Global Power and Pipelines (with GHB friend and once National Security Advisor Brent Scowcroft on the board[43]), along with its Argentinean ally, Pecom Energia, bought a seventy percent stake in the newly privatized Gas del Estado SE. Menem, before the sale, had renamed it as Transportadora de Gas del Sur (TGS). TGS owned the 1.9 billion cubic feet/day capacity, 4,104 miles of natural gas pipelines in Argentina, the largest in South America. Now, gas transport in the Southern Cone was essentially in Enron's hands. Ken Lay said that the purchase of TGS "reflects our continued confidence in Argentina." No wonder: the infrastructure had been built by the Argentinean taxpayers, and purchased by Enron at bargain-basement prices. What the working people of Argentina built up over generations was sold to a Houston upstart thanks to the devastation wrought by IMFunda-mentalism. Lay didn't have to contribute any cash to the IMF to get the job done: they worked for Enron gratis.

But grabbing the gas pipeline was just the beginning. On 4 May 1998, Enron became a full energy partner with Argentina when the Menem regime welcomed Enron Commercializadora de Energia Argentina to be the first power marketer in the country. This meant that this wholly owned subsidiary of Enron could now buy and sell electricity. For Enron International's Scott Porter, this license was "an important step in Enron's strategic efforts to establish marketing operations in Latin America and to further participation in the future integration of the Southern Cone's energy markets." By mid-2000, South American markets accounted for more than half of Enron's $6.5 billion in overseas assets. Enron began to so dominate the energy market in Argentina that in the early days of 2000 the regulatory agency of the country, ENARGAS, asked the company to postpone a rate increase. The reason was clear: since the rate was pegged to the U.S. producer price index, and since the peso was already linked to the dollar, the deflated Argentinean economy meant a large increase in prices and devastation for consumers. Eduardo Ojea Quintana, CEO of TGS and Enron's man in the South, wrote the following to his shareholders in response to the government's entreaty: "We will maintain the firm position of strictly applying the clauses agreed upon in the privatization process. Any violation of them would imply serious damage to the country's credibility."[44]

Don't cry for Enron, Argentina.

During 1997, when $130 billion fled the country (a figure equivalent to the state's debt), Argentina went into a deep recession. By 2001, the economic indicators showed that Argentina, once the economic pride of South America, had entered a depression. One Prime Minister after another took office to stem the meltdown (de La Rua, Saá, Puerta, Camano, then finally Eduardo Duhalde). From mid-December of 2001 to late January 2002, the people filled the streets in what they call *caerolazos*, or pot-banging protests by the *piqueteros*, the picketers. Demanding that the country heed the will of the people and not of firms like Enron one hundred thousand people went to the Plaza de Mayo. These people follow a decade of anti-liberalization movements that developed amongst the unemployed in Argentina's main cities, a movement that took action in the working-class suburbs of Buenos Aires in the late 1990s against the high electric rates charged by Enron.[45] Statistics are imprecise in the midst of such a collapse; stories circulate that the unemployment figure is somewhere between thirty and eighty percent. "We are not Peronists or Radical [Party] members or socialists," said the leader of a Buenos Aires neighborhood assembly. "We are just the hungry people who for the first time have organized themselves and know their strength."[46] In response, Duhalde has freed the peso from the dollar (after he allowed Argentina to default on $142 billion of its debt at a cost of forty percent of the peso's value). He has forbidden banks to raise rates and thereby partly offset the costs of devaluation and he pledged to restart the import-substitution dynamic with the goal to rebuild Argentina's industry. Duhalde is neither Chavez nor Castro, nor does he have the potential of Lula of Brazil. He is an old Peronista forced by Enron-style capitalism to stumble in the dark as Argentina's people try to imagine a future.

They are all Enron. We are all Argentina.

Proclamation of Emaciation:
What's *Free* About the Free Market

India, by far, Enron's worst story and it shows the absolutely complicity of the regional elites to the Enronista stage of history.

In the wake of India's turn to the IMF in 1991, the government released the new Power Policy to "liberalize" the energy sector. The Indian Electricity Act of 1910 and the Electric Supply Act of 1948 came before the legislature for amendment so that foreign investors could hold a majority interest in utility firms. The list of goodies doled out by the Indian government is identical to the list in the Philippines: no tax, few import duties and all manner of regulatory concessions. For three weeks in May and June 1992, the Indian government sent a delegation to garner Foreign Direct Investment. Think of it as akin to an entrepreneur's road show that raises capital for investment. Except this is more like a yard sale with precious gems on sale cheap. During their travels they met with Enron officials to discuss power projects in India. The delegation returned on 10 June. Then on 15 June an Enron, Bechtel and General Electric team descended upon India and five days later the parties signed a Memorandum of Understanding (MoU) to build what would become the Dabhol Power plant in the western state of Maharashtra.[99]

What struck critics immediately was the haste of the MoU, the lack of openness in the process and the complete absence of effort in seeking any competitive bid—for a contract that was worth billions of dollars. Indeed, the deal was so bad that twice the World Bank found the deal "one-sided" to Enron's favor, once on 8 July 1992 and again 26 July 1993. The first note found that Enron had not given "an overall economic justification of this project," and the second note found conclusively that "the Dabhol project as presently formulated is not economically justified and thus could not be financed by the

No oversight

Bank." The Indian Government's Central Electricity Authority (CEA) is authorized by the Indian Electrical Supply Act to protect the public against malfeasance in the power sector, but it did only half its job. The CEA tried to get a breakdown of the costs for the Dabhol project, but Enron balked ("Your request is…not deemed necessary") and the CEA gave the project technical clearance, but preferred to pass the buck on the matter of economic clearance. That, it said, was the responsibility of the Ministry of Finance.

Elements in the government and in the bureaucracy seemed eager, on the other hand, to go forward with "reforms" to draw in capital. Even though Enron's subsidiary, the Dabhol Power Corporation (DPC), was a private sector company under the Companies Act of 1956, the nature of its business in utilities meant that it would be subject to public and judicial scrutiny. The Maharashtra State Electricity Board (MSEB) felt, however, that "this may not be acceptable to foreign promoters," so Enron should be exempt from oversight. In September 1992, the MSEB agreed with Enron's lawyers who wanted to ensure that there be less regulation not only of its contracts but of its accountancy practices as well. In light of later events, limiting oversight of accounting might have been prescient.

The project was fairly straightforward. The DPC planned to build a power plant of between 2,000 and 2,400MW that used liquefied natural gas (LNG) instead of coal. Enron's partner in the DPC included Bechtel and General Electric, although Enron held a majority sixty-five percent share. The DPC would then own and operate the plant for a twenty-year period. Some studies show that India is in need of electrical power, so Enron sold its idea as a windfall for the consumer even though Phase I of the project would only supply 695MW.

In December 1993, the DPC and the Maharashtra State Electricity Board (MSEB) signed a Power Purchase Agreement (PPA) that spelled out the financial and legal aspects of the

between the company (as supplier of power) and
    ___nt (as purchaser of power). Neither side was will-
ing to release the PPA, Enron because it claimed that the PPA
contained trade secrets, and the MSEB because it probably
knew that the deal stunk. Silence all around. Only after repeated court cases did the parties make the PPA public.

As Abhay Mehta, author of *Power Play: A Study of the
Enron Project*, notes, "The only redeeming feature of [the PPA]
was that it pertained only to the first phase of the project for the
supply of 695MW of power."[48] What was wrong with the PPA?
There are six defining issues.

(1) Fixed Payment

The PPA enjoined the MSEB to pay the DPC $430 mil-
lion per year (at the 1993 dollar-rupee exchange rate) regardless
of whether it drew power from Dabhol. With the plant on-line,
the MSEB was obligated to buy the maximum output from
Enron, not what power it actually drew from the power plant. If
the plant did not run, but simply sat idle, the MSEB had to pay
the Capacity Payment (capital recovery, return on equity, maintenance costs, fixed operation costs, debt service on principle
and interest as well as the annual insurance premium). Even as
the Capacity Payment seems fixed it fluctuates with the
exchange rate and with various inflations (rate of Indian inflation, rate of U.S. inflation, U.S. labor inflation index, U.S.
materials inflation index). Furthermore, if there is a "Gas Force
Majeure" (if a terrorist demolishes the pipeline or the plant),
the MSEB will still have to pay Enron its fees. As most critics
point out, few power plants are able to run at capacity, so this
simple point is itself a scam: the Indian government will pay for
power it could never get even if it needed it. Indeed, it is cheaper for the government to pay the fees to keep the plant idle than
to let it run and then have to buy power from it!

(2) Captive Supplier

The MSEB has to forgo cheaper sources of power and first buy the maximum capacity from DPC. In 2000, for instance, the MSEB purchased 16.435 billion units of energy at a cost of Rs. 3,798 crores (just over $1 billion). From DPC, the MSEB bought 4.2 billion units for Rs. 1998 crores ($560 million), and the balance 12.235 billion units for a cost of Rs. 1,800 crores ($500 million). In other words, half of the MSEB expenditure went to buy a quarter of the power (from DPC).[49]

(3) Billed in Dollars

The MSEB had to pay for most of the power in U.S. dollars regardless of the dollar-rupee exchange rate. Initially, the MSEB had to pay 60% of the fees in dollars, then 70% and later 100%. The trend is clear: the dollar is stronger than the rupee, and has become stronger each year. Yet by simply agreeing to pay Enron in dollars the MSEB essentially pledged to assume all the risk of currency fluctuation, even when history suggests that it would no doubt lose over time . The trajectory of the currency gamble is clear: in 1993, the dollar was worth Rs. 32; by 2002 the dollar had climbed to Rs. 47. If the currency continues to devalue at this rate, then India would pay Enron the percentage profit plus another 4.36 points—any Bank would love this scheme.

If we forget that some of this is now the normal practice of business and that it does not appear improper any longer to demand a fixed return on investment, it might still be of interest that the PPA violated several Indian laws:

- That a power company cannot expect payment for generating capacity, but only for actual power generated.

- That the public should only pay for electricity based on the "least cost" whereas Enron charged much more than other power generators.

- That the rate of return on equity in the power sector cannot be more than sixteen percent. The MSEB (and the Government of India counter-guarantee) assured the DPC of a post tax 16% rate of return on capital investment, but many economists who did the numbers argued that its after-tax rate of return would be about 32%.

Abhay Mehta who has studied the numbers carefully offers a much more overwhelming result:

> The payments due on the renegotiated contract constitute one of the largest contracts (civilian or military) in world history, and the single largest contract in [India's] history. Payments amount to about U.S.$1.3 billion in the first year of Phase 2 of the project going online. Total payments amount to about US$ 35 billion (Rs. 1,25,000 crore) over the life of the contract. The payments are linked to various indices including, among other, the oil-price index making exact estimation completely contingent on an assumption of the rate of change in various indices. In any case, a conservative low end estimate of the Net Present Value (NPV) of this stream of payments is about US $17 billion (Rs 70,000 crore) to about US $23 to 25 billion (Rs 1,00,000 to Rs 1,06,000 crore) at the middle end.[50]

As the PPA came on the horizon, the Finance Secretary of the Government of India called a meeting on 3 November 1993 to discuss the DPC's project and "the tariff for power proposed by Enron." The Financial adviser to the MSEB told the Finance Secretary that the PPA's provisions provided DPC's investors with an Internal Rate of Return (IRR) on equity of between 20.6% and 25.22% (approximately, a 32% return on equity). The Chairman of the MSEB said, "In the negotiations they had attempted to bring down this rate but eventually had accepted this figure." Domestic investors generally require a lower IRR, around 17-18.3% in real terms, not the high IRR demanded by

DPC. When asked about the unreasonableness of the rate, the group took up the issue of costs. "The point was made that high rate of return could be obtained by keeping down costs and through efficient operations without any adverse effect on the power cost. It was, therefore, necessary to consider also the validity of the cost estimates. The Financial Adviser, MSEB, stated that they were not competent to comment on capital costs but generally felt that these were not out of line."

That the MSEB claimed ignorance about capital costs is astounding, mainly because the DPC used the canard of high costs to demand a high IRR and high tariffs. Enron refused to reveal the capital costs to anyone, and it took much ferreting by government agencies and activists to produce an estimation of what Enron claimed as its start-up, capital costs—upwards of $4 billion. Enron argued that the costs are high because the technology is superior and that any comparison with other plants is therefore specious. Let's do it anyway.[51]

(4) The Cost of Liquefied Natural Gas (LNG)

Enron's plant at Dabhol required that LNG be imported to India by refrigerated ships (each at $200 million), downloaded at a specially-built LNG terminal on the coast, then rendered into natural gas at Dabhol for power generation. The Godbole Committee, set up to investigate Enron in 2001, argued that Enron ran a scam on the LNG costs. LNG is natural gas liquefied to well below its normal ambient temperature, then made into gas again before it can be rendered into power. Enron attempted to pass off all the charges to the MSEB for the production of LNG and its return to gas (even as Enron would only use 40% of the LNG it imported at Dabhol, the rest being sold to other producers). Furthermore, and here following from its training with Andersen, Enron "double charged" the MSEB for harbor fees, once as capital recovery charges and then as harbor charges. "The total excess payment quantified by the Godbole

Committee is of the order of Rs. 930 crore [$260 million] per year."[52]

(5) Cheaper Local LNG Plants

In Kerala, the National Thermal Power Corporation's LNG plant at Kayamkulam used domestic naphthalene and had start-up costs less than two-thirds of those for the Dabhol plant. Costs of LNG plants in the U.S. and in Africa fell between half and two-thirds of Dabhol.[53] The Government of Maharashtra's own report on the Dabhol project offered the following assessment of comparative costs: "The Committee had the opportunity to peruse the study on comparative capital costs of coal- and gas-based power plants conducted by the U.S.-based Advanced Light Water Reactor Programme (ALWR, Palo Alto, U.S.A.). The draft report is attached at Annexure V. If the findings of this report were applied to the present case, it would be clear that the capital cost of the DPC is on the high side and needs to be considerably reduced. The capital cost of the Enron Project which is gas-based cannot be compared with the capital cost of coal-based plants which could be 50 percent higher depending upon the type of coal used and also whether it is a combined cycle coal-based plant or not. In fact the high capital cost wiped out the main advantage that the Dabhol power was supposed to bring. Because gas-based technology was to be used, the capital cost of the Project should have been much cheaper than a coal-based plant, whereas the running cost would have been higher. In the instant case we have lost the advantage of a lower capital cost from a gas-based plant while still retaining the disadvantages of a higher running cost."[54] Enron/Andersen's famous accounting practices worked hard to jack up prices, but so too did Enron's insistence that everything come from the U.S. Indigenous materials, available at Kayamkulam for example, did not enter the Enron workshop. They needed to import everything. All these inputs guaranteed U.S. exports to India.

(6) The Social Costs of Being Green

On the surface it seems as if natural gas is always a better alternative than coal, even as both are fossil fuels. This is certainly so at the point of consumption, although there are some who say that piped natural gas causes health problems like asthma. At the point of extraction and distribution, the social costs of natural gas are less clear. In the next section, I'll offer some examples from South America of the environmental chaos at the point of extraction, but I could just as well tell the story of the lost fight to stop a natural gas pipeline from Sable Island off the coast of Nova Scotia. The dirt of the process is well hidden when the clean gas comes piped into our stoves. What I don't emphasize enough in the next section, but which is crucial to this point, is that the corporations that pipe natural gas often dispossess very oppressed people from their homelands. The DPC, as I will show, used police power to remove people long resident in the Dabhol region. A clearer example of the social costs of being green can be followed in the aborted adventures of California's Unocal and France's Total/Elfina in Myanmar—where their proposed Yadana ("Jewel") pipeline would not only have displaced the Karen, Mon and Tavoyan peoples, but it would also have disrupted the Tenasserim ecological region. According to one account in 1995, "In constructing the pipeline, Unocal has allied itself with a brutal and illegitimate government in its decades-long war against three ethnic groups, the Mon, the Karen and the Tavoyan peoples. To put a pipeline through the lands of these people—areas never controlled by the central government—will require Unocal and SLORC [the Burmese government which is called State Law and Order Restoration Council] to crush these ethnic groups. The repression is being conducted by the Burmese and Thai armies."[55] I'm no deep ecologist, but if we don't have a debate about the social costs of natural gas taking into consideration all its aspects, then we are lying to each other about its cleanliness.

Enron did not want a debate on anything. Everything had to be a secret, to hide its sweet deal.

The justification made by Enron was that it had these vast capital investments, but no one cared for the investment of U.S. government agencies (almost $400 million from OPIC, over $300 million from the Ex-Im Bank) or from Japanese governmental agencies ($258.2 million from the Japanese Ex-Im Bank, $175 million from the Japanese Ministry of International Trade and Industry), or from the Belgian government ($90.8 million from the Office National du Ducroire) or from the Indian banks (The Industrial Development Bank of India and the State Bank of India lent $1.4 billion to the Enron subsidiary as part of the deal).[56] Enron was not alone in its hustle of the people of Maharashtra and of India, because behind it all the way were loans and grants from public bodies of culpable states across the world. If Enron broke Indian laws, so did they by association.

Meanwhile, the people of India don't even get a dog's breakfast. Their taxes paid for the MSEB's enormous infrastructure over the past fifty years, but Enron did not pay the MSEB rent to send its power along those lines. It took all that for granted. Nor did Enron care that power delivery is not about profit in a social democratic world, but it is about the need for electrification for all. The State Electricity Boards (SEBs) did attempt to create equity by the provision of cheap power to farmers and this, among other reasons, is one of the causes of the SEBs' poor financial record. In ten years, the annual subsidy for agricultural and domestic consumers has risen from $1.2 billion (1990-91) to $5.7 billion (1999-2000). No wonder, then, that in the same period the SEBs registered commercial losses from $850 million (1990-91) to $2.9 billion (1999-2000). In 1998-99, the average rate of return on assets for SEBs was –21%. The state spent money to benefit those who could not otherwise have afforded power as rates spiral upwards. The SEBs did not fail because they are worse at business than Enron. Since Enron cares not a jot for social equity, it is able to maximize its profits with impunity. The lack of a social good in the Enron project was quite baldly stated by a High Court panel of two judges in response to the Center for Indian Trade Union (CITU—the left union) lawsuit against Enron:

> Multinationals who want to invest in developing countries should not indulge in tall talks about educating the people of those countries. The decision of multinationals to invest in that country is based on the security of its investment and lucrative returns on the same. It is not activated by the desire to help resource-starved nations. They do no charity. They move out of their country for greener pastures or better returns. They should, therefore, act and behave like an investor or an industrial house and not a Government.

Enron is out for a killing. The SEBs are charged to provide electrical power at low rates to all customers, a social good irrelevant to Enron. Even the SEBs efforts, however, are insufficient. As writer Arundhati Roy notes:

> There's no doubt that there is a power-shortage crisis in India. But there's another, more serious crisis on hand. Planners in India boast that India consumes twenty times more electricity today than it did fifty years ago. They use it as an index of progress. They omit to mention that seventy percent of rural households still have no electricity. In the poorest states, Bihar, Uttar Pradesh, and Orissa, more than eighty-five percent of the poorest people, mostly Dalit and Adivasi households, have no electricity. What a shameful, shocking record for the world's biggest democracy. Unless this crisis is acknowledged and honestly addressed, generating 'lots and lots of power' (as Mr. Welch [of GE] put it) will only mean that it will be siphoned off by the rich and their endless appetites. It will

require very imaginative, very radical forms of 'structural adjustment' to right this.[57]

Every governmental body complained that the MSEB inevitably would go bust because it was selling electricity to consumers for less than what it paid for it. Enron's PPA guaranteed it a high rate of profit, the MSEB could only raise rates up to a judicially sanctioned level and so the MSEB had to absorb the rise in costs. The citizens lost in two directions: they had to pay the maximum rates and their tax money went toward the preservation of the utility. In the end the taxpayers picked up the tab. Protests across the country against the rip-off led to the collapse of the Congress government in Maharashtra. In April 1995 the right-wing coalition government led by the fascistic Shiv Sena came to power vowing to "throw the [Enron] project into the Arabian Sea." Despite its liability, the new government cancelled the project. But this was a brief respite. On 3 November 1995, Enron International's Rebecca Mark sat down with Shiv Sena supreme leader Bal Thackeray and the Right quickly came to an accommodation with capitalist globalization. Whereas everyone knew the MSEB's political and financial position was hopeless, and whereas it was clear that the GoM did not have the funds to pay Enron (the fees would seize half of Maharashtra's budget, thereby putting pressure on social services), Enron went to the Government of India to seek a counter-guarantee. A right-wing government led by the Bharatiya Janata Party (an electoral and ideological ally of the Shiv Sena in Maharashtra) came to power for only thirteen days in May 1996. While a no-confidence motion was in the works to bring that parliamentary government coalition down, the *one act of parliament passed by this government was Enron's counter-guarantee*!

The Hindu Right made all the right populist noises about imperialism. But when push came to shove it was the Right that was most eager to do the work of the IMF, gaining legitimacy through a cynical and cruel cultural nationalism that serves as cover for its neoliberalism. When the Congress Party lost its legitimacy in 1991 as the bulwark against multinationals, the Hindu Right staked its claim to being the patriotic force in Indian society. As it cloaked itself in patriotism, it opened the doors to the national wealth, especially in the sale of formerly nationalized assets at very low prices to overseas investors like Enron. It even created a Ministry of Disinvestment. The Hindu Right is the Trojan Horse of globalization. In 1998, after the Hindu Right exploded nuclear devices as an act of national self-assertion, it begged for entry into the Club of Five (US, Russia, China, France, England), but it was rebuffed. Undeterred, the Hindu Right government implored the U.S. to allow it full membership in the coalition to topple the Taliban and bin Laden during the Fifth Afghan War. Again, U.S. calculations drew it to Pakistan rather than India. While the Hindu Right leadership tried again and again to beg to stand beside Clinton/Bush/Blair, and to welcome Enron/Coca Cola/Suzuki, it told its cadre to take action outside the U.S. Embassy in New Delhi because GWB's cat is called "India." The protest was no doubt fashionable among a certain section of hard-core activists of the Right, but it was also meaningless. "We are not cats," said one man. "We are lions." Perhaps. But these lions, it seem, are on a tight leash.

Enron, meanwhile, was faced with a round of genuine protests from various peoples' movements and trade unions. The Dabhol region where the plant began to be built was home to almost a hundred thousand people who rely on the land for their livelihood. Enron's environmental record is not impeccable and its disdain for indigenous communities had not fully been realized as yet. At a meeting on 12 March 1993, Enron benefited from the forced migration of part of the population to build the LNG storage tankers. Protests grew from then till the present, with a lull between 1995-96 when the government opposed the project and when the CITU's lawsuit mentioned earlier came before the courts. When the courts dismissed the CITU case, the protests started anew. Enron, according to the fine investigation of Human Rights Watch, colluded with the local police to smash the demonstrators and even gave the police access to company helicopters to conduct surveillance of the crowds. Mahadev Satley, a participant in the 15 May 1997 demonstrations told Human Rights Watch, "There is a popular feeling that the Guhagar police act as employees of Enron and not guardians of law and order on behalf of the state. Not only the local police, but also the local courts are colluding with Enron. Whatever treatment we got from the time we were arrested was to please or appease Enron. The state, police and courts were extremely harsh to show Enron that they were serious."[58] In 1994, Enron invoked Section 47 of the Bombay Police Act to hire the State Reserve Police force from the GoM to suppress dissent at the plant's gates. Between ten and three hundred officers of this force have, at any one time, been at Dabhol. From this and other information, Human Rights Watch argued, "Enron's local entity, the Dabhol Power Corporation, benefited directly from an official policy of suppressing dissent through misuse of the law, harassment of anti-Enron protest leaders and prominent environmental activists, and police practices ranging from arbitrary to brutal."

Phase I, or 740MW, of the Dabhol project went on-line in March 1999. The political pressure on the MSEB was immense, so they requested a twenty percent rate hike (they required at least a twenty-four percent increase in rates to pay their Enron fees). They were allowed short of seven percent, and sent toward bankruptcy. Nonetheless, the hike was a vast amount for most consumers. A host of firms went under, or else they bought private generators to get off the Enron grid. By October 2000, Maharashtra's Minister of Energy noted, "The MSEB is finding it difficult to purchase the entire power from DPC's first phase of the 740MW project," so the MSEB asked for emergency funds. Unable to find the funds, the MSEB refused to pay Enron. In June 2001, the plant went idle.

Overjoyed that the Dabhol plant promised billions of dollars for Enron, CEO Skilling told his employees in the early summer of 2001 that Enron had good times ahead even as Enron's stock profile began to deteriorate. Months later, Enron collapsed. On 26 February 2002, as Skilling was grilled by the Senate Committee on Commerce, Science and Transportation, he defended his promotion of Enron stock to his employees in the early summer of 2001 because "we were potentially going to be resolving the India situation."[59] India, in other words, will work like a Raptor to subsidize Enron's bad trades in the derivatives markets.

Imperialism's Wild Side

While the financial rip-off in India illuminates how money can be sucked away, the case of Enron's environmental destruction is no less crucial. The best example is not from India (although there is something perverse about making the case for an LNG plant as more ecological when the company conducts forced migrations to situate the LNG containers), but from South America. In 1997, the Brazilian and Bolivian government laid the foundation for a $2 billion natural gas pipeline that would begin in Santa Cruz, Bolivia, and carry thirty million cubic meters of gas to the Brazilian eastern seaboard. Petrobas (Brazil) and Yacimentos Petroliferos Fiscales Bolivianos (Bolivia), both government-held concerns, commissioned the thirty-two hundred mile pipeline. Enron was a major stakeholder in the project, along with the usual suspects, British Gas, Tenneco, BHP and El Paso Natural Gas. The slated goal was to open the Amazonian forests to environmentally unsustainable development. The pipeline project would slice a thirty meter wide path through the subtropical dry forest of Gran

Choco Park, the Izozog, Chiquitos and Utoquis swamplands as well as the Santa Cruz la Vieja Park (all in Bolivia for a total of 540 kms), and then onto the Pantanal in Mato Grosso do Sul, the largest wetlands in the world, the mountainous and there-fore erosion-prone Aparrandos of the Serra in Rio Grande do Sul (all in Brazil for a total of 2315 kms).

The *Washington Post*, not normally at the forefront of green stories, reported in early May 2002 on this pipeline and Enron's "Scar on South America." Completed in late 2001, the pipeline and its service roads "have opened the forest to the kind of damage environmental groups had predicted: Poachers travel service roads to log old-growth trees. Hunters prey on wild game and cattle gaze illegally. An abandoned gold mine reopened and its workers camp along the pipeline right-of-way."[60] Enron refused to route the pipeline around the forest because this would have cost an additional $100 million. Meanwhile, precious forest cover has been brought under the heel of heartless development.

Brazil's native people have faced the assault of the fats cats from the U.S. and the running dogs of Brazil for decades. In 1934, Henry Ford founded the poorly named Belterra Rubber Plantation in Amazônia. Brazilian President Getúlio Vargas spoke at that Planation on 5 October 1940 to lay out a strategy for the forest that would have warmed the heart of Enronistas in the 1990s: "Everything which has up to now been done in Amazonas, whether in agriculture or extractive industry, has been an empirical realization, and must be transformed into rational exploitation. What nature offers us here is a magnifi-cent gift, which demands the care and the cultivation of the hand of man. From the regime of sparse colonization, sub-servient to casual interests, consuming energy with but slight profit, we must change over to the concentration and fixation of the human element. Already to arrive are North American industrialists who are interested in collaborating with us in the development of Amazônia, where their capital and technical resources will find a secure and remunerative application."[61]

Vargas had here presciently laid out the game plan for Enron's shenanigans a half century later in the 1990s. But the outdated Lockean nakedness of his message would not have been well received by a sophisticated Enron in consultation with its pollsters and PR agents. The Defense of the Patanal Association, the Brazilian Institute for Cultural Heritage and the trade unions saw the Enron project for what it was and fervently opposed the project. Enron countered by making the case that even this was ecologically good for the planet because the product was natural gas. Gas, indeed.

Enron, in league with Shell and Transredes, was at work on a 390 mile pipeline known as the Cuiaba Pipeline Project that has "brought serious environmental and social problems" to people who lived in the vicinity of the project site, and these people complain of "pollution of local water resources, degradation of local roads, soil and air pollution."[62] When the U.S. government's Overseas Private Investment Corporation felt the heat of people power, Enron announced in 1999 that it would go it alone if OPIC decided not to underwrite the project. Republican Congressman Ron Paul (Texas) said of the $200 million loan from OPIC to Enron, "Big business is in cahoots with government on this one. Government wants to subsidize the attack on the environment."[63] Incidentally, Congressman Paul voted against stronger environmental standards for cars, he voted to open the Arctic National Wildlife Reserve for exploration and he voted against implementation of the Kyoto Protocol. Not an environmentalist by any standard, Congressman Paul was just annoyed by Enron's state-sponsored arrogance. In January 2000, a pipeline owned and operated by Enron and Dutch Shell ruptured to spill 29,000 barrels of crude petroleum. The Uru Morato people who live beside the Poopo Lake in the Andes reported that many acres of their farmland, as well as fish and birds, had been affected by the oil-spill. Enron and its partner, Transredes, have spent $10 million on the clean up which continues to this day.[64]

Enron officials rarely commented on these dirty deals from Brazil, Bolivia and Dabhol. But, when a reporter from *Far Eastern Economic Review*, asked Rebecca Mark of Enron International, the same woman who showed up on the Harley Davidson, about the forced removal of people from the site in India, she got angry. "Enron worked to defuse accusations that the company deprived locals of land," wrote the reporter, "and headed off the formation of a powerful lobby against it. It did so in part by involving locals in community activities meant to help people adversely affected by the project, even giving jobs to some. Mark denies the company bought off local people for the sake of peace. 'There are always ways to include people, to make them productive when they could be counterproductive. That's not corruption, that's economic interest."[65] The "involvement of locals in community activities" included the creation of shell Non-Governmental Organizations (NGOs) funded by Enron to disrupt community solidarity and the use of company funds to hire thugs to dissuade people from their protests. Human Rights Watch documents this at length from the Dabhol project. It shows that DPC's Vice President for Community Relations, Sanjeev Khandekar, offered contracts to the leaders of the rebellion. Sadanand Pawar, one community leader, told HRW, "I would get messages sent through contractors. They repeatedly offered me contracts throughout 1996-97. They would call me and say, 'Take a contract, give work orders, and give up the agitation.'" According to the HRW, Enron's subsidiary hired a member of the Hindu Right's political party, Sushil Velhal to create an NGO to undermine the protests. Velhal had been part of the anti-Enron agitation, but he switched sides. A well-known smuggler and gangster (he was arrested in 1993 for running RDX explosives into Mumbai for the series of bomb blasts), he started the Guhagar Parishad Vikas Manch as part of Enron's "community development" schemes.[66]

Privatizing IMF and USAID Functions

Ms. Powers' testimony that opened this chapter—that the private sector "forces government officials of the country in question to deal with the reforms..." is perversely correct. Her firm succeeds in doing the work of reform where state agencies failed: Enron is more effective at IMFundamentalism than either USAID or the IMF itself. She is saying that while attempts to craft reform via the state fail, private entities motivated by profit are far better at efficiency, and that to be efficient is the goal.

The ideological terrain trumpeted by Ms. Powers is nothing new, but follows in the footsteps trodden by F. A. Hayek and other members of his Austrian Circle. Hayek felt that humans should not try to make a just world because justice "is an adaptation of our ignorance," and justice itself does "not belong to the category of error but to that of nonsense," this principally because to seek justice is to "chase a mirage."[67] Rather than attempt justice through the state form, institutions of state power must be reduced so that corporations, the most effective social agency, can go about their efficient business, and conduct development on their own terms. As Hayek put it, "The system of private property is the most important guaranty of freedom, not only for those who do own property, but scarcely less for those who do not."[68] What Ms. Powers is saying, in effect, is that regardless of the history of colonialism and imperialism, the world can only advance in the hands of corporations who can teach the natives how to reform their institutions.

Three Ingredients in Enron's Recipe for Capitalism

As the leader of the flagship for U.S. transnational corporate power in the 1990s, Ken Lay impressed all his industry cohorts as Enron signed deal after deal from Manila to Mato Grosso do Sul. Enron's style of capitalism, however, was not its alone, but a general theory often learnt more on the job than in business school. Three ingredients of Enron's capitalism illuminate how it was so good at what it did. Enron will no doubt be the subject of case studies in failure. But if the Wharton, Harvard, or Stanford schools were really doing their jobs they would have a course on each of these aspects for their budding Enronistas.

(1) The Revolving Door

There is a scene in one of the Superman movies where our hero moves through a revolving door so quickly you can't see the transformation from Clark Kent into his Superman get up. But you know he's done it. Enron employees could move through that revolving door almost as quickly, changing from the mild-mannered government regulator into costume at Enron before taxpayers knew what hit them. Since the Enron-style of capitalism is to make massive profits through deregulation, having allies in government who kill regulation is an enormous advantage. These allies all too frequently then leave government and take lucrative jobs with the firms they "regulated."

The tale of Wendy Gramm is exemplary in this regard; Enron welcomed her onto its board for her work on the U.S. Commodity Futures Trading Commission. But she is not alone. On 28 October 1997, Enron Oil and Gas (EOG) announced the entry of Frank G. Wisner Jr. onto its board of directors. Forrest Hoglund, Chairman of EOG, noted that Wisner "brings exceptional foreign service experience with international business markets." The media ignored this event and did not make the requisite connection to corporate corruption of the U.S. state (and to the farcical hearings on "campaign finance reform"). For those who follow events in Asia, Frank Wisner's name is familiar. During his tenure as Ambassador in the Philippines (1991-92), Enron lobbied for the Subic Bay and Batangas power plants. When Wisner left Manila in July 1992, Enron won the deal and began to manage the plants in January 1993. Wisner then moved to the ambassadorship in India, where he assisted Enron as it vied for $1.1 billion contract for offshore holdings as well as for consolidation of its interests in the Dabhol plant. When there was renewal of economic nationalism during the winter of 1995-96, Wisner enthusiastically pushed the U.S. advisory to transnational firms to avoid India for six months, and he personally boycotted the "India Power '96—Beyond Dabhol" summit, despite being scheduled to give an address. Wisner sent a clear message: do business with Enron or the U.S. will be very unhappy. Once Enron and the government signed the PPA in August 1996, Wisner began to make preparations to leave India. He returned to the U.S. and joined Enron's EOG board in October 1997.

In 1995, the U.S. Congress passed legislation to make lobbyists report their activities to operate, as President Clinton put it, "in the sunlight of public scrutiny." Prior to this, lobbying rules had not been changed for fifty years! Simultaneously, a group of progressive representatives proposed the Revolving Door Act of 1995 to restrict government servants from immediate employment as lobbyists. Congress roundly defeated the measure, even as its main sponsor, Martin Meehan, labored on with this issue (he left it behind when his tepid Campaign Finance Act took on momentum). There is no popular struggle on this issue, so it is unlikely to have much effect on the legislative agenda and despite the flagrancy of revolving door corruption, the media tends to ignore it (or treat it as normal).

In 1998, the U.S. Treasury Department formulated new regulations to prevent U.S. firms from shifting profits to overseas subsidiaries in countries with lower tax burdens. For many years now, firms had taken advantage of what are known as

action rules," or what is generally called "transfer
ͻsidiaries located in tax-free zones are billed for
ᴡᴏʀᴋ. ᴛʜᴏₛ expends revenues of parent companies with a
high-tax burden, lowering or eliminating the taxable profit.
Treasury sought to close this loophole. The counter attack was
fierce as major U.S. transnational firms (Price Waterhouse-
Coopers, Hallmark Cards, Coca-Cola, Philip Morris, GE and
IBM) ganged up to block the rules. They won. The well-paid
heads of the coalition, Daniel Berman and Kenneth Kies were
recent employees of—the government. Berman had worked for
three years as deputy international tax counsel for the U.S.
Treasury and he quite candidly said that he had helped formulate the law he now successfully blocked.[69] Kies was Chief of
Staff for the Joint Committee on Tax for the U.S. Congress.
Fortune magazine said of Kies, "he is the man to see when it
comes to altering the nation's tax code," and it was said of him
that he "ghosted virtually every line" of the 1997 tax bill.[70]
These two put their contacts to work and, in the absence of
much Congressional resistance, won big for corporate power.

If Kies-Berman came from government to corporations and
used their skills to institutionalize corruption, the Bush cabinet
shows us how people can do the reverse, moving from corporations to government and do the same thing. The revolving door
moves both ways. In April 1998, the overdeveloped world, organized as the Organization for Economic Cooperation and
Development (OECD), urged its member states to constrain the
activities of tax-free havens such as the Cayman Islands. The
Clinton administration began a study of the problem, and
Treasury Secretary Lawrence Summers said that the government
must "name and shame" those countries with no banking regulations. In the aftermath of the well-financed bombings of the U.S.
embassies in Tanzania and Kenya (on 7 August 1998), the target
of such pronouncements was clear. Since the terror networks used
these financial shields, the government noted in December 2000

that one of the guilty parties was any state with "weak financial regulatory systems and lax enforcement measures." The Cayman Islands cut a deal with the Clinton administration just before the July 2000 summit of the G7, and things seemed to be on the road to some sort of transparency of tax havens.

Then the Bush people took over. Even as there is much that is the same between the two governments, the Bush folk are themselves corporate while the Clinton people by and large tried to work on behalf of corporations. Treasury Secretary Paul O'Neill cracked down on the Clinton approach. On 17 February 2001 he told the G7 that the scrutiny of tax havens was "under review"; in May he wrote an op-ed that said that the Bush administration would not "interfere with the internal tax policy decisions of sovereign nations"; and finally on 27 November 2001, after Enron's collapse, the administration signed a deal with the Caymans that mandated more transparency after 2004 but only if the Enron assets and records can be moved to a secret third location.[71] Groups like Public Citizen called the deal a sham.[72]

The most egregious industries that indulge in the revolving door are pharmaceuticals and agriculture, and we should stop and visit with their executive workforce.[73] To simplify things, lets look at two companies, Monsanto and Pharmacia, one from each world. In October 2001, the two firms merged to become one of the most powerful combines in the world of industrial chemical products. In July 2002, Pfizer acquired both firms in a massive merger. In 2001, Monsanto's net sales amounted to $5.5 billion from its wide range of products, from herbicides (Roundup) to seeds (Dekalb and Asgrow), as Pharmacia took in $13.8 billion from its vast array of products such as Celebrex (arthritis), Xalatan (glaucoma), Xanax (panic), Rogaine (hair loss) and Nicorette (nicotine addiction).

Monsanto and Pharmacia embody the idea of the Revolving Door (RD). Here are a few examples:

- Linda J. Fisher: Her career enters the RD radar when she was the Assistant Administrator of the United States Environmental Protection Agency's Office of Pollution Prevention, Pesticides and Toxic Substances in Reagan's second administration, then worked as Chief of Staff for EPA Administrator Lee Thomas (also in Reagan's second spell), before working as Assistant Administrator for Policy, Planning and Evaluation at the EPA and then Assistant Administrator for Prevention, Pesticides, and Toxic Substances during Bush Senior's time in the White House. In 1995, Fisher joined Monsanto as Vice President for Government and Public Affairs, essentially for using her contacts in DC as head lobbyist for the agro-giant. When Bush Junior came to the helm, he called her back to the EPA as Deputy Director, a post she currently holds. Phil Clapp, President of the National Environmental Trust, said Fisher is a "moderate, corporate-style Republican, not a hidebound conservative" and that Fisher was seen as "pretty reasonable by environmentalists" when she headed the EPA's pesticide division. "But afterwards she headed Monsanto's lobbying operation while the company was trying to head off any government oversight of genetically engineered crops."[74] What is not remarked upon in the media is that Fisher developed the EPA's pesticide policy before joining Monsanto, a firm much beholden to the lax regulations created by the EPA in the Reagan-Bush years.

- Michael Friedman: Friedman was the acting commissioner of the Food and Drug Administration who joined Pharmacia as Senior Vice President. On 7 October 1998, Friedman, as acting commissioner, sat before Congress and testified on behalf of a reform of the FDA's practices with regard to pharmaceuticals. He wanted "modernization" and "reform," in other words, an easing up on regulation, something that benefited the firm he then joined. Friedman is the same person who as an FDA official during the Bush administration urged the Pentagon to use the anthrax vaccine in the Gulf War.

- William Ruckelshaus: Harvard-trained Ruckelshaus was the first administrator of the EPA in 1970. He returned to the agency in Reagan's first tour of duty, left government, worked as the top dog at Browing-Ferris Industries, became a strategic director of the Madrona Venture Group and took a seat on Monsanto's board for twelve years. He now warms a board chair for Pharmacia. Even though Ruckelshaus's name appears versus Monsanto in the famous 1984 Supreme Court case on intellectual property (settled on behalf of Monsanto to protect its "intellectual property" on pesticide formulae), Ruckelshaus was a friend of big business and Big Pharma.[75] Incidentally, a fact frequently left out of all his biographies is that Ruckelshaus was acting director of the FBI under Nixon and he ran the notorious COINTELPRO program.

- Mickey Kantor: Kantor served under Clinton as U.S. Trade Representative, then when Ron Brown died, Kantor took his place as Commerce Secretary. A major booster of free trade and of big corporations (such as Monsanto), Kantor left government to join the law firm of Mayer, Brown and Platt, as well as the board of Monsanto, now of Pharmacia. As U.S. Trade Representative, Kantor was a vigorous champion of intellectual property rights (under the Trade Related Intellectual Property Rights or TRIPS regime of the Uruguay Round of GATT). On 8 November 1995, Kantor replied to a stinging letter from Ralph Nader and James Love (Consumer Project on Technology) with a strong defense of intellectual property "particularly with regard to pharmaceutical products." Monsanto and Pharmacia benefit enormously from the TRIPS regime, notably from the watered down provisions for "compulsory licensing" (when a country can move a drug off patent).

- Frank Carlucci: On the board of Pharmacia, Carlucci (a former wrestling teammate of Defense Secretary Donald Rumsfeld) brings the entire weight of the Carlyle Group, a merchant bank and defense contractor with CIA firepower that is worth about $13.5 billion. In the CIA during the Carter years, Carlucci entered the Defense Department of Bush Senior. We tend to forget that Carlucci held the fort in the Congo as the U.S. competed with the Belgians to assassinate Congolese leader Patrice Lumumba (1961). Carlucci is the main arms man for the Carlyle Group, being the center of the so-called reforms of arms procurement in the Pentagon when he was there. His ties with the Bush administration go back to the father (who is a senior adviser at Carlyle), but also to the son, because Bush Junior sat on the board of a Carlyle subsidiary, Caterair, when he was a Texas businessman (1990-1992).[76]

- Parry, Romani, DeConcini and Symms: The DC law firm that lobbies for Pharmacia, but also for Bristol-Myers Squibb and Glaxo-Wellcome. The three senior partners in the law-firm all come from the world of politics. Thomas Parry was Chief of Staff and Chief Counsel for Senator Orrin Hatch. Romano Romani was legislative aide and Staff Director for Senator Vance Hartke and Dennis DeConcini. DeConcini was a U.S. Senator from Arizona and member, along with John McCain of the Savings & Loan scandal's Keating Five. DeConcini's important work on behalf of Big Pharma came in the Judiciary Committee of the Senate, when he chaired the Subcommittee on Patents, Copyrights and Trademarks (fought to tighten intellectual property rights of firms) and on the Subcommittee on Antitrust, Monopolies and Business Rights (fought to maintain the rights of firms to combine into behemoths). For Glaxo-Wellcome, Parry, Romani, DeConcini and Symms fought to keep Glaxo's Zantac on the patent.

Aware of the inappropriateness of the revolving door, Dennis DeConcini told the *Washington Post*, "People who serve in government often go ahead and work for somebody later. I

think that's pretty natural."[77] DeConcini is n~~
Amy Comstock, Director of the Office of Governm~~
(and main ethicist for both the Clinton and Bush admini~~
tions), sat on a panel at the American Enterprise Institute on 14
February 2001 and said, "Our government, in fact, is designed
to turn over at the highest levels every four years, and I generally think it is a good principle to hire people who have experience in the fields that they're going to regulate," and again, "I
do not see it that way as long as they [taking the example of
Colin Powell and Donald Rumsfeld] vigilantly honored the
conflict of interest rules while they were in government, and I
have absolutely no reason to believe that either of them did not.
I do not believe it is inappropriate for people to actually benefit from that experience and growth that they gained in government, and if we prohibited people from doing that, we are
going to have a hard time getting people into government."
Then Comstock tells us, "When people talk about the revolving door in a negative way, they also often refer to not the
access, the actually communicating back, which is what our
rules cover, but they also talk about people financially benefiting from having been in the government. I have to say, I don't
really see what is wrong with that. Entering the government is
not entering the priesthood. It is not a lifetime vow of poverty.
This came up when Secretary Powell was up for confirmation,
as well as [at the confirmation of] Secretary Rumsfeld. They
both made a fair amount of money after they left their first
round of government service and some people referred to that
as using public office for private gain."

A defense of revolving door in terms of the need to hire
experienced personnel fails when you see how blatantly the figures in question worked to benefit the firm in a general way. Few
cases show us that FDA Chief X passed a rule to benefit
Company Y, but we can see that FDA Chief X passed a rule that
worked in the benefit of the entire industry of which Company

is a part. The benefit is not often directed to the firm in question, but it is mostly to corporate interests in general.

(2) Agent 007: Out of the Bedroom and into the Boardroom

When Frank Wisner joined Enron's board in 1997, it was on the back of a series of revealing scandals that the CIA had begun to spy for U.S. corporations. In 1992, CIA Director Robert Gates announced, "Nearly forty percent of the new requirements are economic in nature." Wisner's tour of duty in the Philippines and India, discussed earlier, bears this out. A Wisner aide told Inter Press Services in 1997, "If anybody asked the CIA to help promote U.S. business in India, it was probably Frank." And Mr. Wisner had impeccable credentials, even though he only worked as Under Secretary of Defense for Policy and Under Secretary of State for International Security Affairs before he became Ambassador. But Wisner's father, Frank Senior was a legendary CIA figure who joined in 1947, helping overthrow Arbenz of Guatemala (1954), helping Kermit Roosevelt dispatch Mossadeq of Iran (1953) before Wisner Senior committed suicide in 1965.

Enron was not only in good company; it stood on the shoulders of history.

On 18 September 1997, an Egyptian-American businessman Roger Tamraz (a fugitive from Lebanon accused of embezzlement) sat before a Senate Committee interested in campaign contributions. Tamraz, who contributed $300,000 to the Democratic Party from late 1995 to 1997, had close ties to other petro-luminaries. These included John Connally (Texas Oilman and one time Nixon cabinet member), the Bank of Credit and Commercial International's Ghaith Pharaon (both together at Harvard Business School) and the National Commercial Bank of Saudi Arabia's Khaled bin Mahfouz.[78] When the Senators asked Tamraz why he donated money to the Democrats, he answered brazenly, "The only reason [was] to get access [to the President]. In America, nothing is impossible. Thank God we are a capitalist society and there's nothing wrong in running after money." Tamraz' attitude annoyed the Senators, and Richard Durbin (Democrat-Illinois) exploded, "You put money in the slot, you get a response from the political party in power. I think that is distasteful, at the minimum, and unseemly." Tamraz remained unmoved, for, he argued, what he did was "business as usual."[79]

Tamraz, head of TamOil and Oil Capital Corporation, wanted the U.S. government to intervene on his behalf to reconcile Armenia and Azerbaijan so that his pipeline could be built and secured. On 6 June 1995, Tamraz announced his intention to build a $2 billion pipeline to tap the coveted Caspian Sea oil reserves, with a potential catch of two hundred billion barrels, enough to satisfy the planet's oil needs for decades. A consortium of oil companies signed a series of agreements with the republics in the region, and all understood the problem of getting the oil out. Tamraz wanted to circumvent the land route that contained the twin stumbling blocks of war-torn Chechnya and embargoed Iran, not to mention the bottleneck of the Bosphorus. The Southern California based Unocal had hoped to build the pipeline through Afghanistan, but the turmoil there at the time made that gambit impossible.[80] Tamraz was eager that the CIA and the National Security Council get to work to bring peace between the two neighboring republics of Azerbaijan and Armenia, so that his pipeline could wend its way through the Caucuses into Europe.[81] Even as the NSC and Congressional leaders found Tamraz to be unsavory, the U.S. Ambassador to Armenia (1993-1995) Harry Gilmore tried his best to get Tamraz clearance for his deeds.

Here was a businessman, a representative of corporate power, glibly telling the people's representatives that the public's resources must be brought to bear to facilitate his profit and not the best interests of the taxpayers at large. Genuine peace in Azerbaijan and Armenia is not as important as the ability of a large corporation to build a pipeline through the country. Evidence for this mendacity is the Clinton administration's ties to the Taliban so that Unocal could build its pipeline: anything, even the Taliban, is sufficient as long as the gas flows.

Nothing Tamraz requested was unusual.

None of this is shocking if we recall CIA Directive 10/2 (18 June 1948): the CIA is to conduct, among other things, "propaganda, economic warfare, preventative direct action." The ambassadors, the CIA, the branches of the U.S. government had one mission: to ensure that U.S. fat cats fed first at the trough, and the government conducted all kinds of "warfare" (including the non-metaphorical kind) to make this happen.

With the fall of the USSR, the CIA redefined itself as the provider of economic espionage for big U.S. corporations. Although the CIA cannot do "commercial spying," Director Robert Gates said in 1992, it could "be helpful on economic intelligence, by identifying foreign governments that are involved in unfair practices...where they are colluding with businesses in their country to the disadvantage of the U.S."[82] That summer, the Senate Select Intelligence Committee held hearings on espionage, at which former CIA Director Stansfield Turner candidly asked, "If we spy for military security, why shouldn't we spy for economic security?"[83] Senator Joe Lieberman joined the debate to argue that economic espionage must be used to protect U.S. corporate dominance. "The real economic gain goes to the companies and nations that make the products," he wrote, "not the consumers who buy them. To suggest that America wins because other nations produce, commercialize and now dominate technological products we invented misses the idea of what we need to do to protect our standard of living."[84] Perhaps what we need to do, then, is build an economic missile defense platform to shoot down imports if they diminish our stranglehold on international trade.

None of this was idle pondering. The FBI created the Economic Counter-Intelligence Program in 1994, and the CIA went to work to pilfer technology from around the world. In France, a team of agents tried to steal ATM switching technology from France Telecom, but they were caught. France's Interior Minister noted, "There were transgressions by [US] secret services not only in France, and in other European countries as well."[85] Undeterred, the CIA enabled Raytheon to defeat a Thomson CSF bid to build a $1.4 billion radar system in Brazil.[86] By all indications, the U.S. espionage apparatus, at least before 9/11, had been turned over to the disposal of corporate America. In 1993, the Clinton administration formed the National Economic Council to "plan" U.S. industrial policy. One unnamed CIA official told journalist Robert Dreyfuss rather bitterly, "The National Economic Council is treating the CIA like an extension of its own staff."[87]

Alongside economic espionage, the CIA uses a device known as Non-Official Cover (NOC), by which an agent takes a job with a U.S. transnational corporation, has no contact with the U.S. Embassy and conducts economic espionage on his/her own. The CIA used firms such as RJR Nabisco, Prentice-Hall, Ford, Pan Am, Procter & Gamble, GE, Campbell Soup, IBM, Bank of America, Chase Manhattan Bank, Sears Roebuck and Rockwell International for the NOC program. The firms sponsor the agent (who enters the company payroll), and the agent gets information for them using subterfuge. Robert Dreyfuss who broke this story in 1995, notes, "The CIA's economic spies are currently active in Japan, Western Europe and key developing nations like Mexico, Brazil, India and the countries of the Middle East."[88] The CIA, for instance, is on the road to get data on Japanese auto technology, particularly on blueprints for its "clean cars" and the battery that it would use.

There is no evidence that Enron joined the NOC program, but critics did argue that Enron used the CIA to gain information about its competitors. Frustrated during Enron's fight with Philadelphia utility Peco and by charges that Enron uses intelligence from the government to quash rivals, Ken Lay told the *Philadelphia Inquirer*, "To my knowledge, I don't think we've ever received any information from the CIA. When we go into these countries and bid on these projects, we rely solely on our own intelligence."[89]

A visionary intelligence, no doubt.

(3) Monopoly is Our Game

Markets are insecure, full of the uncertainty of human existence—the weather, intangible demand, and of course, political instability. These are only some of the factors that constrain economic activity. One of the features of the democratic state has been to cushion the populace from the burden of insecurity inherent in these market systems by the creation of social security, subsidies, disaster relief and other such instruments of civilization.

Big firms also seek stability, and a safe harbor from markets, their "free market" rhetoric notwithstanding. Standard devices include state subsidies and attempts to corner markets and create a monopoly situation. If Enron held control of the entire energy market as a wholesaler of power, it would be able to determine prices and shield itself from the wiles of the customers and of the weather, but most importantly from its competitors. In California, this is just what Enron did. Its sheer domination of the market enabled it to manufacture a crisis and then walk away with massive profits. To shield itself from problems, Enron-style firms, contrary to their public claims to desire open markets, try to set-up contracts that secure it a guaranteed price, generally from the state. In effect, the state insures a privately-held transnational against losses. The infamous Power Purchasing Agreement in India, discussed above, is one example. But there are many others such as the December 1999 PPA signed by Enron and the government of Nigeria. (The World Bank objected to the PPA here as well, on the grounds that there was no competitive bidding, very high prices, no penalty for poor performance, secure payment by state insurance and finally excessive contract termination payments—a soup familiar to the Indian Government of Maharashtra and the MSEB).[90]

Enron in Indonesia reveals another look at this cookie-cutter method of using government and corporate muscle power to wring profits from whole countries. Wracked by corruption under the heel of the US-backed President Suharto, Indonesia's economy stumbled forward at great human expense. If the U.S. green light for the coup of 1965 that installed Suharto was not enough interference, and if Nike-type firms haven't created chaos for the working people of the country, then World Bank's Multilateral Investment Guarantee Agency (MIGA) that insured Enron's shenanigans in Indonesia certainly cemented the U.S. entry into the annals of sordidness.[91] Enron, as Enron Java Power Company, bid and won the right to build the 500MW Surabaya power plant at Pasuran, East Java. But government enthusiasm for the deal was squelched by the currency crisis of 1997. When the government was forced by these circumstances to back out of the agreement, Enron pressed on. Perusahaan Listrik Negara (PLN), the government's utility, argued that Enron's rates could not be sustained even in normal times, especially because Enron demanded payment in dollars; and certainly with the crisis it became impossible.

Through MIGA, the World Bank entered the fray, to defend Enron's deal even though it was thirty percent higher than the regular rates in Indonesia. Djiteng Marsudi, former president of PLN, complained after Suharto's regime collapsed in 1998 that "we had no choice [but to accept the Enron deal]" mainly because of political pressure from the government. Suharto's son sat on the board of the Enron subsidiary. The government in turn felt the pressure from an eager Clinton administration (Ron Brown wrote two letters in 1995 to the Indonesian government). "Most of the power plants rely on their connections with Suharto's family and cronies," Marsudi said. "Only one of the twenty-seven private power projects won a contract through a competitive bid." When Enron was forced out, MIGA paid $15 million to the Enron Java Power Company so that it could cover its bills, around the same time as Indonesia had to fork out $290 million to MidAmerican Energy Holdings Company, via the U.S. government's Overseas Private Investment Corporation. The shakedowns of places like Indonesia take place not just by the monopoly condition of the firms, but also by the monopoly over future business deals brokered by MIGA and OPIC. If you don't pay up now, there may never be a chance to do business again. No wonder they're angry in Indonesia.

A scandal that bears recollection in light of the Enron PPA is the largest corporate fine for price fixing. On 18 September 1998, the scion of the Archer Daniels Midland (ADM) Company was convicted of plotting with competitors to fix the price and worldwide sale of lysine (a feed additive that produces lean muscles for chickens and pigs). ADM's total stock value was $9.7 billion (with $417 million in the hands of its owner, Dwayne Andreas) and in the nine months of 1997 prior to the scandal, ADM posted sales of $12.06 billion with profits of $340.9 million (a thirty-four percent increase from 1997). With a lock on the world's ethanol, corn syrup and lysine market, ADM calls itself the "Supermarket of the World" and is one of the most aggressive agro-business outfits around. In 1995, ADM paid $100 million in fines when it was found guilty of fixing the price of citric acid and lysine. In 1998, Andreas' son Michael was convicted of a conspiracy to sell twenty-seven percent of the world's $600 million lysine market (the plot was hatched in Mexico City in 1992). Every few years, ADM fixes prices, gets busted by the Feds, pays a fee that is chickenfeed when compared to the profits (a rare $100 million fine against profit of three times that in just one year isn't so bad), and then sets off again to try to fix prices.[92]

Even as the government went after ADM for fixing prices (and the evidence was conclusive: a whistleblower taped ADM officials and others laughing about prices as they made the deal), the government continued to support ADM through a massive price subsidy on the ethanol market. In May 1998, the U.S. Congress passed a $215 billion transportation bill to enhance the country's deteriorating infrastructure.

That bill contained a massive subsidy for ethanol, a bene-fit that made about $400 million for ADM. In 1997, Michael Andreas confessed, "We have to have tax incentives to make that ethanol program work." The GAO agreed, "Without tax incentives, ethanol-blended gasoline currently cannot be priced to compete with substitute fuels, and ethanol fuel production would largely discontinue." From 1979 till 1998, the subsidy cost the U.S. government $7 billion, and more than $3 billion went to ADM, the dominant force in the market. In those years, ADM donated $3 million to the reelection fund of politi-cians from both parties (as well as underwriting PBS's News Hour with Jim Lehrer), so little was done to either remove the subsidy or challenge ADM's attempt in the late 1990s to domi-nate prices.[93]

Enron, by any other name.

Power Revelations

In 2000, Enronization struck the Indian state of Andhra Pradesh.[94] But this time Enron itself was absent and the only actors on the scene came from the World Bank and the state government. The World Bank had made a brief reputation for itself in the 1990s as the one agency that tended to refuse the PPA-type arrangements made by the Enronistas. But the

Hyderabad story (and the Bolivia one that comes in the next chapter) should give us pause. Even as it has given cover to anti-Enron movements here and there, the World Bank is for the most part an agent of Enronization.

Our story must begin with a crime.

This crime was committed under the shadow of the State Assembly in Hyderabad (capital of Andhra Pradesh, in central India) on 28 August 2000. For three quarters of an hour the guns of the police tore through thousands of people. Hundreds fell, two never to rise again. The streets could not hide the wounded and dead. Images of the slaughter flew across the airwaves into cables, and to the television sets of distant audiences. Nobody hid this crime. This crime was committed in the middle of the day.

And the U.S. papers said nothing. Nor did then U.S. President Bill Clinton, friend of the man whose troops neglected every rule that regulates their actions, Chandrababu Naidu, Chief Minister of Andhra Pradesh, also known as Naidu.com, King of the Indo-Internet of High-Tech Hyderabad.

For three months this state in India had been engulfed with struggles led by a vast and novel coalition of the Left. The Communist Party of India (Marxist) joined with their Left Front partners the Communist Party of India, and both in turn made common cause with two Maoist (or Naxalite) outfits, Communist Party of India (Marxist-Leninist) and the CPIML (New Democracy). To top it off, this Left ensemble allied with the Congress Party (that tired and tattered former monolith whose path down the right was well-crafted by the IMF in the early 1990s). The issue on the table was a rollback in the rates for electricity. Rates had been raised through the roof by the ruling Telugu Desam government who were and are in a rather tenuous alliance with the Hindu Right in New Delhi.

In response, the government was obdurate. Too much is at stake, since the state government has vested its fate in the hands of a kind of Cyber-Structural Adjustment: in 1996 the Andhra Pradesh government signed an agreement with the World Bank called the Andhra Pradesh Economic Restructuring Project. There is nothing special about Andhra Pradesh here, since it is the same old tonic, the same tired medicine from the discredited quack. It asks for the government to withdraw services from the water and power sector and to reduce government employees. The task was to privatize electricity generation and distribution. In February 1999 the World Bank and the Naidu government signed a five-year agreement to get the state Rs. 40 billion ($880 million) in five installments in return for a fifteen percent increase in power rates per year. Since Naidu was up for election, the World Bank agreed to postpone the measures till after the vote (so much for free elections!). After the elections Naidu raised the rates so that consumers were hit with at least a fifteen percent hike in fees per unit of power.[95]

On 24 March 2000, just five months before the police shot fatefully into a crowd of protestors, Bill Clinton met Naidu.com and told him, "The Andhra Pradesh CEO was very much known in the U.S. and very much admired." In these neoliberal times, U.S. presidents not only treat elected officials of other parts as CEOs, but they even call them that.[96] He praised Naidu.Com for his reforms and said, "Little wonder that Hyderabad is now known as Cyberabad." During their mutual love fest, and after his very brief stay in the city, Bill noted, "If you look at the example of this city and this state, you will realize that good governance is also necessary," and "the Chief Minister's role in accomplishing this is evident."[97] What must these people mean by "good governance"? Yes, the Internet monopolies (such as Microsoft, Sun, Intel) have flocked to Cyberabad, but not with the same numbers as these have gone to nearby Bangalore (in the state of Karnataka). But the social indicators in Andhra Pradesh are abhorrent and the "reforms" seem to only produce social misery for the people: thirty percent of its 73 million people live beneath the poverty line, the literacy rate is just about 44%, the female literacy rate is only 33%. The rate of malnutrition among children up to six years old is about 30%, and the infant mortality rate is 73 per thousand live births. For the past six years or so across India, journalist P. Sainath reports, there is "evidence of farmers committing suicide in large numbers." In 1996-97, in a few districts in Andhra Pradesh, four hundred farmers killed themselves, "mainly because they were too burdened in debt and unable to feed their families." In Ananthpur, a district in Andhra Pradesh, "1,826 people, mainly farmers with very smallholdings of two acres or less, committed suicide between 1997 and 2000."[98]

In response to these miseries, chiefly due to rising costs for electricity, many of came out for the agitations led by the Left on August 28, 2000.[99]

And that's when the police opened fire. No warning, no shots in the air, just thirty to forty-five minutes of gunfire toward and around the protestors. This is "good governance." In a further demonstration of what this term really means, the state authorities intervened with TV cable operators to remove the segments of newscasts covering the police barrage. The people marched toward the state assembly, with an agreement to remain peaceful. Women's organizations led the march, and in a report from the All-India Democratic Women's Association (AIDWA), it becomes clear that the police were ruthless.[100] One woman, named Mamta noted, "The male police pulled my kurta [shirt] right up and tore it. I was lifted by them and thrown on the [barbed] wire [fence]." Another, Devi, reported, "The [police] men surrounded me and started pulling my clothes. I protested. They used filthy language and said we will teach you to come to demonstrations and tore my kurta and pulled my salwar [top-cloth]." This is the state that brags about the "empowerment of women."

When the police blocked their march, the people began to court arrest. Things went awry. The bullets started to fly, and two men lay dead. One of them, Vishnu Vardha Reddy, was a Communist Party of India (Marxist) activist. I quote from the AIDWA report about him:

> Vishnu Vardha Reddy was targeted and killed by the police. He was 23 years old. This is what his mother Durgamma said 'Vishnu was a gentle boy. He was working in a factory called Aquapure earning about Rs. 1500 rupees a month [less than $30]. We come from Tufran village of Medak district where we have a little land. We had to come to Hyderabad to stay with Vishnu as my only other son Anji Reddy who was older than Vishnu was killed in a traffic accident a month and a half ago. I do not know whether it was an accident or whether he committed suicide. He was very disturbed. He had taken a loan of a lakh [100,000] of rupees from the moneylender in the village to buy a pump. But the ground water level in our village is very low. The richer people including our neighbour have a more powerful pump at 225 feet which pulls all the water. My elder son had to dig twice to get the water but the pump burned. He said he was ruined. One day he had gone out for some work. Only his dead body came back. He left behind his wife and two little children. We could not stay in the village because the moneylender wanted the money. So we came to Vishnu. He used to work very hard and then he used to do work for the other workers. He used to tell me "we should do good work for the people." On August 28th he went as usual. I did not know that he was going for a demonstration. But later some people came to us and said "amma [mother] come quickly your son is hurt." But he was not hurt. He was dead. They killed him, they killed my gentle son.'

The report continued, "Vishnu did not threaten anyone's life. He did not indulge in any violence. He was shot dead by the police during the indiscriminate firing mentioned above.

The Government has refused to give his family, of which he was the only earning member, having lost his brother only a month earlier, any compensation. This is an urgent issue which needs to be addressed."

The killing has not been addressed, despite the ceaseless struggle of the people's organizations. When the Indian media was outraged by Linda Powers' revelation that Enron spent $20 million to "educate" Indian politicians and the media, there was little of that outrage at the "excesses" in Hyderabad. The running dogs are as complicit in our messes as the fat cats, but they smile, run for "cover" behind the well-known reputation of the fat cats' venality and pray for our votes once in a while. Enron is not just about the one firm or of firms in general. The Enron phenomenon across the planet is about the tight nexus between money and power, of the denigration of democracy by the elected representatives of the people.

Vishnu Vardha Reddy died on the side of the people. This book is dedicated to him.

CHAPTER THREE

The Shape of Sins to Come

The detritus left behind after the collapse of Enron is formidable. In 1997, then Enron's senior executive Jeffery Skilling told a room of business executives at a conference, "You must cut costs ruthlessly by fifty to sixty percent. Depopulate. Get rid of people. They gum up the works."[1] Enron has done just that, and the utter contempt with which the management held the employees should be no surprise. Four thousand Enron workers in Houston join twenty thousand of their neighbors in the unemployment queues, or else resign themselves to a life of part-time jobs without any hope of retirement. "The word Enron raises all kinds of negative things an employer might balk at," said one former Enron employee. When he went for a hard-won interview the new firm "told me directly that the one thing that I'll have to address about my background is the Enron factor. Either be prepared to defend it or at least understand that it is a factor that works against me."[2]

When Enron was on the rise, Houston's developers enjoyed high rents and a spurt of construction activity. In April 2000, as Enron's shares soared at $60, one contractor "poured 11,000 cubic yards of concrete into 1,200 tons of reinforcing steel in a nonstop flow that lasted 16 hours."[3] No longer. Now "To Let" signs go up in downtown Houston, a reminder of an earlier crash for the city. In the 1970s, as the U.S. economy felt the recessionary pressures of the rise in oil prices, the capital of Texas oil, Houston, boomed. Millions of square feet of office space cluttered up the city, only to be emptied out a decade later by the Savings and Loan collapse, the decline in oil prices and the downturn in the Mexican economy (still a major part of the city's trade). Boom-Bust-Boom-Bust: meanwhile the developers made a pretty penny, the city boasts cheap office space and the homeless suffer for lack of shelter.[4]

So it goes.

The anger of Enron's employees pushed some state representatives like Wes Chesboro (Democrat from Arcata, Texas) to demand that the Enron executives face jail time. "Three strikes," he said, "and you're out." What were the three strikes? Price fixing, securities fraud and failure to appear before the state legislature despite receipt of a subpoena. State Senator Debra Bowen (Democrat from Redondo Beach, CA) quipped, "I doubt that Enron will ever send us anything more than a picture postcard from the Cayman Islands," just as Senator Barbara Boxer (Democrat-CA) demanded that Enron's wealth be confiscated by the government and sent to California.[5] On a less prosaic note, but marking a profound shift in attitudes nonetheless, water commissioner Lisa Melyan of Oregon's Tualatin Valley Water District told a receptive hearing of the Public Utility Commission in early March 2002 that a publicly owned power system "is in the best interests of the citizens."[6] Melyan, a musician by trade, ran for the post on the Green Party ticket at the behest of the Citizens for Safe Water to block a water filtration plant that would further pollute the Willamette River. Outrage for the mangled lives of those within the U.S. abounds, but little concern for those on other shores whose destiny has been equally squelched while their present predicaments are much more precarious.

Even that outrage, however, may be little more than posturing. Consider the track record in prosecuting white-collar crime. In only one major case in the last decade has a corporate executive done time in prison: our old friends at Archer Daniels Midland connived on tape to fix prices and laughed at federal regulators; a federal court sentenced the two main culprits to a couple of years in jail, increased to three years by an irate appeals court; then the court felt that the two men should suffer leniency because they had a history of charitable contributions—made, no doubt, with illegal money. Our get tough on crime policy of zero tolerance is for the masses, not the upper classes.

Other examples read like a catalog from a "Ripley's Believe It or Not" comic book. Even as E. F. Hutton accepted that it conducted two thousand felonies in 1985—a number few individual criminals would be capable of—the company paid only $2 million as a fine. Even as Prudential Securities admitted that it committed fraud in the sale of investments worth $1.4 billion and swindled 120,000 people, it only paid $375 million in fines. "How is it that someone is more likely to go to jail for robbing a liquor store than for defrauding the equivalent of the population of a mid-sized city?" asks journalist Kurt Eichenwald. "The answer goes to the nature of business fraud and the demanding standards of evidence in the criminal justice system. It is not enough to prove there are victims, or that some people got rich from others' suffering. Rules of evidence require the proof of several elements of the crime—some of which can look a lot like standard industry practice."[7] Mike Milken stands relatively alone as one who did do jail time, but only because he pleaded guilty of defrauding millions of people during the S&L scandal with his junk bond scheme. The history of the recent past and the corporate-tinged legal system we have makes it unlikely that Enron executives will face any serious criminal repercussions for their domestic behavior. Prosecution for their international behavior remains off the agenda.

And, meanwhile, around the world, as the peasants and workers celebrate the downfall of Enron, its assets sit in limbo—untouchable and yet attractive.

In India, Enron tried to sell its share of the Dabhol Power plant for the first six months of 2002. Due to a dispute with the

MSEB, both took their cases to the International Court of Arbitration. On 6 March 2002, the Bombay High Court ruled that those proceedings must stop because the only body with jurisdiction over the matter is the Maharashtra Electric Regulatory Commission, a government body. Enron is desperate to liquidate the assets and the Indian banks, which forked out the cash for the deal, want to move forward with the eight firms who have tendered bids.[8] Indian firms that at one time expressed interest (such as the Tatas) removed themselves from the high stakes game. Meanwhile the Industrial Development Bank of India, one of the lenders, reported that "Enron officials say they are sorting out their problems at home," an indication that there is no hurry from Houston. Mainly it shows us that the Big Fish of international finance have begun to circle the waters, wait until the country is desperate and then come in with low bids as the price drops. Enron's collapse has given a boost to arguments about sovereignty and nationalism, but the powers know that time will wither those arguments.

The Philippines is in a state of flux. A government without a coherent program to address the economic woes of its population turns to the U.S. for economic assistance in exchange for its entry as a junior partner in the War Against the Planet. Ten years ago the government threw out the U.S. military from Subic Bay and then welcomed Enron in its place. Now that Enron is defunct, the cruel logic of history draws the Filipino government back into an alliance with the Pentagon. Navy ships may soon be seen back in Subic Bay, and one can only guess that the Filipinos in the area may go back to old jobs (such as sex work) that bespeak a general descent into international debt peonage. Enron, therefore, seems low on the government's list of priorities. Besides, no one seems to want to buy the Batangas and the Subic Bay plants. Private sector firms like the Mirant Philippines Corporation await government regulations on the power sector before they make any moves. Mid-

American Energy Holdings Company has shown some interest. The state utility, National Power Corporation (NAPCOR) waits for a reduction in the price, currently at $35 million. In the near future, the government of the Philippines may sell Napocor itself—a firm with assets of $13 billion, with sales of $2 billion, with profits of $175 million and with the current gener- ation of over sixty percent of the country's energy.[9] The fire sale of neoliberalism continues even as Enron's bit part in that drama ends, and the Texas firm makes its exit ungracefully.

Japan, the world's second largest economy, is hard hit by the collapse of Enron. The Japanese Trade Minister Takeo Hiranuma grieved the loss of Enron because it was fated to be a major player in the new government's plans for the deregu- lation of the country's power sector. "Enron was planning to build several large scale projects in Japan to take advantage of deregulation in the Japanese market," he told the press in January 2002, "but this plan is probably being scrapped so I cannot deny that there will be an effect on the deregulation process."[10] Enron's two subsidiaries, E Power Corp (in whole- sale electric power) and Enron Japan (in energy and financial business), had just begun to make their presence felt when the collapse occurred.

But even as Enron, one of the partisans of "reform," has disappeared, the "reform" process goes on. One of the code words for this feast of "privatization" that Enron engorged itself on is "globalization." This dynamic provides an important underpinning of the General Agreement on Trade in Services (GATS), a planetary process pushed by big business. Enron is gone, but GATS remains, and the latter is poised to produce Enrons anew. And globalization makes it all possible.

Globalization as Cannibalism

"Globalization" was born in the 1990s, after the demise of the USSR removed all constraints from transnational corporations. The USSR's presence allowed the two-thirds world to protect itself from corporate rapacity, sometimes by playing the two superpowers off each other or else by drawing help from the Soviets in the United Nations (to create bodies to regulate transnational corporations, for example). For all its problems, the USSR was the defense shield for the formerly colonized zones of Eastern Europe and to a lesser extent around the globe. It made possible a nonaligned movement headed by India, Egypt and Yugoslavia that squeezed itself between the two superpowers.

In the 1990s, the global media championed globalization, a new form of unrestrained existence for capital, and anything that seemed to be a hybrid became an emblem of our new cultural condition: McDonalds in Beijing, Pepsi in Lusaka. The hybrid, frequently, represented a G-7 mass-market commodity in the world of color. Or conversely, it was represented by cultural objects (Indian dance, African singers) to be consumed by an elite audience in the overdeveloped world. To most of the world, globalization did not mean the equality of conditions of exchange. But it meant the entry of G-7 goods and finance into their zones, just as a few of their compatriots could take their own goods to a limited part of the G-7 market.

Of course the world has been connected for millennia, with people and good in transit from one end of the planet to another. Globalization, however, is not simply about inter-connections. Globalization is the current Enron stage of capitalism. Firms are re-entering, not entering for the first time previously sheltered sectors of the two-thirds world's economy and they export themselves for their brand-name ability to carry capital garnered from stock markets and from development agencies. On the list of the push to privatize, made possible by globalization—from water to sewage, and, of course, the big-ticket item, power.

In earlier epochs, transnational corporations did indeed go

forth to conquer the world and they share so much with their descendants, the Enron-type firms. The difference this time, as history circles back to repeat itself, is one important element. The Enron firms try to commodify those elements of the commons held over self-consciously as the charge of the public. While the entire history of capitalism has been about its desire to make everything into a commodity, the contradictory dynamic of nationalism held back certain spheres of life as the social good and therefore to be relatively outside the profit motive. The state provided where the markets could not efficiently succeed. Ken Lay, chief among others however, had a vision: take advantage of the circumstances to demand that even that self-consciously protected sphere, that vast arena of the social good, must come under the sway of the private sector, the profit sector. Privatization is the act of cannibalism made possible by the forces of globalization.

The Enronistas do to the social democratic state what the first transnational corporations did to feudal-like, sprawling states of the early modern epoch. Around the year 1600, northwest Europe gave the world three of these joint-stock (or shareholder financed) firms: the English East India Company, the Dutch VOC and the French Companie des Indes. The East India Company (and those like the Hudson Bay Company in the Americas) burst out of Europe, backed by stakeholders (who rather than being merchants alone were the kings, queens and other rulers of their day) and managed by a ruthlessness that rivaled the Mongol Khans. Jan Pieterszoon Coen, governor general of the Dutch East Indies (1618-1629) spoke for the managers of all three firms when he wrote, "May not a man in Europe do what he likes with his cattle? Even so does the master do with his men, for everywhere, these with all that belongs to them are as much the property of the master, as are brute beasts in the Netherlands. The law of the land is the will of the King and he is King who is strongest."[11] Before sociologist

Herbert Spencer corrupted naturalist Charles Darwin, the East India Companies practiced a version of "survival of the fittest."

In a poetic way, Enron resembles the East India Company (EIC). The EIC went into India, backed by stakeholders, and its managers (then called Nabobs) made vast fortunes. When they bought themselves into Parliament, Edmund Burke impeached the most famous Nabob, Warren Hastings. Nonetheless, the investors came away with decent returns. The harsh conditions of rule guaranteed the profits of the EIC, because any dissent or attempt to prevent the forced entry of EIC (including with opium or for the destruction of the artisans of Bengal) was met with the harshest violence. No student of Indian history can ever forget that the EIC participated in the catastrophe that befell the weavers of Bengal, as epitomized by Agha Shahid Ali in "Dacca Gauzes":

> In history we learned: the hands
> of weavers were amputated,
> the looms of Bengal silenced,
> and the cotton shipped raw
> by the British to England.
> History of little use to her,
> my grandmother just says
> how the muslins of today
> seem so coarse and that only
> in autumn, should one wake up
> at dawn to pray, can one
> feel that same texture again.
> One morning, she says, the air
> was dew-starched: she pulled
> it absently through her ring.[12]

When the firm collapsed due to the uprising of the sub-continental peoples in 1857, the Crown (this time on Victoria's head) came in and bailed out the undertaking by the entry of its military force. Whenever the EIC needed state assistance, the Crown was able and willing to offers its services, here just as the Crown colluded with Parliament to crush the democratic Chartist movement within England in the 1840s, once again with its repressive force.

India and other English colonies became a captive reserve for raw materials, since the English had complete control over what should be grown, who would buy it and then at what price the goods should be sold. Furthermore, the English secured relatively captive markets for their finished products, once again to those who they had colonized. With the fix in on supply and demand, the English began to make the case for "free trade." In 1846 the English parliament repealed the Corn Laws. These laws protected English farmers from the wiles of the market as the state promised to buy their produce at a fixed price (a similar arrangement currently enjoyed by U.S. agri-business and small dairy farmers). With the end of this law, the agrarian sector suffered a deathblow. An EIC publicist at the time wrote of England's new comparative advantage (its "high mission") in industry rather than in agriculture:

> It is clearly seen that to our beloved land Great Britain has been assigned the high mission of manufacturing for her sister nations. Our kin beyond the seas shall send us in our ships their cotton from the Mississippi valley. India shall contribute its jute, Russia its hemp and flax, and ironstone for our factories and workshops, our skilled mechanics and artificers the necessary machinery to weave these materials into fine cloth for the nations; all shall be fashioned by us and made fit for men. Our ships, which reach us laden with raw materials, shall return to all parts of the earth laden. This exchange of raw materials for finished products under the decree of nature makes each nation the servant of the other and proclaims the brotherhood of man. Peace and goodwill shall reign upon

the earth, one nation after another must follow our example and free exchange of commodities shall everywhere
prevail. Their ports shall open wide as ours are open for
their raw materials.[13]

Linda Powers' deposition before Congress in 1995 is
almost identical. But there has been an important shift over the
centuries. England set up the doctrine of "imperial preference"
to further consolidate its hold on the world economy—its
colonies could not trade outside the Empire in competition
with English industry, a good example of what came to be called
"free trade imperialism." By the turn of the 19th century, that
shift was under way, as Henry Brailsford wrote in his 1914 *The
War of Steel and Gold*, that "the old imperialism levied tribute:
the new lends money at interest."[14] Or rather, by 1914, the
English worked the system on three legs. It drew tribute (what
Indian nationalists called the "drain of wealth") by forcing
Indian raw materials to be sold to the British at low prices and
prevented any competition for English goods sold back to India
by preventing it from buying elsewhere. The third leg was the
profits of finance capital. The latter began to get more and more
important in the 20th century. From the 1970s onward, it
became the major form of subjugation of the world's population.

Enron continues to be the normal practice of finance
imperialism, but the phase it belongs to is somewhat different
from that of both the EIC (even as there is that poetic reso-
nance) and of the commercial banks in the mid-20th century.
Enron and similar marauding firms seek to enter the oppressed
regions of the world, cannibalize those sectors of the economy
held in the public's trust and constrain weak states to guarantee
them a high rate of return—all this without putting a gun to the
              e regime. This is the Enron-stage of capitalism. Two
          hat will form the bulk of this chapter show how nor-
           like practices are across the planet. One from the
           transnational firms to take control of the world's

water; the second comes from the attempt by firms to take advantage of the popular prejudice against drugs and terrorism to conduct corporate wars in places such as Colombia and Afghanistan.

Enronism is here to stay, even as Enron is now gone.

To understand these two examples, a brief sense of globalization as an instrumental process produced by big business is imperative. All international bodies prior to the World Trade Organization (WTO) only had an advisory function, with very constrained powers to force sovereign nations to do the will of the planet. Although states can use an adjudication process for disagreements, the WTO is a governmental body with multinational power to sanction states that do not follow its rules. In the process that produced the WTO, the Uruguay Round of the General Agreement of Trade and Tariffs (GATT), there was a broad discussion of various multi-national agreements such as the Multilateral Agreement on Investments (to formulate "rules" for finance markets, a measure defeated in December 1998 due to strong protests across the world), the Trade Related Intellectual Property Rights or the TRIPS regime, and finally GATS (the General Agreement in Trade in Services) formed in 1994 by 140 nations as a part of the WTO. The overall framework of GATT was to "liberalize" the traffic in *goods*, to open markets to transnational corporations and to cutback on the right of states to levy tariffs as a means to manage economic development and equity. It appears that these can be violated by the US, when it suits it, as made clear by its 2002 tariff on imported steel.

GATS sought to "liberalize" the international trade in *services*, from banking regulations to real estate brokerage services to rules for accountancy. GATS arose to manage the most vibrant growth sector in the international economy: services. This sector, which has outgrown merchandise trade for t two decades, accounts for twenty percent of all cros trade and totals, in 1999, $1.35 trillion. While hotels, travel agencies and others are popularly associated with the service sector economy, this arena also includes those services traditionally provided by the government. One of the biggest ones across the planet is health care. GATS takes aim at this juicy target, attempting to privatize it through the export—and forced import—of the disastrous U.S. model around the planet.

Far from being mere opportunists of a global context created by the fall of the USSR and other changes, these global firms do more than just privatize services by purchasing them or building new facilities. They also supersede the democratic process of many countries by taking over the function of writing the rules.

Both Enron and Arthur Andersen were in the thick of the 1990s GATS discussions, even as anti-globalization protests paid little heed to these deliberations. Andersen formed part of the team that drafted the new rules for GATS on accountancy procedures. There is no indication that its role in the Enron scandal that brought it disgrace and dissolution will provoke any reconsideration of those rules.[15]

The main group that lobbies for "liberalization" in GATS is the U.S. Coalition of Service Industries, all of whose members hoped to gain immeasurably from the privatization of services around the planet. Enron was a member—and a top sponsor—of the 1999 World Services Congress in Atlanta that set in motion the GATS 2000 round of lobbying. Enron has also been a major player in the two umbrella groups that work almost full-time on GATS—U.S. Trade (the strongest proponent of Fast Track, or Trade Promotion Authority, for the President) and USTR Industry Consultation Program—Industry Sector Advisory Committee on Energy. Enron is on the board of the National Foreign Trade Council and a member of the U.S. Council for International Business—both major forces within U.S. Trade. As a mark of how seriously Enron takes these issues, for USTR, Enron deputized its Executive Vice President Terry Thorn to be its representative. In addition, Enron was part of the U.S. Energy Service Coalition whose mandate is to ensure that oil and gas drilling is seen as a service within GATS.

These instruments of globalization are filled with Enron/Andersen staff, and it is likely that many of the things they wanted prior to their bankruptcy phase will continue to form the agenda of the overdeveloped world through GATS and GATT. These policies will be an important part of Enron's legacy. Policies that enable the Second Enclosure Movement. A movement of money dealers addicting the world to dollars and nonsense, just as they snatch their livelihood from it.

The Second Enclosure Movement

The battlefield of the Second Enclosure Movement is being most spectacularly fought in the world of water and oil. In May 2000, *Fortune* noted, "Water promises to be to the 21st century what oil was to the 20th century: the precious commodity that determines the wealth of nations."[16] As with oil, the global trade in water is now in the trillions of dollars with the two giants, Vivendi and Suez, in domination of the market. Oil is not yesterday's game, however, because the corporate war over energy reserves (natural gas and oil) continues in Colombia, Afghanistan and elsewhere. Often this Great Game is played between corporate power and those whom it designates as drug-lords or terrorists. The people are made into the planet's enemy so that the superpower corporation can do what it wants with our resources. Those areas of human life hitherto held in trust for the people's good are now fair game for giant corporations.

The First Enclosure Movement took place in Europe from the late 16th century into the early 18th century. Karl Marx, whom economic historian Robert Heilbroner called the "angry genius,"[17] provides one of the best summaries of this long process:

> The spoliation of the church's property, the fraudu-
> lent alienation of the State domains, the robbery of the
> common lands, the usurpation of feudal and clan proper-
> ty, and its transformation into modern private property
> under circumstances of reckless terrorism, were just so
> many idyllic methods of originary accumulation. They
> conquered the field for capitalist agriculture, made the soil
> part and parcel of capital, and created for the town indus-
> tries the necessary supply of a 'free' and outlawed prole-
> tariat.[18]

In other words, the world of private property we know
today wasn't always that way. Property once held by the church,
the state, feudal lords, or by ordinary people in a common trust,
entered the world of the market and became, in effect, property for the first time. In other words, just because I hold something doesn't mean it is property: to become property the good
should be a commodity, should be able to be bought and sold.
The first enclosure movement took land that had been held and
transferred, but not bought and sold at will, and made that land
into the private property of large land-owners. A secondary
effect of the first enclosure movement was that vast amounts of
people who had been ejected by these early agro-business cartels
had to find other work. They went to the new factories and sold
their labor as workers. Capital, gained from the accumulated
land and from the colonial adventures of north-western Europe,
hired these workers in factories whose labor now provided the
commodities that capital sold around the planet. Early industrial capital, thanks to labor in the colonies and in the factories, is
the closest thing to resemble the perpetual motion machine—
with money ceaselessly entering the ravenous accounts of the
capitalists.[19]

The Second Enclosure Movement begins in the 1990s as
an echo of the first, a massive move to privatization. This time,

transnational firms go after all those sectors that have been protected by state sovereignty and power as a public trust in the name of the people. Globalization opens these sectors to the rapaciousness of the profit motive. But even as massive profiteering is under way, the votaries of the Second Enclosure Movement eschew bald terms like profit. Instead, the "reckless terrorism" of globalization cloaks itself behind code words like "efficiency," "drug war" and "terrorism," as they rob the planet's peoples of our right to existence.

(1) The Water Wars

> ¡¡El Agua es Nuestra y las Decisiones Tambien!
> The Water is Ours and the Decisions Too!!
> —A slogan from Cochabamba, Bolivia

> Water has moved from being an endless commodity
> that may be taken for granted to a rationed necessity that may be taken by force.
> —(A statement from Global H2O,
> previously Global Water Corporation).[20]

In July 1998, Enron's water firm, Azurix made its international debut when it acquired England-based Wessex Water and the water concession in Rio de Janeiro, Brazil. It appears that Enron won the bid for Wessex Water partly due to its enormous financial contributions to the Labour government and to the assistance it then received from the secretary of state for trade and industry Peter Mandelson. The revolving door worked well for a few months in Europe, as Azurix hired former UK regulator of the gas industry Calre Spottiswoode to be its Senior Vice President of Regulatory Affairs in Europe. Spottiswoode quit after four months in 1999 with concerns about the financial viability of a firm that paid huge amounts to buy international water firms and contracts to deliver water.

Rebecca Mark, the prophet's main agent in India via

Enron International, took over Azurix. Then, in late 2000, she quit in frustration (she remained on the Enron board). When she took over the water world, she noted, "Enron's water subsidiary initially will pursue the development of water projects in Europe, Latin America and Asia—markets in which privatization is occurring and in which Enron already has gained significant international experience and has established a substantial operating presence." But water is not quite the same as power. People have a palpable fear that financial pressure may cutback on safety and lead to water pollution. Even as Enron hoped that people would surrender those fears before the temple of efficiency, the sentiment that certain public utilities must be outside the profit motive stubbornly remains. Aware that the water industry is not as unregulated as power, Mark told *Global Water Report* in June 2000, "Since buying our Wessex Water operating base, we have learned a lot and become more understanding of the opportunities and restrictions in the industry." [21]

Wessex Water, Enron hoped, would provide vast revenues that would help it underwrite its adventures elsewhere in the world of water. (Hence Mark's comment about Wessex being the "operating base.") Azurix expected Wessex to provide almost three quarters of its revenues, but this was not to be mainly because of popular resistance to a rise in the rates for water, which we still see as a human right rather than a commodity. Unable to garner the necessary profits, Azurix extended itself in Eastern Europe, Argentina and Ghana. In May 1999, Azurix failed to win a contract in Sofia, Bulgaria because officials there felt that the firm was too inexperienced. A year later Azurix pulled its bid for the Bucharest water contract because of "internal strategic decisions concerning reallocation of capital to priority areas." What might that term "reallocation of capital to priority areas" mean? Azurix had just fired a third of its workforce in London and Houston, a savings of capital. But three of its executives who left in this period earned $7.4 million in severance packages with an additional $3 million in stock options—these are priority areas.

Elsewhere in the two-thirds world, Azurix tried out Enron's tested strategies. In Argentina, Azurix won a thirty-year concession to run the water supply for a section of Buenos Aires in June 1999 for the astronomical bid of $438.6 million, ten times that of its competitors. After Wessex Water, this was Azurix' prize possession. However, even as Azurix announced its contract, experts wondered how it would be able to cover its down-payment and do the two things it needed to do: first, deliver clean water to two and a half million people, increase the population's access to drinking water from 52% to 82% and to sewage lines from 38% to 68%—in five years; second, to raise the rates for water from a population already wracked by debt and neoliberal ruin.

Of course Azurix failed and it had to break its thirty-year contract after two years. The immediate cause of its departure was its failure to provide clean water. Residents of Bahia Blanca complained that city water smelled and hurt their skin. "I've worked here for twenty-five years," said Bahia Blanca's health chief, Ana Maria Reimers, "and this is the worst crisis I've ever seen."[22] When the city tests showed that the problem might have stemmed from excessive algae in their water reservoir, Azurix pinned the blame on the municipality. Nevertheless, the stigma did not leave the foreign company. Problems with unions and a restriction on rate increases made Azurix lose heart in the project. In January 2001, the government and Azurix began to talk about the cancellation of the contract, but Argentina's Economy Minister, Jose Luis Machinea worried that a cancellation would destroy one of the country's banks that had fronted Azurix the money for the investment. The largess of the world to see to Enron's rise is replicated here. Eventually, Azurix took the case to the World Bank's International Center for Settlement of Investment Disputes and it agreed to continue to provide services through half of 2002 before it departs.

How did Azurix get the concession when it offered such an inflated price? What mechanism might it have used to sway the authorities? Unfortunately, the accounts we have of the deal are from the business press and none of them do the kind of investigative journalism that may reveal the rationale of the officials.[23] But from Azurix' strategy in Ghana, we might get some idea of how the business operates. In Ghana, Azurix won a contract to deliver water to Accra's citizens by defeating bids from Suez and Vivendi, the world's largest water companies. The Azurix-Accra deal of $285 million was funded by the World Bank ($100 million loan) and the terms of the contract said that the company would provide water at the rate of 95 cents per cubic meter, at least one-third more than the average in Accra until then. An investigation by the World Bank led to its withdrawal from the project and its representative, Peter Harrold, wrote at that time to Ghana's Vice President, "The arrangement you have reached with Azurix is one that has been arrived at on a completely non-transparent basis."[24] Then, in February 2002, Harrold acknowledged further, "There were suspicions of corruption, and a draft schedule of payments by Azurix showed a $5 million upfront payment. I concluded that the only way they thought they could get contracts was through the back door, not through the front."[25] If in Ghana, why not in Argentina?

The failure of Enron's Azurix in capturing the water resources of the planet does not herald the assurance that the water is safe from privatization. As Enron collapsed around them U.S. Senators Bob Graham (Democrat-Florida), James Jeffords (Independent-Vermont), Michael Crapo (Republican-Idaho) and Robert Smith (Republican-New Hampshire) introduced the Water Investment Act of 2002 (S. 1961) "to make federal funding conditional on the recipient's consideration of privatization."[26]

In the summer of 2000, one hundred million people and sixty million cattle experienced a horrible drought in the western part of India. Some of this had to do with poor monsoon rain. But a junior cabinet minister admitted that the bulk of the blame must rest on what he so nicely called "administrative failure." So rarely do government officials accept culpability for their errors that one hopes that this man (incompetent perhaps, but at least honest) was promoted for his candor. Sureshwar Sinha of the activist group Pani Morcha (Water Front) said, "We owe the drought to the government's disastrous policy during the past fifty years, when a hundred dams and canals were built. There is evidence to show that as much as fifty-five percent of this water goes to waste through evaporation and other means."[27]

The people thirst, but if they have no water, at least they have Pepsi and Coke. Government water tankers visited the villages once a fortnight to distribute a few liters of water per head. In these very villages, shopkeepers eagerly inflated the price of their bottled treats and awaited their parched fellow citizens. In most of non-drought India, a bottle of Pepsi sold for about Rs. 9 (23 cents). Where the drought was severe, each bottle could be found for not less than Rs. 16 (30 cents). For a day's work on the government drought relief works, the wage earned Rs. 23 (53 cents). Let them drink Pepsi!

In the *maquiladora* zones of Mexico, Canadian activists Barlow and Clarke report, "clean water is so scarce that babies and children drink Coke and Pepsi instead."[28] From the Coca Cola Company, we hear that "every single one of the world's 5.6 billion people will get thirsty [each] day. If we make it impossible for these 5.6 billion people to escape Coca Cola, then we assure our future success for many years to come. Doing anything else is not an option."[29]

In late 2001, news comes from Maharashtra, still embroiled in the Dabhol dispute, that Coca-Cola has taken control of a lake in Wada for a bottling plant. The traditional source of water for the residents has been abruptly cut off. These are the water wars. In India, the old advertising phrases "The Pepsi Generation" and " Coke, It's the Real Thing," may come to pack a new, more sinister punch.

In 2000, the frontlines of the water wars lay in Bolivia, where the people took to the streets to protest a thirty-five percent water hike in the Cochabamba municipality.[30] Aguas del Tunari, a consortium led by International Water Limited, a London firm jointly owned by Edison (an Italian company) and Bechtel (a U.S. company, and Enron's old pal from the Dabhol deal), purchased the $200 million concession in Cochabamba and was as eager as Azurix to use these investments in the two-thirds world to draw vast profits that could be recycled through the financial dynamos in the City of London and on Wall Street. Bechtel, whose 1998 revenues were $12.6 billion ($2.4 billion in Latin America alone), works through Aguas del Tunari in the water business, "presently providing water and wastewater services to nearly six million customers in the Philippines, Australia, Scotland, and Bolivia and completing agreements in India, Poland and Scotland for facilities that will serve an additional one million customers."

Cochabambinos formed the Coordiadora de Defense de Agua y la Vida (CDAV, Coalition in Defense of Water and Life) that represented all the groups and individuals outraged by the assault on their water sources. Led by a machinist, Oscar Olivera, CDAV held out against the outrages of former dictator (1971-1978) and then president (elected in August 1997 with twenty-two percent of the vote) Hugo Banzer. Banzer responded by invoking martial law to smash protestors (one hundred and seventy five injured and two blinded during the wars in early February 2000). Banzer and his two associates in the emergency committee "to protect law and order" trained at Fort Benning, Georgia's notorious School of the Americas. But in this Guerra por El Agua, the CDAV held out through street battles, nighttime arrests of organizers, and military on the highways to remove barricades in five of the nine provinces of Bolivia. Eventually, militant people on the streets armed with agrarian and kitchen implements defeated both the consortium and the government. The war for water resembled the French Revolution.

What had Bechtel in mind for Bolivia? Nothing that the World Bank and the U.S. government did not see as quite normal, the need for what they call "reform." In June 1999, the World Bank reported on the Cochabamba sale and noted, "No subsidies should be given to ameliorate the increase in water tariffs in Cochabamba." Families that earn an average of $100 per month now will have to pay $20 for water. This while those, like World Bank economists who live in the suburbs of Washington, DC, notes Jim Schulz of the US-based Democracy Center, currently pay less than that for their water! The World Bank pushed Bolivia to sell the concession, and it did not object here when what amounts to a PPA ensured that Aguas del Tunari would earn an average of 16 percent rate of return on its investment.[31] Given that the U.S. stock market historically earns a rate akin to 11 or 12 percent, a lock in of 16 percent would indeed constitute "efficiency" for the investors—and a boondoggle for consumers.

When the Cochabambinos eventually won and Aguas del Tunari had to leave, the company sued the Bolivian government in the Court for the Settlement of International Disputes (a World Bank body) for $40 million to cover their own bad investment, another part of the Enron culture that is normal in our times. Although not germane to the problem of this book, the strategy used by Bechtel to sue Bolivia is also ingenious. Bolivia and Holland signed a Bilateral Investment Treaty in 1992. These treaties offer concessions that should remind any historian of the famous Extra-Territorial protections demanded by the 18th and 19th century empires for their citizens in the periphery of nominally independent states like China. The Bilateral Investment Treaties protect the rights of investors and place restrictions on governmental actions (such as regulation or the withdrawal of a contract by popular pressure). In 1999, Bechtel moved the holding company for Aguas del Tunari from the Cayman Islands to Holland, just when the firm began to operate in Bolivia. Being a *Dutch* company now, Bechtel then used the 1992 treaty to sue Bolivia. The Bolivians argue that the transfer of shares does not invalidate Bechtel's U.S. roots. The conflict continues.[32]

Bolivia registered a victory for the people, and on 8 December 2000, CDAV hosted a conference called "Water: Globalization, Privatization and the Search for Alternatives" that produced the Cochabamba Declaration:

> We, citizens of Bolivia, Canada, United States, India, Brazil:
>
> Farmers, workers, indigenous people, students, professionals, environmentalists, educators, nongovernmental organizations, retired people, gather together today in solidarity to combine forces in the defense of the vital right to water.
>
> Here, in this city which has been an inspiration to the world for its retaking of that right through civil action, courage and sacrifice standing as heroes and heroines against corporate, institutional and governmental abuse, and trade agreements which destroy that right, in use of our freedom and dignity, we declare the following:
>
> For the right to life, for the respect of nature and the uses and traditions of our ancestors and our peoples, for all time the following shall be declared as inviolable rights with regard to the uses of water given us by the earth:
>
> Water belongs to the earth and all species and is sacred to life, therefore, the world's water must be conserved, reclaimed and protected for all future generations

and its natural patterns respected.

Water is a fundamental human right and a public trust to be guarded by all levels of government, therefore, it should not be commodified, privatized or traded for commercial purposes. These rights must be enshrined at all levels of government. In particular, an international treaty must ensure these principles are noncontrovertable.

Water is best protected by local communities and citizens who must be respected as equal partners with governments in the protection and regulation of water. Peoples of the earth are the only vehicle to promote earth democracy and save water.

When Bechtel fled Bolivia, the company shredded its documents, emptied its bank accounts and left behind unpaid bills of $150,000. The court case to gain damages is its latest salvo against the people. Meanwhile, the people of Cochabamba celebrate their victory and try hard to reconstruct their water resources through the debt-ridden local utility, SEMAPA.

Water, sewage, air, power, heat, health care, education— these are all elements of the public good that had hitherto been held in trust by the social democratic state and sometimes by the dictatorial state, outside the rapaciousness of profit, in the people's interest. The Enron stage of capitalism demands that even these domains come under the enclosure of corporations that will run them "efficiently," make vast profits for insatiable investors, all the while depleting the world's resources of nature and nurture. This is the Second Enclosure Movement.

Well aware of the setbacks in Bolivia and elsewhere, firms like Bechtel retooled their ideological arsenal for the next assault. Protesters, the claim goes, are underwritten by the drug trade. Already in Bolivia, Bechtel tried that strategy out, but it was not as coherent as it might have been. On 8 April 2000, Victor Hugo Daza, a teenage protestor, was shot in the face and killed. "The blood spilled in Cochabamba," said CDAV's

Olivera, "carries the fingerprints of Bechtel."[33] Bechtel, in its defense, argued, "A number of other water, social and political issues are the root causes of this civil unrest," and the Bolivian government stated that the protests were "absolutely politically financed by narcotraffickers." Bechtel further accused the opposition of being supported by the coca growers. The combined specter of drugs and terrorism enables corporations to cloak their own acts as benevolent opposition to the evil of those who argue against corporate power. That this ruse even needs to be answered is a terrible sign of our times. But Jim Schultz provides the words of Franz Pedrazas as an adequate rejoinder. Pedrazas is a taxi driver in the town whose water rates doubled when Bechtel came to town. "I'm not a narcotrafficker," he said, "If I were, why would I be driving a cab? The farmers aren't narcotraffickers either."

(2) The Lubricants of Capitalism: Drugs, Oil and Blood

[Free Market Capitalism] could not exist for any length of time without annihilating the human and natural substance of society; it would have physically destroyed man and transformed his surroundings into a wilderness.
—Karl Polanyi, *The Great Transformation*, 1944[34]

Behind the raging talk of the Colombian drug war is a little known fact: the U.S. currently imports almost as much oil from Colombia, Ecuador and Venezuela than from the entire Middle East (minus Iraq). Colombia is the front-line of a new oil war. The United States military is active in the Andes, but we are told they have no brief there for oil. Their main mission is to end drug production (the War on Drugs) and to crush the left-wing insurgency (the War on Terrorism). Alongside the military travel the barons of transnational capital, mainly the oil lords. They are the stealth element in the U.S. arsenal—representatives of finance and extractive capital who enjoy the cover of the U.S. military to transform the Andes into a real wilderness, a barren expanse of oil wells and pipelines devoid of people, but filled with docile labor.

In June 2000, just as Colombian officials announced their largest discovery of an oil cache, President Clinton announced that the U.S. government would send $1.3 billion in aid to Colombia to fight the war on drugs. Called Plan Colombia, the aid is to go toward fighting what the Colombian and U.S. governments call "narco-guerrillas" and eradicating the coca crop. Almost all (90%) of the funds go toward the armed forces, both the military and the police, with a provision that these agencies will buy forty-two Huey and eighteen Blackhawk helicopters (from private arms manufacturers, Sikorsky Aircraft, a subsidiary of United Technologies, and Bell Helicopter Textron— another subsidy from the government). President Clinton announced at the time of the signing, "A condition of this aid is that we are not going to get into a shooting war. This is not Vietnam, neither is it Yankee imperialism. I reject the idea that we must choose between supporting peace and fighting drugs." The stated aim of Plan Colombia is to combat the homelands for coca, to take the War on Drugs to the supply side.

The bill especially noted that the vast funds would help the Colombian armed forces "push into the south," that is, into the terrain held by the armed revolutionary groups, Revolutionary Armed Forces of Colombia-People's Army (also known as FARC) and the National Liberation Army (ELN). Formed as the military wing of the Colombian Communist Party in 1966, FARC has spent the past three decades to become one of those "two, three…many Vietnams," called for by Che Guevara in April 1967. In control of almost 43,500 square kilometers of Colombian territory, FARC (along with the ELN zones) controls almost half of the Colombian landmass. FARC's growth intensified U.S. counter-insurgency funds to the Colombian government. In the 1999 U.S. federal budget, President Clinton provided for $208 million to the

Colombians to fight its War on Drugs and it warned Colombian President Andres Pastrana's government not to make a deal with FARC. When the government revealed that it would allow FARC to control a demilitarized zone as part of its peace talks, one U.S. state department official noted that "the peace process has frightened the heck out of people" in Washington.[35]

Why were people in Washington frightened by the peace process set in motion once again in January 1999?[36] Was Washington really serious about the War on Drugs and did it go after all the combatants in this period? Well, the answer is no. One small illustration of this is the tale of Raul Salinas, the brother of Mexican President Carlos Salinas de Gotari (1988-1994).

In 1995, the Swiss authorities revealed that Raul Salinas had siphoned more than $130 million of drug-money into secret bank accounts (the sum was later increased to between $500 million and $1 billion).[37] Initially, the only scandal in the story was for the Salinas family and for the Mexican plutocracy. Soon, however, details of the story drew in the financial power of Citibank who, it seems, worked to clean-up Salinas' money and make it relatively untraceable. While his brother was President of Mexico, Raul Salinas worked for the Mexican government's grain monopoly, Conasupo, and drew an annual salary of $160,000. Yet he was able to get his hands on hundreds of millions of dollars that he took to Citibank in Mexico City who transferred it via New York to Swiss banks. Amy Elliot, the agent in charge of the Salinas money, vouched for the money and oversaw Citibank "specialists" who created Swiss accounts in the names of fictitious Cayman Island corporations. When the scandal broke, Citibank quickly said that it had done nothing illegal. Indeed, Elliot claimed that to doubt the Salinases "would be like asking the Rockefellers where they had got their money." In the context of how the global system works, she had a point: the money of robber barons is above suspicion.

Especially when they are so closely connected to our power structure. Citibank chairman John Reed had a close friendship with the Salinases, spending his visits in Mexico under the presidential roof of Carlos Salinas.

Should we be upset over this taking of $500 million to $1 billion? In proportion to other crimes, this serves as an emblem of the problems but is only one example. Over $70 billion left Mexico in 1994 from the personal accounts of the elite, mainly because of the insurgency of the Zapatistas in southern Mexico as well as their lack of faith in the Mexican peso as it entered the NAFTA regime under the sway even more of Wall Street. This departure of funds dwarfs Salinas' theft of hard currency. In 1994-5 Mexico faced a major debt problem, and the U.S. lent the country $57 billion towards its stabilization. The crisis was clearly caused by this drain.

Let us offer some facts against Elliot's own supposed naiveté as she funneled Salinas' cash through Citibank's Confidas scheme (housed in Panama with offices in Switzerland). First, Citibank accepted cheques from Raul Salinas drawn on Banco Cremi, a bank owned since 1992 by Carlos Cabal Peniche who was previously involved with the crooked dealings of BCCI. (He was sued by BCCI's Prince Khalid bin Maffouz in New York City for absconding with $70 million.)[38] This, we are told, did not raise the suspicion of Citibank. Second, Mr. Salinas' small salary did not raise questions about where he could have gotten so much cash, nor was there much discussion about Salinas' acquaintance with two drug lords, Juan Garcia Abrego (of the Gulf cartel) and Joaquin Guzman (of the Sinaloa cartel).[39] Third, Citibank's Elliot was well aware of some level of illegality, since she advised the Salinas' to take evasive action in late 1995 (as reported by Salinas to Swiss authorities). Her advice came in her capacity as a "relationship banker" for Raul Salinas' Confidas accounts. Citibank currently runs about two hundred and fifty such accounts in Mexico for those depositors who hold more than $5 million. This policy is not only for Mexico, since in 1991 investigations revealed Citibank's Ernest Liu ran similar accounts for the Hong Kong narco-Triads. But the scandal does not end here. In February 1992 Citibank entered into an agreement with the U.S. Federal Reserve Bank to help regulate the bank's operations until February 1994. Therefore, during the entire Salinas scandal, the U.S. government officials scrutinized and said nothing about these transactions! This particular aspect of the case received no investigation.[40]

No one is bombing Citibank.

But they are bombing Colombia.

Colombia does, of course, produce a vast quantity of drugs which, like its oil, are largely shipped to the U.S. Long an important crop, cocaine was once controlled by the Inca rulers. But when the Spanish arrived, the conquistadors grew it on plantations and sold it for enormous profits to the survivors of the conquest in order to make them work harder and with less complaint in the massive silver mines. The mine at Pótosi sent the bullion to Europe that enabled the growth of mercantile capitalism and eventually Europe's colonial empire and the industrial revolution. Rich in a wide variety of natural resources (such as oil, coal, gold, emeralds, platinum, uranium, sugar, bananas, coffee), Colombia has the ability to move out of its terrible present. Until the 1970s, the region of Medellin was a producer of textiles and it covered much of the internal market in Colombia. Three decades ago, globalization wiped out the development of the Colombian textile industry and produced distress in the province of Medellin. The emerald mafia of the state of Boyaca moved into prime agricultural land and began to grow coca so as to manufacture cocaine for the markets of the north. In these past decades, Colombia's cocaine production has grown dramatically, so that the region now provides 80 percent of the cocaine that reaches the U.S. It also produces 60 percent of the heroin.

Since the U.S. is the world's final source of demand for most things (including drugs), the place of Colombia in the world's drug economy has become central. At last count, the Cali cartel alone takes in an estimated $7 billion per year (of the world's total drug market of $400 billion). Compare this one gang's take to the $70 billion size of the annual Colombian economy! To create protection for their racket, the cocaine cartels have made inroads into the ruling elite of Colombia. For his 1994 election victory, President Ernesto Samper Pizano drew upon $6 million from the Cali cartel. The money was funneled in by Samper's future Minister of Defense, a scandal that led to the fall of the Samper regime in mid-1998. Pastrana, who followed Samper, seemed eager to end the reign of cocaine over Colombia, but the cocaine cartel's paramilitary forces and the narco-greed that permeates the ruling circles of Colombia (the *gamonales*) hampered any attempt at a solution.[41]

Between 1993-5, the Cocaine State made a pretense of a crackdown against the cartels of Medellin and Cali, but as even journalist Mark Bowden's popular history shows us, the state's intervention seemed designed to recompose the trade under smaller barons, take out some leaders (such as Pablo Escobar of Medellin, assassinated with the connivance and intelligence of U.S. agents) and let other remain in power (or, like Jose Santacruz Londono of Cali, escaped "mysteriously" from jail in 1996).[42] The crackdown did not transform the countryside, for the state did not seize land held by the cocaine cartels nor did it conduct any kind of land reform. About three percent of Colombians hold onto seventy percent of its arable land with the drug cartels in control of close to five million hectares of this land (which is about forty percent of all arable land). The rate of growth of the Colombian economy has never been a problem, particularly since narco-dollars financed much of it. However, only the *gamonales* benefited from the growth, while the multitude worked the land in an atmosphere of violence.[43]

The official unemployment rate of 15 percent masks the widespread discontent in the countryside, much of it fueled into FARC and the ELN.

We shouldn't be surprised to learn that Escobar's killers had U.S. intelligence or that they acted with U.S. advice. Alexander Cockburn and Jeffrey St. Clair's *Whiteout* makes a compelling case for the role of the CIA and the Nicaraguan Contras in the dramatic growth of the cocaine economy in South America, thus putting the lie to the claim that the U.S. is serious about eradicating Colombia's drug exports.[44] The Medellin cartel's headmen, Escobar and Jorge Ocho worked in close quarters with CIA agent Felix Rodriguez to help finance the Contras (for whom the U.S. Congress refused military aid in their early years). Rodriguez, incidentally, was present at the murder of Che in Bolivia, just as he was at the Bay of Pigs invasion. The CIA, the U.S. mafia and the cocaine cartels profited from the expansion of cocaine use, while the poor in the U.S. became targets of a crack epidemic that has destroyed the fabric of many working-class communities in U.S. cities.

Under cover of its concern for the drug problem, the U.S. government launched the War on Drugs in the 1980s. The targets of this War are not the main cocaine cartels or the banks that launder drug money, as we've seen. Instead, they are the urban poor in the US, as Christian Parenti shows us in *Lockdown America*, [45] and those who are in the midst of insurgency campaigns against repressive regimes in South America. In February 2002, GWB pledged an additional $98 million to fight "drug traffickers," the Bush administration's name for FARC. Then in March 2002, at a meeting of Andean leaders, GWB said of the trade of "drug traffickers" and "terrorists," "We must stop it." Despite Clinton's guarantee that no U.S. troops will be in Colombia, in April 2002 the State Department accepted that the Pentagon has four hundred U.S. military "trainers" and four hundred civilian contractors already in place, but Marc Grossman, a junior State Department official promised, "Not one of us here is talking about U.S. troops in a combat role. The Colombians need to take the brunt of this, but we need to be there to help them."[46] The "this" in his statement is plainly the war against FARC, and by all indications it seems that the U.S. government wants FARC out of the picture so that control of oil can be consummated.[47]

Don't take my word for it, but listen to the "experts" from within the Empire's power structure.

In 1998, head of the U.S. Southern Command General Charles Wilhelm told Congress that the potential of oil in Colombia had increased the country's "strategic importance."[48] Scientists and prospectors agree that the known reserves in Colombia total only 2.6 billion barrels, a tiny amount compared to Saudi Arabia's 264.2 billion barrels (a quarter of the world's reserves) and Texas' 190 billion barrels. But the number comes from explorations done in only a fifth of the oil region. The capture of vast tracks of the area by the left-wing insurgency forces makes exploration next to impossible. Companies can only speculate about how much oil exists in the country. In April 2000, Senator Bob Graham (Democrat-Florida) and former National Security Advisor Brent Scowcroft bemoaned the loss of access to Colombia's oil fields and noted that they would "remain untapped unless stability is restored."[49] Graham and Scowcroft co-chaired an "independent task force" that lobbied Congress for passage of Plan Colombia. That Scowcroft was on the board of an Enron subsidiary (and therefore an interested party) and that Graham represents the hometown of Occidental Petroleum, another interested party, went unsaid in the process.

On 10 April 2000, the late Senator Paul Coverdell (Republican-Georgia) wrote, "The necessity of protecting the oil interests in Venezuela justifies the U.S. intervention in Colombia." More ominously, Coverdell argued, "In fact, the oil picture in Latin America is strikingly similar to that of the Middle East, except that Colombia provides us more oil today than Kuwait did then. The crisis, like the one in Kuwait, threatens to spill over into many nations, all of which are allies."[50] Occidental Petroleum's Vice-President Lawrence Meriage joined Coverdell as he sat before the Congress and asked the legislators to extend the war beyond Colombia to "augment security for oil development operations."[51] Coverdell revealed that the U.S. concerns over Venezuelan President Hugo Chavez' left-populist moves are a threat to U.S. security interests. Chavez, a political wildcard, has attempted to create a Third Worldist atmosphere in OPEC, of which Venezuela is a member. He failed because he could not sway Saudi Arabia and its bloc, even as Venezuela sells oil to cash-starved states at a cut rate. He also attempted to create a South American-Caribbean alliance against U.S. hegemony (his links with Castro are crucial here). The noises about Venezuelan troops in eastern Colombia reported in mid-October 2000 seemed to set the stage for an expansion of the U.S. into the region beyond Colombia. Indeed, the "Andean Regional Initiative" to follow after Plan Colombia has already made its appearance in policy deliberations on the region. The new U.S. bases in Manta, Ecuador and in Aruba and Curaçao seem to suggest that someone awaits the go-ahead to enter Venezuela as well.[52] The US-backed failed coup against Chavez in mid-2002 may have been part of the plan to pacify the Andean oil fields in the service of US-based transnationals.[53]

All speculation about U.S. motivations should have ended when Sergeant Stan Goff, former U.S. Special Forces, told the Bolivian press, "The main interest of the United States is oil." Goff told stories of how his unit trained Colombian anti-narcotics troops, but the techniques they learnt suggested that there real purpose is to defend "the operations of Occidental, British Petroleum and Texas Petroleum and securing control of future Colombian fields."[54]

Indeed, the fingerprints on Plan Colombia reveal the heavy hand of the US-Colombia Business Partnership (USCBP). Founded in 1996 by BP Amoco, Occidental and Enron, the USCBP has lobbied Congress to create "stability" not only in Colombia, but also in the entire northern part of South America. Even as the media feed us the canard that the war is against drugs, the USCBP and military officials speak very frankly of their oil needs.

In October 1999, Pastrana traveled to Houston, Texas to meet with the executives from the oil, gas and electricity industry (represented by Enron, Reliant and others). Pastrana asked for their assistance to dispatch FARC, offering generous concessions in Colombia for their troubles. Enron was part of the talks. In 1996, Enron entered Colombia as the owner of the Centragas natural gas pipeline project and as an advisor to Empresa Colombiana de Petroleos (Ecopetrol), the state oil firm. The World Bank lavishly funded the Enron venture with $65 million in loans. Enron went into the deal with majority control, while Japan's Tomen Corporation and Colombia's Promigas, S. A., held minor shares. The 357-mile pipeline built by Enron carried gas from the Barrancabermeja gas complex to the port for Ecopetrol. President Ernesto Samper Pizano made it very attractive for firms to do business in Colombia: in 1996 he welcomed Texaco into a project with Ecopetrol, with no stipulation that the state take over the project; soon, Samper allowed foreign firms to hold three quarters of the stake in energy projects, an unheard of bonus for firms generally happy to hold a minority share along with the state's oil company. Pastrana carried forward Samper's pro-corporate stance and in 2000-01 Ecopetrol signed more than fifty such contracts with the major oil firms. The London-based BP Amoco controls the 1.5 billion barrel Casiana-Cupiagua oil-field, the largest in the country, while Los Angeles-based Occidental controls the 1 billion barrel Caño Limón oilfields, the second largest. Both firms take their oil by over four hundred-mile pipelines to Coveñas, where ships then transport it, mainly to the U.S.[55] Canadian Occidental Petroleum controls the third largest oil reserve, an oilfield known as Boqueron with a capacity of three hundred million barrels.

FARC and ELN treated the transnational oil firms as the enemy when they began to buy up the fields and build their pipelines. Since 1986, the two groups bombed pipelines over a thousand times (the Ecopetrol line over four hundred times) and they continue to kidnap oil company executives who work in the field. The ransom money allowed the guerrilla groups to arm themselves with the latest technology to match the Colombian army. The government claims that FARC and ELN generate about $140 million per year from their extortion rackets.

Terrified by the power of the FARC and the ELN, the oil companies funneled money to lobby for Plan Colombia, to bolster the Colombian military, and to arm the right-wing paramilitary groups that terrorize the countryside. Human Rights Watch argued in 1996 that the CIA assisted cocaine cartels and large farmers with the creation of the paramilitary formations in 1991.[56] "The most atrocious violence that we are experiencing comes from the state and its secret affiliates, which are the paramilitary groups," noted Father Javier Giraldo (of the Inter-Congregational Commission for Justice and Peace) who was equally upset that "the United States continues sending military aid to our government without human rights conditions."[57] But if the U.S. is party to the violence, there is no reason for those conditions. Indeed, the peace talks broke down several times in the past five years because of the relentless stream of murders conducted by the paramilitary groups without concern for the state troops, because of the government's accord with the U.S.

In the late 1990s, Carlos Castrano formed th₍
Autodefensas Unidas de Colombia (AUC), the umbrella group
for the paramilitary units. Since then, the groups have been on
a rampage against human rights activists, trade unionists and
the peasantry. In late January 1998, paramilitary formations kid-
napped four employees of the Instituto Popular de Capacitacion
and they told others in the office that they would "not permit
the growth of Communism" in Colombia. In late April of that
same year, these groups assassinated Eduardo Umana Mendoza,
a human rights attorney, who was in the midst of working for
the oil workers' Union Sindical Obrera. In response, Colombia's
public sector workers went on a one-day strike. Ten years earlier, state Decree No. 180 branded trade unionists as "terrorists."
As a consequence, 2,300 organizers of the Central Unitaria de
Trabajadores (CUT), the trade union federation, have been
killed since the late 1980s. Only one suspect has ever been
charged. The Colombian Army's Twentieth Brigade and Naval
Intelligence Network No. 7 act with impunity against the population, just as the Air Force bombs entire villages (as it did in
March of 1998 in Cartegena de Chaira). But the police did little in response. As the guerrillas go after the oil concessions, the
petro-conglomerates have made a tacit alliance with the paramilitary and military groups.

Human rights groups, such as Human Rights Watch, and
regional organizations, such as the Organization of American
States' Inter-American Commission on Human Rights as well
as the UN Commissioner for Human Rights, say that oil companies have given millions of dollars to the paramilitary to protect the pipelines. As the biggest investor in Colombia,
London-based BP Amoco is the most heavily involved with the
para-military racket.[58] In 1992, BP hired Defense Systems
Limited to guard its pipelines and train a five hundred-person
unit of the Colombian National Police. In 1996, the Police
signed a $2 million, three-year deal with BP to take care of its

red General Hernán Guzmán Rodríguez, a U.S. .mericas graduate, to help its operations.[59] The Commission cited Guzmán in 1992 for 149 murders between 1987 and 1990. Sitting before the UK's Parliamentary Select Committee on International Development on 20 October 1998, Chris Gibson-Smith, Managing Director of BP, said that two years before, "We were building a pipeline through the most guerrilla-infested area of Colombia and a field security contractor was looking at options. Among the options he looked at, offered by an Israeli contractor, was attack helicopters and other things." When management got wind of this, the security contractor was fired, went to Venezuela, and then returned, after a brief hiatus, to the BP payroll. When asked directly about what BP provided to the paramilitary and the police, Gibson-Smith said, "The short answer actually is night vision goggles were supplied to the brigade because the pipelines get attacked at night and the brigade did not have any way of seeing the attackers."

BP is not alone. In December 1998, Occidental Petroleum joined with AirScan, a private paramilitary formation, and the Colombian military to bomb a village called Santo Domingo and killed eighteen people suspected of being "narco-terrorists." It took an enormous effort to break this story, so it is likely that there are many other Santo Domingos that we will never hear about. Senator Patrick Leahy (Democrat-Vermont) noted, "Three years have passed, and we have yet to see anyone prosecuted for the needless death of eighteen people or the flagrant attempts by Colombian military officers to cover up the crime."[60]

The U.S. government isn't innocent in this game. Until Pastrana came to power in mid-1998, the Colombian state has been tutored effectively in counter-insurgency by the U.S. military. On 7 October 1996, the Western Hemisphere military leaders met at Bariloche (Argentina) to coordinate activity against "narco-guerrillas."[61] The U.S. suggested that an international center to fight drugs be located in Panama, just at the same time as U.S. military operations were being forced to vacate that country. "Panama is located right on the edge of some of the most substantial narco-trafficking that exists anywhere in the hemisphere," argued U.S. Defense Secretary William Perry. Two weeks later, the U.S. military tested an airborne jungle-penetration sensor to scan Colombian jungles for "narco-guerrillas." The Colombian military used US-supplied A-37 fighter-bombers and Blackhawk helicopters to strafe villages in the "liberated areas." In this context, the military and the U.S. began chemical warfare against the Colombian peasantry. Dow Chemical (makers of Agent Orange) supplied the U.S. and the Colombians with tebuthiuron (a hazardous herbicide) until 1998, which was sprayed in large doses over Colombia. In 1998, the military sprayed 45,000 acres, but the acreage of coca increased by eighteen percent. Over the past four years despite the spraying, coca acreage increased by fifty-six percent, so it begs the question of what is being sprayed, the coca or the FARC? In September 1996, Colombian peasants began a campaign against the defoliation tactics and Pastrana joined them in 1999 to put an end to the spraying. The War on Drugs continues unabated, however, and the U.S. funnels in more expertise each year. In March 1998, General Charles Wilhelm told Congress, "The Colombian military to date provide little cause for optimism" in their war against FARC and ELN. Apart from money and hardware, the U.S. continues to train Colombian personnel at the School of the Americas (Fort Benning, Georgia) in counter-insurgency tactics. The scale of U.S. action perplexed Colombia's National Police Chief, Rosso Jose Serrano. "You can't say it's a police operation," he noted about the War on Drugs, since by his estimation, "it's a Vietnam-type operation."[62] This time, however, the enemy is not Communism, but those who won't allow the petro-conglomerates access to their drug of choice.

While the U.S. and the Colombian government pin the blame on the guerrillas, groups such as Human Rights Watch and the Centro de Investigación y Educación Popular show that about seventy-five percent of the killings are done by the right-wing paramilitaries, about fifteen percent by the guerrillas and ten percent by state forces. In its March 1998 Report, the Bogatá-based United Nations High Commission for Human Rights noted, "Witnesses frequently state that [massacres] were perpetuated by members of the armed forces passing themselves off as paramilitaries, joint actions by members of the armed forces or police and paramilitaries, or actions by paramilitaries enjoying the complicity, support or acquiescence of the regular forces."[63]

Savvy about the context, FARC argued that the U.S. increased its War on Drugs money in 1998 during the talks to sabotage the government's credibility. There is a hint of truth to this. "While the money [to Colombia] has been designated for use against drug crop growers and drug traffickers," the *New York Times* commented, "much of the equipment could easily be used against the guerrillas."[64] When the U.S. waived its tepid sanctions against Colombia in 1998, U.S. State Department official Rand Beers noted, "the growth of Colombian guerrillas threatens the country's democracy as well as U.S. investments," especially U.S. petro-conglomerates.[65] In January 1999, FARC noted, "The accords with respect to military support reached between the Pastrana government and the North American administration represent an unacceptable intervention in Colombia by the United States to reinforce the counterinsurgency under the pretext of the fight against drugs." Shortly thereafter the head of the governmental Peace Commission, Victor G. Ricardo gave FARC documents that detailed Pastrana's links with the right-wing paramilitary groups and cocaine barons. The most effective way to go after FARC was to label it as a "narco-terrorist" organization and then use the anti-drug money to intervene in Colombia's civil war. *El Espectador* columnist Alberto Molano notes that FARC entered the drug economy hesitantly in the 1970s. "The guerrilla leadership soon realized that banning coca would mean losing peasant support to the authorities. This realization marked the birth of the infamous *gramaje*, a coca-trade tax that is nothing less than guerrilla-imposed extortion of drug traffickers and prosperous coca farmers. The guerrillas' rapprochement with coca also led to the belief that they are traffickers-narco-guerrillas. That notion is false, however."[66] The U.S. Drug Enforcement Agency (DEA) accepts this view, as its Chief of Operations, Donnie Marshall told Congress on 9 July 1997, "To date, there is little to indicate that insurgent groups are trafficking in cocaine themselves, either by producing cocaine HCL and selling it to Mexican syndicates, or by establishing their own distribution networks in the United States."[67] Evidence from the DEA and elsewhere suggests that the right-wing paramilitary groups are knee-deep in cocaine. The U.S. State Department calls one of the leaders of a right-wing group, Carlos Castrano, a "known drug trafficker," but these groups don't get the brunt of Plan Colombia.[68] Rather they benefit from it.

In a 1997 cable from his embassy to Washington, DC, U.S. Ambassador Myles Frechette noted that the allegations of a "FARC Cartel" were "put together by the Colombian military to obtain U.S. assistance in the counterinsurgency."[69] Frechette pinned the blame on the Colombian military, but he should not have neglected the U.S. Congress, the U.S. military and, most importantly, the oil barons who benefit most from the removal of FARC.

In the midst of all this, FARC is not ready to lay down arms without concessions, and it is these concessions that spell out in no uncertain terms just why FARC is a threat to our brand of capitalism. In 1993, the guerrillas adopted a 10-point

Platform for Reconstruction and National Reconciliation, the model for the now aborted talks. The document calls for a political solution to the Colombian crisis, with the reconstruction of the armed forces, the judiciary and the political process as well as the reorientation of the economy in which "the State should be the principal proprietor and administrator of the strategic sectors." Translation: the State, not the private foreign companies, must control the oil.

(3) A Tyrant Speaks of Terror and Spits on Our Hopes

> The hidden hand of the market will never work without a hidden fist. McDonald's cannot flourish without McDonnell Douglas, the designer of F-15s. And the hidden fist that keeps the world safe for Silicon Valley's technologies is called the United States Army, Air Force, Navy and Marine Corps.
> —Thomas Friedman, *New York Times*, 1999[70]

If the War on Drugs is an adequate cover for the petro-war in the Andean region, the War on Terrorism is a sufficient ideological mask for the U.S. presence over the oil lands of the Gulf and Central Asia. The Unocal stakes in Afghanistan alert us to the corporate interests behind the war against the planet that emanates from the Bush White House. First Afghanistan, then Iraq, next Colombia, and then, who knows? Globalization reigns supreme, bolstered by the largest corporate mercenary army in the world—the U.S. armed forces.

The Fifth Afghan War (2001-2002) spluttered to a stop when the US-backed government of Hamid Karzai took power in Kabul, but then soon thereafter it began again.[71] The mountains that barely divide Afghanistan from Pakistan faced a barrage of firepower as the U.S. tested various incendiary bombs and other techniques against bands of suspected al-Qa'ida and Taliban forces. Afghanistan gave Vieques a respite. In Tora Bora, then south of Gardez, U.S. Special Forces joined the new Afghan army in massive assaults against the strongholds of the Taliban. The enormous scale of the assault that comprises "Phase 2," of the war raised the eyebrows of many. The Bush administration answered with this: "If you have any doubt about the depth of our commitment, look at Afghanistan and what we did there."[72] Just as with Iraq, the U.S. wants to send a message to the world that it is serious about any resistance to its power, that it does not let any straggler go, that it takes no prisoners (only "unlawful combatants"). According to Marc Herrold of the University of New Hampshire, the U.S. military killed about 100-200 civilians per Taliban/al-Qa'ida leader. This is quite a kill ratio!

The bombs are retaliation for the terrorist attacks of 9/11, because the U.S. government claims that the organizers of that attack plotted and trained in Afghanistan. The full-scale bombardment and the overthrow of the Taliban occurred to disrupt the networks of terror and to take-out, according to the newly enunciated Bush Doctrine, "those who harbor them."

The U.S. government, however, has not always seen the Taliban as the instantiation of Evil. Formed in 1994 in the Pakistani refugee camps, the Taliban (literally, students) earned the support of the Pakistani establishment as their factor of stability in war-torn Afghanistan. Backed by the Pakistani intelligence services (ISI), the Taliban made rapid strides against the other factions. The rapid assent of the Taliban led many to suspect that it was being backed by the CIA as well, mainly because of the Taliban's anti-Iran posture and because of the CIA's covert war to destabilize and marginalize Iran (with $20 million authorized by Congress). In April 1996, when U.S. Assistant Secretary of State Robin Raphel visited Pakistan, she denied this, "We do not favor one faction over another nor do we give any group or individual support."[73] Nevertheless, when the Taliban took Kabul on 27 September 1996, both the Pakistani establishment and the U.S. government welcomed the move. When the Taliban announced that it would impose Islamic Law (as interpreted by in its most orthodox and culturally cruel manner), the State Department said it saw "nothing objectionable." U.S. Senator Hank Brown (Republican-Colorado) noted, "The good part of what has happened is that one of the factions at last seems capable of developing a government in Afghanistan."[74]

Why was the United States so eager to see a stable government in Afghanistan, particularly after it had abandoned the region when the Soviets withdrew and the warlords began a process to devastate the country? What brought the U.S. back to the forefront of Afghan affairs in 1996, particularly when its current adversary Osama bin Laden had only just arrived there from Sudan (May 1996) and he had not yet been able to create his web of camps to train the al-Qa'ida network? On 21 April 1996, before bin Laden gets to Kandahar and when the Taliban did not look like it would take Kabul, Robin Raphel told the press in Islamabad, "We have an American company which is interested in building a pipeline through to Pakistan. This pipeline project will be good for Turkmenistan, for Pakistan and for Afghanistan as it will offer job opportunities but also energy in Afghanistan."[75] A U.S. diplomat told Ahmed Rashid, "The Taliban will probably develop like the Saudis did. There will be Aramco, pipelines, an emir, no parliament and lots of Sharia law. We can live with that."[76]

The US-based corporations, some claim, did not take a passive role in the growth of the Taliban. Afghanistan expert Oliver Roy argues that the Taliban's rise to power in so short a time "was largely orchestrated by the Pakistani secret service and the oil company Unocal, with its Saudi ally Delta."[77] Journalist Michael Griffin maintains that U.S. law forbids oil companies like Unocal to directly give money to groups like the Taliban. The Bin Mahfouz's National Commercial Bank in Saudi Arabia owns Delta-Nimri, Unocal's partner in Azerbaijan and in Central Asia, and there are indications that they may have financed the Taliban.[78] But why would two oil companies be interested in the rise of the Taliban, particularly when Afghanistan itself has hardly any oil (perhaps 95 million barrels) and a fair amount of natural gas (perhaps five trillion cubic feet)? The real jewel is not Afghanistan itself, but its location in the pipeline wars in Central Asia.

On 12 February 1998, John Maresca, International head of Unocal, sat before a U.S. Congressional committee and testified about Afghanistan's centrality in Central Asia's oil game:

> The Caspian region contains tremendous untapped hydrocarbon reserves, much of them located in the Caspian Sea basin itself. Proven natural gas reserves within Azerbaijan, Uzbekistan, Turkmenistan and Kazakhstan equal more than 236 trillion cubic feet. The region's total oil reserves may reach more than 60 billion barrels of oil— enough to service Europe's oil needs for 11 years. Some estimates are as high as 200 billion barrels. In 1995, the region was producing only 870,000 barrels per day (44 million tons per year [Mt/y]). By 2010, Western companies could increase production to about 4.5 million barrels a day (Mb/d)—an increase of more than 500 percent in only 15 years. If this occurs, the region would represent about five percent of the world's total oil production, and almost 20 percent of oil produced among non-OPEC countries. One major problem has yet to be resolved: how to get the region's vast energy resources to the markets where they are needed. There are few, if any, other areas of the world where there can be such a dramatic increase in the supply of oil and gas to the world market. The solution seems simple: build a "new" Silk Road. Implementing this solution, however, is far from simple. The risks are high, but so are the rewards.

Maresca rejects Iran as the transit terrain for the pipeline and settles on Afghanistan:

> The only other possible route option is across Afghanistan, which has its own unique challenges. The country has been involved in bitter warfare for almost two decades. The territory across which the pipeline would extend is controlled by the Taliban, an Islamic movement that is not recognized as a government by most other nations. From the outset, we have made it clear that construction of our proposed pipeline cannot begin until a recognized government is in place that has the confidence of governments, lenders and our company. In spite of this, a route through Afghanistan appears to be the best option with the fewest technical obstacles. It is the shortest route to the sea and has relatively favorable terrain for a pipeline. The route through Afghanistan is the one that would bring Central Asian oil closest to Asian markets and thus would be the cheapest in terms of transporting the oil.

The U.S. government concurs. In December 2000, the U.S. Government Energy Information Factsheet on Afghanistan reported, "Afghanistan's significance from an energy standpoint stems from its geographical position as a potential transit route for oil and natural gas exports from Central Asia to the Arabia Sea. This potential includes proposed multi-billion dollar oil and gas export pipelines through Afghanistan."[79] The region in question, we are told, bears oil and natural gas resources worth $4 billion, a vast ransom. In 1998, Cheney (then head of the major oil player Halliburton) said, "I cannot think of a time when we have had a region emerge as suddenly to become as strategically significant as the Caspian."

Central Asia has proven oil reserves of more than thirty-three billion barrels and a possible reserve of two hundred and thirty three billion barrels. Its natural gas is proven to be almost two hundred trillion cubic feet and its possible reserves include an addition of almost three hundred trillion cubic feet. This could be an enormous stockpile of energy. For this reason there are currently fourteen oil pipeline projects and six natural gas pipeline projects in the region. The U.S. is not eager to support any pipeline that runs southwards through Iran, or to share control of the pipeline with China (eastwards) or Russia (northwards). The pipelines backed by the U.S. take the energy reserves west under the Caspian Sea (at great cost) or south through Afghanistan. This is the reason why Afghanistan is such a prize, and for this reason Unocal hired top lobbyists like former U.S. Ambassador to Pakistan and main liaison with the *mujahideen*, Robert Oakley as well as former U.S. Secretary of State Henry Kissinger, and it joined forces with Saudi Arabia's Delta-Nimri (whose boss, Badr al-Aiban has the ear of King Faud, and so had influence with the Saudi-backed Taliban). Sleaze all the way.

When the Taliban took power in 1996, Marty Miller, head of Unocal, expressed some satisfaction that finally the region would be in the kind of peace necessary for pipeline construction. The construction of the pipeline, Miller said at the time, was a "conflict resolution process."[80] Miller worried that the continuation of instability from the North, mainly from troops loyal to Ahmed Shah Masud and others who now make up the Northern Alliance, would increase the costs of the pipeline. On 5 June 1997, with the Taliban in power and the Northern Alliance on the move, Miller said, "It's uncertain when this project will start. It depends on peace in Afghanistan and a government we can work with. That may be the end of the year, next year, or three years from now, or this may be a dry hole if the fighting continues." Some leaders among the Northern Alliance speculated, Ahmed Rashid recounts, that Unocal gave covert support to the Taliban to push the Northern Alliance away from the route of the pipeline.

Meanwhile, Unocal welcomed a delegation of the Taliban

under Mullah Mohammed Ghous in November 1997 to the U.S. The Taliban visited NASA, a zoo as well as the home of Marty Miller.[81] Unocal paid close to a million dollars for the Afghan Studies Center at the University of Nebraska to train over four hundred Afghans in various pipeline construction skills.

In 1998, when Clinton bombed Afghanistan in retaliation for the terrorist attacks on U.S. embassies in East Africa, Unocal was forced to cut its ties with the project, although its partner and proxy, Saudi Arabia's Delta continued to push on. But hope emerged on 29 April 1999 when the energy ministers from Afghanistan, Pakistan and Turkmenistan met to pledge their commitment to the tripartite gas pipeline project.

When the terrorists bombed the World Trade Center, and the U.S. started the Fifth Afghan War, the pipeline returned on the agenda. In January 2002, Richard Butler of the Council of Foreign Relations wrote, "The war in Afghanistan has made the construction of a pipeline across Afghanistan and Pakistan politically possible for the first time since Unocal and the Argentinean company Bridas competed for the Afghan rights in the mid-1990s."[82] The bombs were not solely retaliation for 9/11; they sound a 911 for the intensification of capitalist imperialism against the active will of most of us on the planet.

And if Enron had not collapsed in late 2001, it might have joined the gathering of corporate hawks over Central Asia. In 1996, Enron entered the Uzbek gas market thanks to $400 million guaranteed OPIC insurance. Associated Press reported that in April 1997 Lay called then Texas governor GWB, "about Enron's negotiations for a $2 billion joint venture to develop Uzbekistan's natural gas fields. According to the letter Bush was scheduled to meet with Uzbekistan's ambassador to the United States just a few days later."[83] But in 1998, the deal fell through when Enron could not secure its investment. That year, Enron conducted a feasibility study for the government of

Turkmenistan on the Trans-Caspian Gas Pipeline. The 1,680 kilometer pipeline was to run from eastern Turkmenistan to Turkey, and Enron would have been a major player in the construction had the Central Asian states not fallen out between themselves over percentages.

As the war in Afghanistan wound down, attention began to turn toward Iraq. Here, too, the focus is on the oil spoils as much as on the rule of Saddam Hussein. Even as the French and the Russians, Iraq's major oil trading partners, balk at the question of an invasion, the U.S. puppet, the Iraqi National Congress (INC), is already selling concessions. A senior Iraqi National Congress official told investigative reporter Seymour Hersh that the French and the Russians "would be given access to the extraordinarily rich oil fields in southern Iraq. [INC leader Ahmed Chalabi] has been in contact with American oil companies, the official added, in an effort to insure that the fields get into quick production and provide a source of revenue for the new interim government that the INC hopes to lead. The French and Russian oil companies 'would have to go as junior partners to Americans.'"[84]

In Afghanistan, an indication that the oil game is on again is from the personnel selected by the U.S. to take power there once the U.S. guns went silent. Hamid Karzai, President of Afghanistan, won the support of the U.S. establishment despite his shady past. Karzai, scion of an important Pashtu clan, the Popalzai, left Afghanistan during the civil war and moved to the U.S. His family ran a successful chain of Afghan restaurants as Karzai sought work for the CIA and, after a donation, tried to be the Taliban's representative in the UN. Most strikingly, Karzai worked as "a consultant for the American oil company, Unocal, at the time when it considered building an oil pipeline in Afghanistan."[85] Not only is Karzai an alumnus of Unocal, but he also has enduring ties with the U.S. government. When Karzai was chosen as head of state, Christina Rocca, assistant

secretary of state for South Asia and former foreign policy adviser to Senator Sam Brownback (Republican-Kansas), said of
him, "To us, he is still Hamid, a man we've dealt with for some
time."[86]

Unocal's other Afghan is Zalmay Khalilzad, U.S. Special
Envoy to Afghanistan and before 9/11, the National Security
Council's advisor and only Afghan specialist in the Bush White
House. Born in Mazar-e-Sharif, Khalilzad left Afghanistan to
study at the American University in Beirut in the 1970s, did a
PhD at the University of Chicago, then joined Columbia
University's faculty of political science (to work beside former
Carter man, Zbigniew Brzezinski). In 1984, Khalilzad took a
post at the State Department and became its resident expert on
Afghanistan as the CIA-backed jihad against the Soviets inten-
sified. He worked with ultra-hawk Paul Wolfowitz, left the
Reagan administration for the Rand Corporation and then
returned to the state department in the policy-planning depart-
ment under Wolfowitz during GHB's administration.

In the mid-1990s, Khalilzad worked as a consultant for the
Cambridge Energy Research Associates (CERA) and he conducted a risk assessment of an Afghan pipeline for Unocal
under this auspices. While on retainer from CERAs and
Unocal, Khalilzad defended the Taliban in the *Washington Post*
(October 1996), "The Taliban does not practice the anti-U.S.
style of fundamentalism practiced in Iran."[87] The next year, he
entertained Unocal's Taliban guests ("Four years ago," the *Post*
reported in November of 2001, "at a luxury Houston hotel, oil
company adviser Zalmay Khalilzad was chatting pleasantly over
dinner with leaders of Afghanistan's Taliban regime about their
shared enthusiasm for a proposed multi-billion dollar pipeline
deal").[88] When the Taliban lost favor in 1998, Khalilzad joined
with RAND colleague Daniel Byman to co-author
"Afghanistan: The Consolidation of a Rogue State." While
they argued, "Afghanistan is ruled by a rogue regime, the

Taliban" (already a departure from Khalilzad's 1996-7 assessments), the authors returned to the world of oil:

> Afghanistan itself occupies a vital geostrategic position, near such critical but unstable regions as the Persian Gulf and the Indo-Pakistani border. Indeed, the importance of Afghanistan may grow in the coming years, as Central Asia's oil and gas reserves, which are estimated to rival those of the North Sea, begin to play a major role in the world energy market. Afghanistan could prove a valuable corridor for this energy as well as for access to markets in Central Asia.[89]

That same year, in denial of his work for Unocal, Khalilzad told the Los Angeles World Affairs Council, "A California company called Unocal was interested in exploring that option [of the Afghan pipeline], but because of the war in Afghanistan, because of the instability that's there, those options, or that option, at least has not materialized."[90]

As the U.S. returned to Kabul, Khalilzad returned as Special Envoy. Karzai, another Unocal veteran, came in as head of state. In June 2002, the Loya Jirga (tribal council) gathered in Kabul to elect a new head of state because Karzai's tenure as Interim leader had come to an end. As the delegates from across this diverse country gathered in the city's university, the mood shifted from a renewal of Karzai to the enthronement of the King Zahir Shah (recently back from his close to three decade exile in a Roman suburb). As news of Karzai's impending exit leaked out, "U.S. special envoy Zalmay Khalilzad and Hamid Karzai, the present leader whom Western governments prefer, raced to Zahir Shah's villa and separately urged him to back Mr. Karzai publicly to continue as leader." Flanked by Khalilzad and Karzai, the King listened to his press aide read his statement renouncing the throne at a press conference on 10 June 2002. Khalilzad "made the U.S. pressure public by calling a mid-afternoon press conference to announce that Zahir Shah would renounce his candidacy."[91]

Unocal's people, with U.S. insistence, remain in power in Afghanistan. Meanwhile, behind the scenes and largely unreported, on 30 May 2002, Pakistan, Afghanistan and Turkmenistan signed a $2 billion agreement to construct the gas pipeline from Dauletabad gas fields to Gwadar port in Pakistan. Pakistan's President Musharraf took time out from the tense situation at the border with India to join Karzai and Turkmenistan's Niyazov in Islamabad to sign the agreement.

Hastily, after 9/11, Unocal put the following note on their website: "Unocal has received inquires about a previously proposed pipeline that, if built, would have crossed a part of Afghanistan. We withdrew from that project in 1998, and do not have, nor plan to have, any projects in that country. We do not support the Taliban in any way whatsoever." Under pressure from 9/11, this has to be the official lie. On the continent of sleaze, the military men and the corporate men spill blood to install in Maresca of Unocal's terms a "recognized government in place that has the confidence of governments, lenders and our company."

Karzai's is that government, and Enron's old pal from Colombia, Unocal, is back in the game, subsidized by the U.S. military once more.

Under the regime of globalization, we seem to go forward into the past—eager to move ahead, we return to the days of Empire. Enron's pals, like Unocal, are protected from its collapse. The shape of sins to come is by now clear by the indulgences already committed.

CHAPTER FOUR

Moving on the Contradictions

> Some are willing to play the villain, they just chillin'
> To pass the time, pass the information
> Or pass the wine
> Pass the buck or pass the baton
> But you can't pass the police or the Pentagon,
> The IRS or the upper echelon.
> I think it's time to make a move on the contradiction.
> —Michael Franti, 2001.[1]

Enron's collapse precipitated the rise of Enronism's defenders. Alan Greenspan, head of the Federal Reserve Bank and acolyte of right-wing thinker Ayn Rand, addressed business students in early March 2002, where he noted, "After considerable soul-searching and many Congressional hearings, the current CEO-dominated paradigm, with all its faults, will likely continue to be viewed as the most viable form of governance for today's world. Corporate governance has doubtless already measurably improved as a result of this greater market discipline in the wake of recent events."[2] Always the standard setter for audacity, arch conservative writer and most frequently quoted author by Ronald Reagan, George Gilder boldly claimed on CNN that Enron is "a success story" because the system worked: a corrupt company hiding all that debt in the end paid the ultimate price of bankruptcy. He might be right for the wrong reasons; Enron's failure is no success story for the investors and workers who lost millions. But if the collapse has in any small measure slowed the privatization of the public good around the globe, this might be termed a success. Events suggest that even on this score, the collapse of Enron has not been a success.

While the Enron fiasco broke out, the South Korean power workers took on the Second Enclosure Movement as they fought their government's attempt to sell the power plants to the private sector, the profit sector. Four thousand workers of the five subsidiaries of the Korea Electric Power Corporation struck work on 25 February 2002, but in early April the workers' union, the Korean Confederation of Trade Unions announced that their heroic stand had failed. As the strike ended with an undisclosed agreement, the Commerce and Energy Minister Shin Kook-hwan and Labor Minister Bang Yong-seok told the media, "The government will proceed with the privatization of the power companies as planned since the government and the KCTU agreed to exclude the power industry's privatization from the agenda of future negotiations."[3]

On 31 May 2002, the government of Delhi, India's capital city signed a memorandum of understanding with two private power firms to sell electricity to New Delhi's residents. The government took this move, it claimed, because it loses as much as $245 million each year due to unpaid bills and theft. "Democracy allows us to be strict to a certain extent only," complained Delhi's Power Minister Ajay Maken. The Confederation of Indian Industry, a major chamber of commerce, welcomed the move as "a step in the right direction." The left demurred. The Communist Party of India [Marxist], the main opposition to the deal in Delhi, argued that the capital city would go the way of the eastern Indian state of Orissa. When that state came under its Electricity Reform Act of 1995, private firms descended on it, made short-term profits, obdurately refused to pay the state its arrears when the expectations of profits petered out (the firms owe upwards of $306 million to the state of Orissa), and then relied upon the state to forgive it its debts.[4]

The capture of the commons remains on the front burner of capitalism, even as Enron itself vanishes into the ash heap of historic greed.

In the United States, a jury finds Arthur Andersen guilty of obstruction of justice, but it does not go after its accountancy shields for Enron's crimes. Andersen's partners seek new jobs in the other large accountancy firms as its old hand, Pitt at the SEC, tries to paper over the systemic ills with talk of reform and acts of regret.

Corporate theology, the abiding belief that profit by any means constitutes justice, continues unabated and unchallenged. The failure of Enron does not demand that corporate theology repent or reassess itself. On the contrary, corporate failure often produces an enthusiasm to continue the same old policies of the past.

What did we have before Enron collapsed? In May 2001, the GWB administration released the Cheney Plan ("National Energy Policy: Report of the National Energy Policy Group") that promoted an increase in the domestic production of energy from coal, gas, and oil as well as an expanded use of nuclear power. The government admonished radical environmentalism and advocated exploration in such places as the 1.5 million acres of the Arctic National Wildlife Refuge. After 9/11, after the oil wars came to the U.S. shores, in January 2002, GWB could only bring himself to say that cars might have hydrogen fuel cells in a few decades, this while he extended the limits for pollution as a counter-weight to the Kyoto Protocols.

After Enron's demise, none of these elements of the GWB agenda have shifted. From the Democratic Party, we have much of the same as well. Senators Daschle (South Dakota) and Bingaman (New Mexico) co-authored S. 517, the Energy Policy Act, in February 2002. The Daschle-Bingaman act attempts, among other things, to repeal the 1935 Public Utilities Holding Company Act, a crucial part of the regulatory system to prevent private utilities from gaining monopoly power. The utility firms went along with the government because the bargain suited them: they gained an exclusive service territory in exchange for government oversight and a regulated rate for electricity service. The 1935 Act, then, did not so much end monopoly control as it brought the monopoly power of the utility under governmental control. The 1992 Energy Policy Act (following from allowances made to firms in the 1978 Public Utility Regulatory Policies Act) "unbundled" (or broke up the separate components of) the utilities and let the "market" (or corporate intrigues) determine prices rather than governmental regulation. It isn't as if the Daschle-Bingaman team was unaware of what their 1935 forefathers had figured out. Keep in mind they were legislating after Enron had devastated California, which had only been made possible because Enron, in 1994, won exemption from its regulations and acted as a monopoly. Repeal of this valuable act would be vital to a repeat. No repentance here.

Another avenue of justice, if not repentance, this time in the service of the aggrieved employees and customers of Enron, was the class action suit. But here too the U.S. Congress in its HR 2341/S. 2341 Class Action Fairness Act of 2002 attempts to squelch the power of a disorganized people to collectively act in the courts against corporate malfeasance. (As of this writing, it is currently in the Judiciary Committee and is poised to once again make mischief in the Congress.)

In early January 2002, the U.S. government started a criminal probe of Enron. But to make criminals of employers is against the hallowed traditions of Yankeedom, where the employer has become *primus inter pares*, first among equals, and the firm has become a citizen. Neoliberalism is now the self-evident philosophy of the planetary ruling class, and most of its members thank their various gods for the stars and stripes, for the protective armor of the U.S. armed forces and political muscle.

Lord of All Things: U.S. Imperialism

Midnight is the hour when men desperately seek to obey the eleventh commandment, 'Thou shalt not get caught.' According to the ethic of midnight, the cardinal sin is to be caught and the cardinal virtue is to get by. It is all right to lie, but one must lie with real finesse...The Darwinian concept of the survival of the fittest has been substituted by a philosophy of the survival of the slickest. This mentality has brought a tragic breakdown of moral standards, and the midnight of moral degeneration deepens.

—Martin Luther King, Jr., 1963.[5]

In 2000, when the House of Enron seemed firm and able, Harvard University Press released Antonio Negri and Michael Hardt's *Empire*. In the Preface, the authors (both well-known leftists) informed us, "The United States does not, and indeed no nation-state can today, form the center of an imperialist project. Imperialism is over."[6] Those of us who are system breakers don't appreciate the fact that the world has changed, that power is diffuse, that there is no center and that we all hold the reins of power one way or another. Rather than battle an adversary who does not exist, Hardt and Negri argue, we need to engage with globalization and reconfigure it in the interests of the people over profit. But, as the Enron story teaches us, the Fortune 500 firms are nothing without the rules of the G-8, and the G-8 is nothing without the F-15 and B-1. If imperialism is over, why does the hell of Wal-Mart always seem to follow the smell of napalm?

If there is no U.S. imperialism how should we understand the bombardment of Afghanistan, Iraq, Yugoslavia, Colombia, and elsewhere? Yes, say Hardt and Negri, the U.S. military interventions are "dictated unilaterally by the United States," but "the U.S. world police acts not in imperialist interest but in imperial interest."[7] In other words, the U.S. military, the largest in the world, acts not so much in U.S. national interest, but in the interest of the global Empire that is far too diffuse to be seen in classical left terms. "Even if it were reluctant," the authors insist, "the U.S. military would have to answer the call in the name of peace and order."[8]

Among the many problems with this line of argument, two need to be addressed in light of the Enron story. First, imperialisms of the 19th century (the classical variety) did not operate for the benefit of the entire population of the homeland. English domination of India, for instance, hardly brought prosperity for *all* the English, but it certainly did wonders for the financial and industrial elites. In the 20th century, U.S. imperialism worked cheek by jowl with US-based firms to devastate, for example, both Latin American agriculture and the hopes and aspirations of U.S. workers. The English and U.S. workers may have gained some of the perks of being in the homeland of the Empire, but they did not profit by this location to a great extent. So, to say that the new imperialism does not operate in the national interest of the main power is to obfuscate the way imperialism has functioned for the past two hundred years—essentially as the iron fist of global capital. Second, diminished role of the U.S. military in *Empire* conceals the way US-based transnational firms (such as Enron) gain an enormous advantage from their association with the war machine. The Bush Boys and Baker on assignment for Enron in Kuwait or else Cheney for Halliburton in the entire region after the Gulf War offer an indication of how US-housed capitalists (for Cayman Island-sheltered capital) operate in the wake of US-taxpayer funded bombardments.

Let's stay with the bombardments for a moment. In the budget for 2003, the GWB administration slated $396 billion on the U.S. military, about $45.5 billion above the budget for 2002 (an increase of 13 percent). The War Resisters League takes this figure and adds 80 percent of the national debt to the amount and conclude that almost half the outlay of funds ($1.6 trillion) will be swallowed by the military.[9] At almost $400 billion, the U.S. spends six times more than Russia, the second largest weapons hoarder on the planet and more than twenty-six times as much as the seven "rogue states" (Cuba, Iran, Iraq, Libya, North Korea, Sudan and Syria). The combined military budgets of Russia and China are $117 billion, less than a third of the U.S. military funds. Of all incredible facts, while the planet's military expenditure dropped from $1.2 trillion (1985) to $812 billion (2000), the U.S. share of the total military spending increased from thirty-one percent to thirty-six percent.[10]

The military is not without its industrial twin. The U.S. arms merchants are now in control of more than half the world market. When the U.S. arms merchants became the dominant force in the planet, the government renamed its Office of Munitions Control to the Center of Defense Trade—a sure-fire way to signal the commercial values of the Pentagon. This is, of course, given corporate sanction, and the political parties lick their chops at the rather evenly distributed $10 million from arms dealers in campaign contributions (not to speak of lobbying investments of over $50 million). Arms are still attractive for states that want to "defend" themselves against neighbors, even though both live under the shadow of cruise missiles and hyperspectral imaging satellites. But the principal reason, it seems to me, that the bedraggled states of the world want arms is to prove their nationalist credentials before their populations. It's also true that the U.S. sometimes dictates the defense needs and what will be purchased to meet those needs, in Saudi Arabia and Israel, to name two examples. As IMFundamentalism and capitalist globalization takes charge of the world, the largely compromised leadership of the former Third World (whether India, Indonesia, Ghana or Brazil) must somehow prove its commitment to state sovereignty even as it signs trade accords that undermine its own states. Neoliberalism + Nationalism = Occasional Jingoism + Well-armed Military. If there is too much jingoism, then the states of the G-8 worry about the "reasonableness" of the regime and urge it to act in "consensus" with the powers. If there is no jingoism, then the regime loses the only card it has to earn legitimacy on the "street." If there is insufficient militarism to accompany the occasional jingoism, then the U.S. arms merchants are dissatisfied and make noises about border disputes, missile defense shields and joint-military exercises with U.S. forces—all reasons to bulk up on imports of US-made arms.

And the G-8 welcomes a strong military because this amounts to an international regressive tax on the bedraggled states and to super profits for the monopoly military contractors. (Consider that the merger frenzy has not left this sector untouched and operates as in other business areas to reduce rather than enhance competition: Lockheed Martin comprises Lockheed, Martin Marietta, Loral and General Dynamics; Boeing is paired with McDonnell Douglas; Raytheon with Hughes). World expenditure on munitions is in excess of $800 billion, with the Pentagon absorbing a third of the produce. The U.S. stockpiles for "Full Spectrum Domination" (including the now vastly funded Space Command, and the 527th Space Aggressor Squadron based in Colorado, but with an eye to the sky) are enormous, and they will act as the ultimate force to secure the warrant of the Dollar.

The U.S. government pushes the hegemony of global capital, counted in Dollars, through the idea of "free trade," for example in such diverse venues as:

- The North American Free Trade Agreement of 1994, to absorb Canada and Mexico.

- The Africa Growth and Opportunity Act of 2000 to divide and conquer the raw materials and productive capacity of the African continent.

- The Asia Pacific Economic Cooperation Forum made up of twenty-one states that rim the Pacific Ocean, but at work to ensure a U.S. presence in East Asia.

- The World Economic Forum, a business-government partnership set-up in 1970, but since 1996 hosted in Davos, Switzerland and held in New York City in 2002, at work to ensure that global, mainly US, capital dominates policy discussions around the globe.

- The World Trade Organization, whose mandate is complex and contradictory, but whose ambit is being shaped by global capital, and pushed by the U.S. government to cut down the sovereignty of states to regulate capital (for example, while the much more stringent International Labor Organization passed a slew of over a hundred amendments to regulate capital-labor relations, the U.S. Congress has only ratified a handful—and it is this handful that the U.S. has now pushed forward in the WTO as the planet's "core labor standards").

The U.S. economy remains stable despite the global downturn in fortunes mainly because of its role at the core of an imperialist world system. A first indication of this is that the U.S. draws in the world's capital by vast amounts: in 1999, a country with only four and a half percent of the world's population absorbed almost three quarters of the world's profits and personal savings. Hundreds of billions of dollars enter the U.S. annually, some petrodollars, but most of it investments from Europe and Japan (and elsewhere) in high technology, communications, real estate and other ventures. Some of this inflow of capital comes from an interest in speculation on the U.S. economy. But significant amounts come in as tribute to maintain the singular place of the Dollar (still the world's main reserve and intermediary currency, despite the appearance of the Euro) and as payment to the world's policeman.[11] As the world's manufacturing is being crushed by leveraged buyouts and Russian-style predatory capitalism, the U.S. remains, after a brief drought, as an industrial powerhouse. The World Bank estimates that almost a quarter of the world's industrial capacity, or its ability to produce finished products, has declined since 1991, whereas the US's industrial plant has been regenerated (by greater mechanization and taylorized streamlined production).[12]

When Enron's Linda Powers sits before Congress and sells her company as the best way to further U.S. corporate ends as well as to teach the rest of the world to buy American, it might be a good idea to pay attention to her and not to Hardt and Negri. Or, when the U.S. bombers pummel Afghanistan from Halliburton-built bases and then when Unocal renews its ties to the new US-backed regime, we may once more want to consult the *Wall Street Journal* for the 411 and not the idealism of Hardt and Negri. The lord of all things is global capital, backed in this instantiation, by the U.S. military and by the U.S. government, eager as it is to ensure the dominance of the Dollar as the hard currency of the planet.

The Diggers of the Twenty-First Century

> We're here and we're not alone. Together we're going to change the world. If you're in the way, get in step, because we're coming.
>
> —Janet Robideau, Indian People's Action,
> Montana, 2001.[13]

It is late March 2002. I decided to stop in at a lecture given by Jagdish Bhagwati, a Columbia University economist picked by his Swedish peers to win the Nobel Prize in the near future. An enigmatic man, Bhagwati not only trumpets free trade in his academic work, but he advises both the World Trade Organization *and* Human Rights Watch. He offers a defense of globalization as a progressive and enlightened force, just as he worries about the rapacious instincts of speculative "hot money" gamblers. He opened his talk by damning all those who don't agree with the tendency of globalization to the outer reaches of hell. They are not stake holders, he argued, but they want to drive a stake through the system and therefore are not worthy of serious dialogue. Only a technocracy with expertise in global management is equipped to have this conversation even as these experts must rule with a sense of enlightened despotism. Like most of the WTO and Enron types, intellectuals like Bhagwati talk about democracy when it suits them, but they much prefer the rule of the suits. I wanted to ask him, why should we, as citizens of the planet, trust the rule of the oligarchs when Mr. Moneybags so frequently wants to take us for a ride at all costs? The story of Enron is not the tale of incompetence, for it offers us a window into the only currency that matters to the suits—profits and power...not social justice. Why trust those who want to truss us?

And do they want to get us! As Marx unfurled the mendacity of global capital, he quoted from T. J. Dunning's 1860 tract, *Trades' Unions and Strikes*, "With adequate profit, capital is very bold. A certain 10 percent will ensure its employment anywhere; 20 percent will produce eagerness; 50 percent positive audacity; 100 percent will make it ready to trample on all human laws; and 300 percent and there is not a crime at which it will scruple, nor a risk it will not run, even to the chance of its owner being hanged."[14] Neoliberalism is the condition of the three hundred percent return, and within this structural moment the international people's movement is at a disadvantage. In 2000, Ken Lay promised what might as well have amounted to a three hundred percent increase in Enron's fortunes. Hubris may yet be the price of avarice. But social change should not be left to the Fates. There is much to be done by us mortals here on the planet.

One of the tasks of the Enron stage of capital is to recapture the commons. Here we are in the company of Hardt and Negri, who note, "Capitalism sets in motion a continuous cycle of private reappropriation of public goods: the expropriation of what is common." Furthermore, and here drawing from philosopher Jean-Jacques Rousseau, "The first person who wanted a piece of nature as his or her own exclusive possession and transformed it into a transcendent form of private property was the one who invented evil. Good, on the contrary, is what is common." "The commons," they argue, "is the incarnation, the production, and the liberation of the multitude."[15] Hard to argue with that.

Between 1649 and 1650, a group of agrarian communards under the leadership of Gerrard Winstanley and William Everard challenged the First Enclosure Movement. Fashioned as the Diggers, these peasants convened at St. George's Hill, Surrey, in April 1649 to protest the betrayal of the hopes of the English Civil War. Why else did they overthrow the monarchy if not to gather the land and distribute it among the poor? Why had the fruit of the execution of Charles I turned out to be the end of the commons? On 20 April 1649, in their first manifesto *The True Leveler's Standard Advanced*, they explained their acts: "The Work we are going about is this. To dig up Georges-Hill and the waste Ground thereabouts, and to Sow Corn, and to eat our bread together by the sweat of our brows. And the First Reason is this, That we may work in righteousness, and lay the Foundation of making the Earth a Common Treasury for all, both Rich and Poor, That every one that is born in the land, may be fed by the Earth his Mother that brought him forth, according to the Reason that rules in the Creation."[16]

By 1 June 1649, in their second manifesto *A Declaration from the Poor Oppressed People of England*, the Diggers directly challenged the value of enclosure with their own sense of a moral economy, "that we must neither buy nor sell. Money must not any longer (after our work of the Earth's Community is advanced) be the great god that hedges in some and hedges out others, for money is but part of the Earth; for after our work of the Earthly Community is advanced, we must make use of gold and silver as we do of other metals but not to buy or sell." As the movement grew among a landless peasantry burdened by an increase in the price of foodstuffs, the government of Cromwell cracked down on the settlement and by March 1650 destroyed it. The original Diggers put a stake in the ground against acts of enclosure that impoverished the multitude, but even as they took such bold positions, they could not stop one of the poles of the development of capitalism, the expropriation of the European peasantry.[17]

Three hundred years later, the Diggers took birth in name among the children of the post-scarcity suburbs of the United States who formed an urban commune in the Haight-Ashbury zone of San Francisco. Peter Berg, its auteur from the San Francisco Mime Troupe, wrote of the Diggers conception of freedom and the free stores, "First free the space, goods and services, then let theories of economics follow social facts. Once a free store is assumed, human wanting and giving, needing and taking, become wide open to improvisation. No owner, no manager, no employees and no cash register. When materials are free, imagination becomes currency for spirit. The question of a free store is simple: What would you have?"[18] While the Diggers self-consciously drew from their English forbearers, their politics remained at the level of circulation, of distribution, and they did not take much account of the problem of labor and production. Their origins in the white, suburban, middle-class intoxicated with the lures of consumerism constrained their political vision, since they did not think it important to interrogate the continued exploitation of labor around them. "Give up jobs so computers can do them. Computers render the principles of wage labor obsolete by incorporating them," the

Diggers wrote as their contribution to a critique of political economy. In a decade, they argued, "machines and computers will do most of the work," hence all that the flower people needed to worry about was mental liberation.[19] The Diggers practiced "garbage yoga," the collection of useful waste and the distribution of it via Free Stores to anyone who wanted it. They emblazoned Marx's famous dictum ("take what you need, give what you can") on their politics without making any attempt to undermine the power relations that made this seem altogether like a hip form of charity.

Now, the Diggers of the new millennium share little with their San Francisco counterparts. But they do share a great deal in an emotive way with the English rebels. The Second Enclosure Movement called forth its opposition in the guise of people around the world who work for a living, and who find that all their resources are being seized. The St. George's Hill of this movement is Porto Alegre in Brazil,[20] from where Hebe de Bonafini (of Argentina's Madres de la Plaza de Mayo) said to George Soros in a 2001 trans-Atlantic debate between the World Social Forum (WSF) and the World Economic Forum (Davos), "Mr. Soros, you are a hypocrite. How many children's deaths are you responsible for?" "Another World is Possible," says the WSF, and indeed it is already been formed both on the frontlines of the anti-globalization struggle and in several experimental pockets held one way or another by left governments. If neoliberalism comes in three aspects (weak social regulation, strong repressive apparatus, cultural conservatism), the opposition can also be arrayed along these lines:

(1) Build a People's Economy

In Brazil, the Moviemento dos Trabalhadores Sem Terra (MST), the movement of the landless, grabs land under the banner of slogans such as "Land is not earned but conquered" or "Occupy and Produce." They are not alone, joined in West Asia by the New Intifada, in Mexico by the EZLN, in Zimbabwe by the social classes unleashed by Mugabe, and in South Africa by the Landless People's Movement (with their slogan, *Phambili ngo mzabalazo wa mhlaba! Izwe lethu!* Bring Back the Land! Enough is Enough!). João Pedro Stédile, of the MST, argued, in 1999,

> The MST has only managed to survive because it has matched private, corporate interests with class interests. We were aware that although the struggle for land and agrarian reform has a peasant based social core, it will only progress if it forms part of the class struggle. Right from the start, we were well aware that we were not fighting against *grileiros* [squatters] illegally taking over unclaimed or ownerless lands for re-sale. We were fighting an entire class, the large-scale landowners. We were not battling merely the Land Act, but rather against a bourgeois state.[21]

Alongside the fervor of the peasantry, stands the resilience of a trade union movement battered by neoliberalism, but in many quarters still defiant. In South Africa, the Coalition of South African Trade Unions (COSATU) and South African Communist Party (SACP) emain the bulwark against the neoliberal GEAR policy that drives the government. A vigorous challenge from the SACP and COSATU (two legs of the tripartite alliance with the African National Congress) has galvanized large elements of the people against the government's claim that neoliberalism is inevitable. Drawing from the SACP's 1995 slogan, "Socialism is the Future, Build it Now," COSATU engaged the government's Department of Public Enterprises with a manifesto during its strike wave in mid-August 2001 that aimed to drive a stake into the vampire heart of the Enron stage of capitalism:

> Privatisation has imposed great hardship on poor South Africans, both as members of the public and as

workers. Privatisation of government services has meant rising prices and worse provision for the poor and working people. It undermines the capacity of our government to overcome the legacy of apartheid, which left our communities with poor roads and a shortage of housing, piped water, electricity, refuse removal and sanitation. Our schools and hospitals were in poor condition and understaffed. Privatisation reduces government's capacity to overcome these shortfalls. It aggravates the inequalities between rich and poor. It means the rich can pay for improved services, like education, health and transport, while the poor are left to face cut offs and soaring bills. It is an illusion to think that private interests will bring better services to the poor. Our experiences already show that government regulators do not have the capacity to set up or implement regulatory frameworks that work to serve working and poor communities. For workers, privatisation has spelled job losses, in a country where unemployment is already the main economic problem. Unemployment rose from 16 percent to 25 percent between 1995 and 1999, and has probably risen since then. And that is only using the narrow definition of unemployment. Using the extended vision that counts the discouraged workers this figure rises to 38 percent. Over a hundred thousand job losses can be traced to commercialisation and privatisation in the state-owned enterprises, the public service and local government. Where jobs have been outsourced, workers have been moved outside their bargaining unit and faced reduced pay, benefits and job security. The majority of those who face retrenchment are lower skilled Africans from the rural areas—workers who will not easily find new jobs. For every worker who loses their job, a minimum of five and up to ten people lose their livelihood. We did not fight for liberation so that we can sell every thing we won to the highest bidder! We remain in full support of the Freedom Charter, which declared that "the people shall share in the country's wealth."

Much maligned unions are a crucial element of the Diggers of the new millennium. And there are new forms of unionism, such as Los Angeles's Bus Riders Union (BRU), a formation that organizes workers to fight to improve the conditions that make their lives possible—in this case to defend and extend public transportation. The BRU is a remarkable consumer movement of the working-class: Ricardo Zelada, a Salvadorian immigrant remarks, "I wear two hats for two unions—UNITE for my workplace and the Sindicato de Pasejeros for my civil rights and my transportation." As Eric Mann, the lead organizer of the BRU/SdP, notes, "These tactics of organizing the industrial and service working class through a city-wide struggle over public services allows us to re-enter the trade union movement through a new form of working-class union."[22]

Alongside the unusual ways to organize workers across the planet, the dismissal of organized workers in favor of disorganized workers in degraded work has led to the generation of movements of the unemployed, whether in the Moviemento de Trabajadores Desocupados (MTD) in Argentina or the Agir Ensemble Contre Le Chomage (AC!) or the Mouvement National des Chômeurs et Précaires in France. These organized unemployed workers brought down the Argentine government in early 2002, they bolster the populist regime of Chavez in Venezuela and they give direction to the anti-racist struggle in the U.S. (through the welfare rights work of the ensemble, Grassroots Organized for Welfare Leadership or GROWL). "Road blockades of the unemployed," James Petras notes in a stimulating study of the MTD, "are the functional equivalent of the industrial workers stopping the machines and production line: one blocks the realization of profit, the other, the creation of value."[23]

These struggles to build a people's economy are the best education for the future. Petra Mata, a member of the anti-Levis

Fuerza Unida in El Paso, Texas, told Mariam Ching Louie, "I learned so much at Fuerza Unida. This is the best school you could have, working with people, listening, chairing meetings—all the things you have to understand to carry out the struggle. Here we are not just individuals. We go to support and participate in all struggles in the movement. We work with Asian, Filipino, African American, Mexican, white. We are part of the same vision, the same movement."[24]

(2) Dare to Stop Police Brutality

On 11 August 1928, President Herbert Hoover predicted, "Unemployment in the sense of distress is widely disappearing. We in America today are nearer to the final triumph over poverty than ever before in the history of any land. The poorhouse is vanishing from among us. We have not yet reached the goal, but given a chance to go forward with the policies of the last eight years, and we shall soon with the help of God be within sight of the day when poverty will be banished from this nation." Indeed, Hoover was right: poverty has been banished—the poor now live out of sight, in jail or in the hovels of highly repressed public housing. The United States jails more of its population, spends more money on its police force (and on the FBI) and enjoys a larger military than any other country on the planet. In the early 1990s, some hoped for a "peace dividend," for a transformation between the relations of guns and butter in the wake of the conclusion of the Cold War, but while the social democratic agenda of the state withered, the repressive apparatus grew. In 1994, the communist writer Libero Della Piana wrote, "Our society is reaching the point where there are only two classes of citizens: those in prisons, and the police."[25] If Della Piana was concerned about the increase in inmates and in the police force, Morris Thigpen, the Director of the National Institute of Corrections, was more sanguine: "People joke [that] we seem to be heading toward the day when you're either going to be in prison or working in some sort of way with corrections."[26] "Imprisonment has become the response of first resort to far too many of the social problems that burden people who are ensconced in poverty," wrote Angela Davis, former political prisoner, currently professor of philosophy and founder of Critical Resistance (a group committed to the abolition of prisons). With the end of welfare programs, the state has rendered the poor into criminals through the elevation in punishment for everyday minor offenses. The new reserve army of labor lives behind bars.[27] Social problems, Angela Davis argues, "are veiled by being conveniently grouped together under the category 'crime' and by the automatic attribution of criminal behavior to people of color. Homelessness, unemployment, drug addiction, mental illness, and illiteracy are only a few of the problems that disappear from public view when the human beings contending with them are relegated to cages."

For those who are not in jail, the lockdown conditions of life in the zones of working-class life are matched by the new anti-terrorism ordinances that keep people afraid of everyday existence. The warrant given to the police to harass, arrest and hold ordinary people whether in the streets of the US, India, France or in the Occupied Territories of Palestine, is enough to constrain the ability of people to live. In the Parisian suburbs, where the North African immigrants reside, the police hold them in lockdown conditions. Groups such as the Mouvement De l'Immigration et des Banlieues fight the police with such slogans as "Police Partout, Justice Nulle Part" or "Police Everywhere, Justice Nowhere." In 1997, the national secretary of the Refuse and Resist Network in the U.S. offered a wide-ranging analysis of the problem:

> The cruel and scapegoating political agenda designed help retain America's economic primacy is tearing our county apart. On one side are the promoters of this politics of cruelty and its supporters. On the other side are

those millions of mainly poor people of color, who are being denied a safety net and being blamed for all that is wrong in this country. By taking the role of enforcers of this politics of cruelty, the police have shown which side they support. It is the climate created by the politics of cruelty that is responsible for the rise in police brutality. No one orders the police to brutalize citizens because no one has to. The politics of cruelty divides this county into a division of us versus them. The hysteria over violent crime has created a war zone mentality where any crime against the enemy is acceptable. The police are also encouraged to brutalize citizens by the battlefield mentality conjured by such terms as the War on Drugs. Blaming the poor and people of color for the problems of this country exacerbates the racism which in instilled in police during their training. The idea of inherent criminality, the belief that people who commit crimes are animals and incapable of rehabilitation, leads police to treat people brutally. By refusing to prosecute police, the justice system promotes police brutality.[28]

(3) Assault on Reason

No body wants to live in a state of repression, without a program for social betterment, unless there is good ideological reason to do so. The neoliberal state seeks to gain legitimacy among its relatively impoverished population by the promotion of cruel cultural practices like jingoism or else such as the encouragement of orthodox religion. Women, frequently, become the targets of such strategies, as the regime turns its male population into policemen of the women and thereby conducts the easiest divide-and-rule ploy against all the people. Crude nationalism or theology suffice to numb the courage of a broke, but disorganized population. Across the planet, however, people take heart and protest this assault on reason. The sharp attack on women's rights as a result of the new cultural conservatism engendered the creation of groups like the France-based Women Living Under Muslim Laws, the Pakistan-based Women Against Fundamentalism (and its subsection, War Against Rape),[29] the India-based All India Democratic Women's Association, and Revolutionary Association of the Women of Afghanistan (RAWA). On 10 December 2000, RAWA offered this denunciation of cultural conservatism:

> No religion in the world can ever condone the Taliban's inhuman, misogynist, science-hating, technology-hating liberty-hating and democracy-hating values and practices. Amongst criminal fundamentalist regimes in the world, the Taliban excel marvelously in execrable misuse of the people's religious beliefs. They can in no way qualify to be guardians of our noble culture and traditions. To the Taliban and those who believe in their pretensions, we issue the challenge to answer a simple question: In the past, were Afghan women totally alien with vestiges of human rights and freedoms including the right to education, the right to work, the right to choose their clothing, etc.? Do the annals of history in any land ever have on record such a shameful, miserable farce played out on a national-historical-ideological scale in regard to women's apparel and men's beards and whiskers! Can such burlesque, medieval edicts and restrictions in any way help in providing food, shelter, work, security, progress and happiness to a people ruthlessly and relentlessly being driven with each passing day to the depths of pauperisation, starvation, desperation and degradation? Is it possible to abstract Afghanistan from the real, living world, from the enlightenment, progress and aspirations of the twenty first century, and to deprive the Afghan people forever from liberty and democracy, the vital breath of life for any nation on the face of the earth?[30]

The outrageousness of the Taliban is not logically far from the U.S. theocrats fulminations about Creationism for the school curriculum, or how lesbianism and homosexuality caused 9/11. It is further still, but not by much, from the urgency of the faith-based this and that of GWB and Lieberman, or else the Pat Buchanan-inspired but Attorney General John Ashcroft enabled anti-immigrant patriotism. Close to the Taliban sits the Hindutva Right, the organs of intolerance that rule, by coalition, the vast diversity of India. To counter its eagerness to welcome globalization and the "free play of market forces," the Hindutva Right accommodates the frustrations of many dispossessed Hindus with the outrageousness of its assault on Muslims and the Left. It foists textbooks on the schools that snuff out any hope of a rational discussion of the past, and it anoints "Vedic Astrology" into the curriculum of colleges and schools across the country.[31]

The captains of contemporary imperialism, like their forbearers, twist words around so that war is called defense and greed is called freedom, as the hand that throttles the poor is painted invisible and as unreasonable hopes get sanctified as science. As hard science is needed to devise missiles and launch smart bombs, the mass of humanity is asked to indulge in a fog of unreason—in such arts as astrology.

In Scottsdale, Arizona, base of the right-wing giant Barry Goldwater, the U.S. Department of Education gave accreditation to the Astrological Institute in 2001. Joyce Jensen, the school's founder and a Scorpio, told the media that "this was a good time" because the school's stars were favorably aligned. Students will learn to write horoscopes and offer their clients a glimpse of the future: they will take courses in astrology and psychology, and earn a diploma that allows them to work at such places as holistic healing centers, cruise ships and spas. Psychology is a must, one can only surmise, because the astrologer will need to study the personality of their clients to find the best method for delusion.

With "Full Spectrum Domination," Ronald Reagan's Star

Wars have now become a reality, and our students are enjoined to turn away from the real star wars and take refuge in the warring star signs—we are in a postmodern nightmare now, where the sign of the star is more hearty than the star itself, where the signifier is all and the signified is beyond reach.

The three legs of neoliberalism (weak social regulation, strong repressive apparatus, cultural conservatism) conjoin to hamper the will of the multitude. A lack of socio-economic regulation impoverishes the pocket-book of the masses, and makes the everyday tasks of organization much more difficult; a tough political police necessarily discourages any attempt to join together in an anti-systemic manner; and, finally, the ideological weight of cultural cruelty, whether jingoism or theocracy, cuts down the legitimacy of the ideas of the Left.

But nonetheless, the Diggers of the new millennium soldier on, fighting to undermine the tripartite architecture of neoliberalism and the Second Enclosure Movement. It is not enough to take on one or another of these three legs. The best of our movement fights them all simultaneously, building from one victory to another, reaching out to each other in the fervent hope that soon, perhaps in a lifetime, we will prevail.

Enron has collapsed. We won that battle. Let the war continue.

It's time to make a move on the contradictions.

Notes

Introduction

1   An exception, apart from brief mentions here and there of the Indian case, is John Nichols, "Enron's Global Crusade," *The Nation*, 4 March 2002 and the best study is by the Sustainable Energy and Economy Network of the Institute for Policy Studies, *Enron's Pawns: How Public Institutions Bankrolled Enron's Globalization Game*, Washington, DC: IPS, 22 March 2002.

2   Subcomandante Marcos, *Our Word is Our Weapon*, London: Serpent's Tail, 2001.

3   The first two legs of neoliberalism are well developed in Saskia Sassen, *Losing Control? Sovereignty in an Age of Globalization*, New York: Columbia University Press, 1996. The element of cultural conservatism as the third leg of globalization appears at some length as McJihad in my study of the Fifth Afghan War: *War Against the Planet: The Fifth Afghan War, U.S. Imperialism and Other Assorted Fundamentalisms*, New Delhi: Leftword Books, 2002, Chapter 3.

4   Don Van Natta, Jr., and Neela Banerjee, "Top GOP Donors in Energy Industry Met Cheney Panel," *New York Times*, 1 March 2002.

5   Don Van Natta, Jr., "Donor Won Praise in Energy Report," *New York Times*, 24 March 2002.

6   John Locke, *Two Treatises of Government*, ed. Peter Laslett, Cambridge: Cambridge University Press, 1960, p. 294.

7   Peter Linebaugh and Marcus Rediker, *The Many-Headed Hydra*, Boston: Beacon Press, 2000, p. 40.

8   Arundhati Roy, *The Algebra of Infinite Justice*, New Delhi: Viking, 2001, pp. 150-151.

9   Diane Elson, "Micro, Meso, Macro: Gender and Economic Analysis in the Context of Policy Reform," *Strategic Silence: Gender and Economic Policy*, ed. Isabella Baker, London: Zed Books, 1994.

10   Vandana Shiva, *Water Wars: Privatization, Pollution and Profit*, Boston: South End Press, 2002, p. xiv.

11   The right to the planet is a battle over the terrain we generally call the social. The general argument is offered by Henri Lefebvre in *Le Droit a la Ville*, Paris: Editions Anthropos, 1968.

Chapter 1

1   "Kenneth Lay: The Energetic Messiah," *The Economist*, 1 June 2000.

2   There is an excellent survey of Lay's finances in Nancy Rivera Brooks, David Streitfeld and Lee Romney, "Enron's Chairman Kenneth Lay Ousted," *Los Angeles Times*, 24 January 2002.

3   Patrick Smyth, "Lay Sold $100m in Enron Stock," *Irish Times*, 18 February 2002.

4   William Greider, "Crime in the Suites," *The Nation*, 4 February 2002, p. 12. I'm not naïve about unions and pension funds, mainly because we have the experience of the theft of the Teamsters' pension by the Hoffa leadership—money used to finance the crooked sprawl of Las Vegas's casinos and hotels. Sally Denton and Roger Morris, *The Money and the Power. The Making of Las Vegas and Its Hold on America*, New York: Vintage Books, 2001, pp. 227-235.

5   Public Citizen's Critical Mass Energy & Environment Program, *Blind Faith: How Deregulation and Enron's Influence Over Government Looted Billions from Americans* Washington DC: Public Citizen, December 2001.

6   Phil Gramm knows a thing or two about energy scandals. Phil Gramm and S. C. Maurice, "The Real Teapot Dome Scandal," *Oil World*, September 1975.

7   Doug Henwood, *Wall Street*, London: Verso, 1997, p. 28.

8   World Trade Organization, *International Trade Statistics 2001*, Geneva: WTO, 25 October 2001.

9   Michael Binstein and Charles Bowden, *Trust Me. Keating and the Missing Billions*, New York: Random House, 1993; Stephen Pizzo, Mary Fricker and Paul Muolo, *Inside Job: The Looting of America's Savings and Loans*, New York: McGraw Hill, 1989.

10   John Byrne, "Andersen's Other Headache: Sunbeam," *Business Week*, 29 January 2002.

11   *Wall Street Journal*, 16 January 2002.

12   Kurt Eichenwald, "A Guilty Plea from Andersen's Enron Auditor," *New York Times*, 10 April 2002.

13   Gaenor Lipson, "Auditors up against the wall after Enron breach," *Sunday Times* (South Africa), 20 January 2002.

14   James Ridgeway, "Enron Update: SEC Chief Has Potential Conflict of Interest," *Village Voice*, 16 January 2002.

15   John Lancaster, "Lieberman Placed in Awkward Spot: Senator Not Immune to Enron Problem," *Washington Post*, 2 February 2002.

16   Floyd Norris, "Andersen Told to Split Audits and Consulting," *New York Times*, 12 March 2002.

17   Louis Uchitelle, "Volcker Will Continue His Push for Change in Auditing Standards," *New York Times*, 15 March 2002.

18   Kurt Eichenwald, "Arthur Andersen Is Indicted on a Count of Obstruction of Justice in Enron Case," *New York Times*, 15 March 2002.

19   Kurt Eichenwald, "Andersen Misreads Depths of Government's Anger," *New York Times*, 18 March 2002.

20   Kurt Eichenwald and Michael Brick, "Enron Investors Say Lenders Took Part in Fraud Scheme," *New York Times*, 8 April 2002.

21   Peter Behr, "Enron's Lenders Face Huge Losses: Big Banks May Have Billions at Risk," *Washington Post*, 30 November 2001.

22   Henwood, *Wall Street*, p. 31.

23   For the Citron story, see Pat Reeder, "Third Eye," *The Skeptic*, vol. 10, no. 4, April 1996.

24   Doug Henwood, "Casualties: Enron..." *Left Business Observer*, No. 99, 28 January 2002, p. 2.

25   I have elaborated on this data in *The American Scheme: Three Essays*, New Delhi: Three Essays Press, 2002. This book will be published in a revised and updated form by Boston's South End Press in the Spring of 2003.

26   Henwood, *Wall Street*, p. 65.

27   An enormous number of people find that their money is in the stock market, so that it appears as if the "investor class" is very large. However, they do not exercise control over their funds. Those who do so are a small and influential com-

munity.

28   There is good background in Francois Godement, *The Downsizing of Asia*, London: Routledge, 1999, Chapter 1.

29   Peter Gowan, *The Global Gamble: Washington's Faustian Bid for World Dominance*, London: Verso, 1999, pp. 21-22 and A. A. Kuburi and S. Mansur, "The Political Economy of Middle Eastern Oil," *Political Economy and the Changing Global Order*, ed. G. R. D. Underhill and R. Stubbs, London: Macmillan, 1994.

30   Institute for Policy Studies/Sustainable Energy & Economy Network, *Enron's Pawns: How Public Institutions Bankrolled Enron's Globalization Game*, Washington, DC: IPS/SEEN, 22 March 2002.

31   Until 1997, Jeffrey Skilling ran Enron's trading operation and he told his troops there, "Cash flow doesn't matter." This was partly because of a practice known as "blending and extending"—traders reported higher profits on a deal by adding all the future profits in one go, so that a reasonably good trade became a wonderful loan! The other way "cash flow doesn't matter" is by Enron's hustle to gain public funds for massive projects in the Third World. Michael Brick, "What Was the Heart of Enron Keeps Shrinking," *New York Times*, 6 April 2002.

32   Stephen P. Cohen, *Failed Crusade: America and the Tragedy of Post-Communist Russia*, New York: Norton, 2000.

33   Sabrina Tavernise, "U.S. Grant to Gazprom Partner Is Questioned," *New York Times*, 27 March 2002.

34   Cited in Michel Chossudovsky, "El apartheid se translada al África subsahariana," *Revisita Del Sur*, no. 65, March 1997; for more context, see Joseph Hanlon, "Strangling Mozambique: International Monetary Fund 'Stabilization' in the World's Poorest Country," *Multinational Monitor*, vol. 17, nos. 7-8, July/August 1996.

35   John Fleming, "U.S. Foreign Aid was Lever that Moved Enron Deal," *Houston Chronicle*. November 1, 1995.

36   P. Epstein and A. Epstein, "Mozambique Reorganizes," *Southern Africa*, June 1980, p. 16.

37   David E. Sanger, "How Washington Inc. Makes a Sale," *New York Times*, 19 February, 1995.

38   Tom Zeller, "The Tao of Enron: Well, It Sounded Good," *New York Times*, 24 February 2002.

39   Neela Banerjee, et. al., "At Enron, Lavish Excess Often Came Before Success," *New York Times*, 26 February 2002.

40   Eric Hanson, "Medical Examiner Rules Death Suicide," *Houston Chronicle*, 27 January 2002.

41   S. K. Bardwell, Mike Glenn and Ruth Rendon, "Investigator: Mother described methodical drowning of 5 kids," *Houston Chronicle*, 21 June 2001.

42   Eric Hanson and Mary Flood, "Police Examine note in apparent suicide," *Houston Chronicle*, 26 January 2002.

43   "Man's Body Discovered in Van Confirmed as Suicide Victim," *Rocky Mountain News*, 12 December 2001.

44   "Executive of energy firm dies in apparent suicide," *Boston Globe*, 4 June 2002 and Laura Goldberg, "Turmoil follows a tragedy," *Houston Chronicle*, 4 June

2002.

45   Gregory Palast, "Enron: not the only bad apple," *The Guardian*, 1 February 2002.

46   "Japan's Executive Suicide Crisis," *Financial Times*, 20 October 2000. In 1950, Japan ranked fifth among the world's nations in terms of suicides, but it has moved to tenth by the end of the 1990s. Maurice Pinguet, *La Mort Volontaire au Japon*, Tokyo: Tsukuma Shobo, 1986, p. 57.

47   Denton and Morris show quite conclusively that the multi-ethnic Syndicate exists in the warp and weft of U.S. capitalism. *The Money and the Power*, pp. 118-119.

48   B. Becker, C. Carner, K. Duarte, W. Keene, K. Kincel, S. Loats, B. Rush, C. Smith and T. Varley, *The Changing Structure of the Electric Power Industry. Mergers and Other Corporate Combinations*, Washington: U.S. Department of Energy, 1999.

49   Richard A. Oppel, "Army Secretary Discloses More Phone Calls on Enron," *New York Times*, 26 March 2002.

50   Don Van Natta, Jr., and Neela Banerjee, "Top GOP Donors in Energy Industry Met Cheney Panel," *New York Times*, 1 March 2002.

51   Joseph Kahn, "Bush Advisers on Energy Report Ties to Industry," *New York Times*, 3 June 2001.

52   Citizens for Tax Justice, *Less Than Zero: Enron's Income Tax Payments, 1996-2000*, Washington, DC: CTJ, 17 January 2002.

53   Public Citizen, *Blind Faith and The Foundation for Taxpayer and Consumer Rights, Hoax. How Deregulation Let the Power Industry Steal $71 Billion from California*, Santa Monica: FTCR, 2002.

54   Daniel M. Berman, "The Confederate Cartel's War Against California," *San Francisco Bay Guardian*, 5 January 2001.

55   The phrase "jailhouse confession" comes from California State Senator Joseph Dunn. Joseph Kahn, "Californians Call Enron Documents the Smoking Gun," *New York Times*, 8 May 2002.

56   Richard Stevenson, "Enron Trading Gave Prices Artificial Lift, Panel is Told," *New York Times*, 12 April 2002.

57   Christian Berthelsen, "How Energy Giant Tried to Cut a Deal," *San Francisco Chronicle*, 3 May 2001.

58   Harvey Weisman, "Power Struggle. California's Engineered Energy Crisis and the Potential of Public Power," *Multinational Monitor*, vol. 22, no. 6, June 2001.

59   Stevenson, "Enron Trading."

60   Aaron Glantz, "Few Lessons Learned from California's Energy Debacle," *Corpwatch*, 15 April 2001.

61   Joseph Kahn, "Californians."

62   Robert Rosenblatt and Richard Simon, "Federal Pact Would Give Utilities More Time to Pay Power," *Los Angeles Times*, 10 January 2001.

63   Eric Berger, "Lay's influence seen in interview," *Houston Chronicle*, 1 February 2002.

64   Tariq Ali, *The Clash of Fundamentalisms*, London: Verso, 2002.

65   Seymour Hersh, "The Spoils of the Gulf War," *New Yorker*, 6 September 1993.

66   These troops provoked the ire of bin Laden and his confederates and it is their main animus against the U.S. The weapons-oil elite, in other words, is part and

parcel of the *causes* of 9/11. For more on this line of argument, see my *War Against the Planet: The Fifth Afghan War, U.S. Imperialism and Other Assorted Fundamentalisms*, New Delhi: Leftword Books, 2002.

67   Steven Wilmsen, *Silverado. Neil Bush and the Savings and Loan Scandal*, Washington: National Press Books, 1991 and Louis Dubose, "O Brother! Where Art Thou?" *Austin Chronicle*, 16 March 2001.

68   Sydney P. Freedberg, "Miami Mystery," *Wall Street Journal*, 9 August 1988 and Stephen Pizzo, "Bush Family Value$," *Mother Jones*, September/October 1992.

69   Mike Schneider, "Columba Bush says she's ashamed about run-in with U.S. Customs," *Naples Daily News*, 29 July 1999.

70   Leslie Wayne, "Enron scandal touches another Bush in Florida," *New York Times*, 27 January 2002.

71   David Corn, "Bush's Enron Deal," *The Nation*, 25 March 2002.

72   George Lardner, Jr., "The Harken-Bahrain Deal: A Baseless Suspicion," *Washington Post*, 30 July 1999.

73   Pizzo, "Bush Family Value$."

74   Geoffrey Gray, "Dick Cheney's Pipe Dream," *Village Voice*, 19 October 2001.

75   Dana Milbank, "Targeting Another Texas Connection," *Washington Post*, 29 January 2002 and Jordan Green, "Halliburton: To the Victors go the Markets," *Facing South*, 1 February 2002.

76   Alex Berenson, "Halliburton and Inquiry by the SEC," *New York Times*, 30 May 2002.

77   Eleanor Clift, "Cheney's Enron troubles are far from over," *Newsweek*, 11 January 2002; Mike Allen and Dana Milbank, "Cheney's Role in Energy Plan Offers Strengths and Liabilities," *Washington Post*, 17 May 2001.

78   For an insightful analysis of this corruption, see Syed Hussein Alatas, *Corruption and the Destiny of Asia*, Selangor Darul Ehasan: Prentice Hall, 1999.

79   Ken Silverstein, *Washington on $10 Million a Day: How Lobbyists Plunder the Nation*, Monroe: Common Courage, 1998, p. 4.

80   Public Interest Research Group, *Phantom Fixes*, Washington, DC: USPIRG, 2002.

81   Greg Guma, "Enron We Hardly Knew Ye," *ZNET* and *Towards Freedom*, 13 January 2002.

Chapter 2

1   Powers' testimony is quoted at length in the fine article by Vivek Monteiro, "Unaffordable is Unviable: The Brown Out of the New Power Policy," *The Marxist*, vol. XVI, no. 1, January-March 2000, pp. 31-33.

2   For a summary, S. Padmanabhan, "Dabhol Project: Politics of Power," *Business Line*, 28 May 2001.

3   Brody Mullins, "NAFTA Issue Prompted Enron Support for Jackson Lee," *Congressional Daily*, 15 January 2002.

4   Mike Davis, *Late Victorian Holocausts: El Niño Famines and the Making of the Third World*, London: Verso, 2001, p. 162.

5   *The Asian-African Conferenc:. Bandung, Indonesia, April 1955*, ed. George M. Kahin, Ithaca: Cornell University Press, 1956, p. 44.

6 Prebisch's study was published in Spanish in 1949, offered in an English translation in May 1950, legendary by mimeograph and word of mouth, but only widely available when it was published in the *Economic Bulletin of Latin America*, vol. VII, no. 1, February 1962. This book is in the debt of L. S. Stavrianos' mammoth account, *Global Rift: The Third World Comes of Age*, New York: William Morrow, 1981. Stavrianos's book offer a history lesson along the lines of Prebisch's economics theory.

7 Eugene Black, *The Diplomacy of Economic Development*, Cambridge: Harvard University Press, 1960, p. 45.

8 Eduardo Galeano, *Open Veins of Latin America*, New York: Monthly Review Press, 1973, p. 144. For details see Celso Furtado, *Economic Development of Latin Ameica*, Cambridge: Cambridge University Press, 1970.

9 Shirley Jenkins, *American Economic Policy Toward the Philippines*, Palo Alto: Stanford University Press, 1954 offers the complete story of the Act, while Stanley Karnow, *In Our Image: America's Empire in the Philippines*, New York: Random House, 1989 details the consequences.

10 In the aftermath of India's entry into IMFundamentalism, a senior IMF economist wrote that despite India's "reputation for heavy-handed interventionism, which also extended to blocking foreign investment, India has nevertheless also established a long track record of macroeconomic stability based on generally cautious fiscal deficit policies." Ranjit S. Teja, "IMF-supported program helps India emerge from crisis," *IMF Survey*, 21 September 1992, p. 285.

11 Raúl Prebisch, "North-South Dialogue," *Third World Quarterly*, vol. II, January 1980, pp. 15-18.

12 Hal Lary, et. al., *The United States in the World Economy*, U.S. Department of Commerce, Economic Series, no. 23, Washington DC: Department of Commerce, 1943.

13 Galeano, *Open Veins*, p. 144.

14 BRD, *The Assault on World Poverty*, Baltimore: Johns Hopkins Press, 1975, p. 215.

15 Renato Constantino, *The Making of a Filipino*, Quezon City: Malaya Books, 1969, pp. 23-24.

16 Sunil Khilnani, *The Idea of India*, New York: Farrar, Straus and Giroux, 1999, p. 79.

17 *Papers Relating to the Formulation of the Second Five Year Plan*, New Delhi: Government of India, 1956, p. 558.

18 A. Vaidyanathan, "The Indian Economy since Independence (1947-1970), *The Cambridge Economic History of India*, volume 2: c. 1757-1970, ed. Dharma Kumar, Hyderabad: Orient Longman, 1984, p. 956.

19 Of course, the Communists returned to power in Kerala many times and have now put in place a system of decentralization of power that should stand as an example of the way forward. T. M. Thomas Isaac (with Richard W. Franke), *Local Democracy and Development: People's Campaign for Decentralized Planning in Kerala*. New Delhi: LeftWord Books, 2000 and Vijay Prashad, "The Small Voice of Socialism: Kerala, Once Again," *Critical Asian Studies*, vol. 33, no. 2, 2001.

20 Albert F. Celoza, *Ferdinand Marcos and the Philippines: The Political Economy of Authoritarianism*, Westport: Praeger, 1997.

21   Vijay Prashad, "Emergency Assessments," *Social Scientist*, vol. 24, nos. 9-10, September-October 1996, pp. 49-50.

22   Hilda López Laval, *Autoritarismo y cultura: Argentina, 1976-1983*, Madrid: Editorial Fundamentos, 1995.

23   United Nations Conference on Trade and Development, *Least Developed Countries 2000 Report*, Geneva: UNCTAD, 2001 has all the necessary data.

24   Mohsin Hamid, *Moth Smoke*, New York: Picador, 2000, pp. 102-3.

25   Children's Defense Fund, *Rescuing The American Dream for Young Families*, Washington, DC: CDF, 1997.

26   Kavaljit Singh, *A Citizen's Guide to the Globalisation of Finance*, New Delhi: Madhyam Books, 1998, p. 85.

27   "The IMF in Action," *Wall Street Journal* (Asian Edition), 19 May 1998.

28   Ammar Siamwalla, "Two and a Half Cheers for Economic Growth: An Assessment of Long-Term Changes in the Thai Economy," *Thai Development Research Institute Quarterly Review*, vol. 11, no. 1, March 1996.

29   François Godement, *The Downsizing of Asia*, London: Routledge, 1999, p. 75.

30   Martin Feldstein, "Refocusing the IMF," *Foreign Affairs*, vol. 77, no. 2, March-April 1998, p. 27.

31   Jagdish Bhagwati, "The Capital Myth," *Foreign Affairs*, vol. 77, no. 3, May-June 1998.

32   Mohsin Khan, "The Macroeconomic Effects of Fund-Supported Adjustment Programs," *IMF Staff Papers*, vol. 37, no. 2, June 1990, p. 215.

33   United Nations Development Program, *Human Development Report*, New York: UNDP, 1992, p. 75.

34   Douglass North, *Institutions, Institutional Change and Economic Performance*, Cambridge: Cambridge University Press, 1990.

35   World Bank, *Governance and Development*, Washington, DC: World Bank, 1992.

36   David Corn, "Enron and the Bushes," *The Nation*, 21 November 1994.

37   The figures are from UNCTAD, *Least Developed Countries*.

38   Yoshikara Kunio, *The Rise of Ersatz Capitalism in South-east Asia*, Manila: Manila University Press, 1988 offers the pre-history of the crisis.

39   United Nations Development Program, *Human Development Report*, New York: UNDP, 1992, p. 59.

40   Vijay Prashad, "On the Periphery of Asia: Thoughts on U.S. Imperialism," *The Marxist*, vol. XV, nos. 2-3, April-September 1999, p. 83.

41   Maria Teresa Diokno-Pascual, "Understanding the New Philippine Debt Situation," *Philippines International Review*, vol. 1, no. 3, Winter 1998.

42   The details are in *Manila Times* and *Mindanao Times*, from the 1990s.

43   Scowcroft, once National Security Adviser to Bush Senior, is now the head of the Scowcroft group, a trustee of the Rand Corporation, a front-man for Pennzoil, on the circle of the Carlyle Group and a member of Kissinger Associates. On the Carlyle Group, see Tim Shorrock, "Crony Capitalism Goes Global," *The Nation*, 1 April 2002.

44   The details are in *La Nacion*, several daily reports in late January and early February 2002.

45   James Petras, "The Unemployed Workers Movement in Argentina," *Monthly Review*, vol. 53, no. 8, January 2002.

46 *Agence France Presse*, 26 January 2002.

47 The story is well covered in a number of places, notably in Abhay Mehta, *Power Play*, Delhi: Orient Longman, 2000; Human Rights Watch, *The Enron Corporation. Corporate Complicity in Human Rights Violations*, New York: HRW, 1999; and Arundhati Roy, *Infinite Justice*, New Delhi: Viking, 2001.

48 Abhay Mehta, "Power In, Power Out," *Himal*, March 2002, p. 24.

49 Monteiro, "Unaffordable is Unviable," p. 34.

50 Mehta, *Power Play*, Introduction.

51 Certainly, the government could have used coal from the nearby and vast Chandrapur fields, because this would have cut the cost, according to the government, by a fourth. But set that aside, mainly because coal's poor environmental record undercuts a demand for it.

52 Prabir Purkayastha, "Hard Decisions on Enron," *People's Democracy*, 29 April 2001.

53 Prabir Purkayastha, "A Disastrous Deal," *Frontline*, 2 March 2001.

54 Appendix B of Human Rights Watch, *The Enron Corporation*.

55 R. Strider, "Blood in the Pipeline," *Multinational Monitor*, January/February 1995.

56 Information on the foreign funds is in *Enron's Pawns*, p. 31.

57 Arundhati Roy, *Power Politics*, Boston: South End Press, 2001, p. 59. The current power shortage, according to the government, is about 11.3% of peak load and 8.3% of energy supply. The government wants to increase by 47, 000MW by 2002 and then by 111, 500 by 2007 (or double the generating capacity in 1999). As of now, it appears that less than 25, 000MW will be added by the end of 2002. The real issue, however, is not just raw MW numbers, but what the power will be used for—social development or affluent waste?

58 Human Rights Watch, *The Enron Corporation*, Chapter V.

59 "Excerpts from Testimony Before Senate Panel Investigating Enron," *New York Times*, 27 February 2002, p. C9.

60 James V. Grimaldi, "Enron Pipeline Leaves Scar on South America," *Washington Post*, 6 May 2002.

61 Shelton Davis, *Victims of the Miracle: Development and the Indians of Brazil*, Cambridge: Cambridge University Press, 1977, pp. 22-23.

62 *A World Class Disaster: The Case of the Bolivia-Cuiaba Pipeline. A Report on the Failures of Enron International to Comply with Bolivian Environmental Laws and OPIC Loan Conditions in the Construction of the Lateral Ipias-Cuiaba Gas Pipeline*, 8 December 1999.

63 David Ivanovich, "Enron Pipeline in Bolivia gets U.S. loan guarantee," *Houston Chronicle*, 15 June 1999.

64 Jorge Aramayo Montes, "Por fin se aclara el ingreso irregular de Enron a Bolivia," *El Diario* (Bolivia), 2 February 2002.

65 Shiraz Sidhwa, "Alive and Well: Against the Odds, Enron Makes a Go of it in India," *Far Eastern Economic Review*, 11 December 1997.

66 Human Rights Watch, *The Enron Corporation*, Chapter V.

67 F. A. Hayek, *Law, Legislation and Liberty II: The Mirage of Social Justice*, London: Routledge, 1976, pp. 39 and 78 and F. A. Hayek, *Studies in Philosophy, Politics and Economics*, London: Routledge, 1967, p. 171.

68 F. A. Hayek, *The Road to Serfdom*, London: Routledge & Kegan Paul, 1979, p. 78.

69 Jonathan D. Salant, "Ex-Government officials lobby for industries they used to regulate," *Hannibal Courier-Post*, 6 July 1998.

70 Silverstein, *Washington*, p. 31.

71 Howard Gleckman, "Laughing all the way to an offshore bank?" *Business Week*, 19 June 2001; David Cay Johnston, "Manhattan Prosecutor Criticizes Caymans Tax Pact," *New York Times*, 8 December 2001; Paul O'Neill, "Confronting OECD's Notions of Taxation," *Washington Times*, 10 May 2001.

72 Joan Claybrook, President of Public Citizen, wrote a very critical letter to Treasury Secretary Paul O'Neill on 18 January 2002. The letter is available at the Public Citizen website, www.citizen.org.

73 Public Citizen, *The Other Drug War: Big Pharma's 625 Lobbyists*, Washington: Public Citizen, 2001.

74 Katharine Q. Seelye, "Bush Picks Industry Insiders to Fill Environmental Posts," *New York Times*, 12 May 2001.

75 For more on the biotech industry, see John Vidal, "Biotech food giant wields power in Washington," *Guardian*, 18 February 1999.

76 Francis Schor, "The Strange Career of Frank Carlucci," *Counterpunch*, 1 February 2002; Oliver Burkeman and Julian Borger, "Ex-President's Club," *The Guardian*, 31 October 2001.

77 "Revolving Doors," *Multinational Monitor*, vol. 17, no. 5, May 1996.

78 The relationship is well-documented in "Ciller's Consultant Tamraz May Testify in Congress," *Turkish Daily News*, 18 April 1997.

79 Edward Walsh, "Tamraz Defends Political Gifts for Clinton Access," *Washington Post*, 19 September 1997.

80 Vicken Cheterian, "Grand jeu pétrolier en Transcaucasie," *Le Monde Diplomatique*, October 1997 and Sophie Shihab, "Russes et Américains s'opposent sur le trace du grand oléoduc de la Caspienne," *Le Monde*, 15 November 1997.

81 "Roger Tamraz Case, Released in Georgia," *Lebanon Business Weekly*, 17 June 1997.

82 "We See a World of More, Not Fewer, Mysteries," *Time*, 20 April 1992; Elaine Sciolino, "CIA Casting about for New Missions," *New York Times*, 4 February 1992.

83 Gerald Seib, "Some Urge CIA to Go Further in Gathering Economic Intelligence," *Wall Street Journal*, 4 August 1992.

84 Joseph I. Lieberman, "New Technologies, Government Should Help," *Washington Post*, 17 April 1992.

85 Craig. R. Whitney, "France Accuses Five Americans of Spying: Asks They Leave," *New York Times*, 23 February 1995; Tim Weiner, "CIA Confirms Blunder During Economic Spying on France," *New York Times*, 12 March 1996.

86 Dominique Dhombres, "La CIA aurait déjoué une tentative de corruption menée par Thomson au Brésil en 1994," *Le Monde*, 25 February 1995; Jacques Isnard, "La CIA et la NSA justifient les missions du réseau d'espionnage Echelon," *Le Monde*, 10 March 2000.

87 Robert Dreyfuss, "Company Spies," *Mother Jones*, May-June 1994.

88   Robert Dreyfuss, "The CIA Crosses Over," *Mother Jones*, January-February 1995.

89   Rich Heidorn, "Peco vs. Enron: Energy giant faces tenacious rival," *Philadelphia Inquirer*, 14 October 1997.

90   Fola Adekeye, "Nigeria Business: Let There Be Light," *Africa News*, 7 August 2000; "Rocky Road for Enron," *Africa Energy and Mining*, 29 March 2000.

91   For an excellent overview, Tim Shorrock, "Enron's Asian Misadventure," *Asia Times*, 29 January 2002.

92   Gregory Palast, "How a few little piggies tried to rig the market," *Guardian*, 25 October 1998.

93   James Lieber, *Rats in the Grain: The Dirty Tricks and Trails of Archer Daniels Midland—The Supermarket to the World*, New York: Four Walls, Eight Windows Press, 2000.

94   For an excellent overview of the issues, B. V. Raghavulu, "Power Sector Reforms in Andhra Pradesh and the Resistance Movement," *The Marxist*, vol. XVII, no. 1, January-March 2001.

95   T. Lakshmipathi, "A Rude Shock in Andhra Pradesh," *Frontline*, vol. 17, issue 12, 10-23 June 2000.

96   The World Bank Briefing Book in November 2000 says, "Andhra Pradesh is known as India's first reforming state. Its Chief Minister, Chandrababu Naidu, has earned a well-deserved reputation as one of India's top reformists and development-oriented politicians, known as Andhra's CEO."

97   All this blather while Naidu funneled almost $4 million for the construction and restoration of three hundred sixty two temples across the state of Andhra Pradesh. B.V. Raghavulu, a CPM leader in the state, noted, "It is ridiculous that a chief minister who claims to be forward thinking and tech-savvy indulges in this kind of misuse of the state's precious funds." Part of the diversion of funds is planned to generate a decent rate of return for Naidu, since these temples are extraordinarily wealthy (Tirupati temple has an annual revenue of $25.5 million and assets of at least 500 kilograms of gold), and the wealthy come in use for election funds and other kickbacks. If the temple workers at Madurai can be members of the CPM's union, then why can't the head priests at Tirupati act like fat cats. George Iype, "Chandrababu Naidu seeks divine help for state's economic growth," *India Abroad*, 7 September 2001.

98   P. Sainath, "None So Blind as Those Who Will Not See," *UNESCO Courier*, June 2001.

99   V. Sridhar, "Brutal Crackdown," *Frontline*, vol. 17, issue 19, 16-29 September 2000.

100   The report is available at www.aidwa.org, but also excerpted in "Targeting Women," *Frontline*, vol. 17, issue 19, 16-29 September 2000.

Chapter 3

1   "Enron President: 'People Gum Up the Works,'" *Seattle Times*, 5 April 1997.

2   Jim Yardley, "Big Burden for Ex-Workers of Enron," *New York Times*, 3 March 2002.

3   Michael Brick, "With Enron's Collapse, Houston Has Lots of Space," *New York*

        Times, 24 April 2002.
4   Joe R. Feagin, *Free Enterprise City: Houston in Political-Economic Perspective*, New
        Brunswick: Rutgers University Press, 1988.
5   Tim Wheeler, "Arrest Enron Executives: Houston Workers Demand Justice,"
        People's Weekly World, 16 February 2002.
6   Tim Wheeler, "Oregonians urge public takeover of Enron unit," *People's Weekly
        World*, 9 March 2002.
7   Kurt Eichenwald, "White Collar Defense Stance: The Criminal-less Crime,"
        New York Times, 3 March 2002.
8   "Sale By Enron Set Back in India," *New York Times*, 7 March 2002.
9   Honey Madrilejos-Reyes, "Napocor acquisition of Enron plant looms," *The
        Manila Times*, 27 December 2001 and Honey Madrilejos-Reyes, "Napocor to buy
        Enron project," *The Manila Times*, 5 December 2001.
10   Tom Fowler, "Enron Stops Funding Overseas Operations," *Houston Chronicle*, 17
        January 2002; "Enron's Failure Fuels Japanese concern over power projects,"
        Daily Star, 5 December 2001.
11   K. N. Panikkar, *Asia and Western Dominance*, New York: John Day, 1953, p. 111.
12   Agha Shahid Ali, "Dacca Gauzes," *The Half-Inch Himalayas*, Middletown:
        Wesleyan University Press, 1987, pp. 15-16.
13   L. C. A. Knowles, *The Industrial and Commercial Revolution in Britain during the
        Nineteenth Century*, London: Routledge, 1921, p. 128.
14   A. P. Thornton, *The Imperial Idea and its Enemies: A Study in British Power*,
        London: MacMillan & Co., 1959, p. 275.
15   Anthony DePalma, "WTO Pact Would Set Global Accounting Rules," *New
        York Times*, 1 March 2002.
16   Maude Barlow and Tony Clarke, *Blue Gold: The Fight to Stop the Corporate Theft
        of the World's Water*, New York: The New Press, 2002, p. 104.
17   Robert Heilbroner, *The Wordly Philosophers*, New York: Touchstone Books, 1972,
        p. 136.
18   Karl Marx, *Capital I*, New York: Penguin, 1976, p. 895 [translation modified].
19   For a good summary, see Ellen Meiksins Wood, *The Origin of Capitalism: A
        Longer View*, London: Verso, 2002. My analysis mirrors that of Susan George,
        "Preface," *Privatizing Nature: Political Struggles for the Global Commons*, Michael
        Goldman, Ed., London: Transnational Institute/Pluto Press, 1998.
20   Barlow and Clarke, *Blue Gold*, p. 130.
21   Most of my information comes from the wonderful summary of *Global Water
        Report*'s decade-long investigation of Enron and Azurix, "Azurix: The Roller-
        Coaster Years," *Global Water Report*, 25 January 2002.
22   Public Citizen, *Liquid Assets: Enron's Dip Into Water Business Highlights Pitfalls of
        Privatization*, Washington, DC: Public Citizen, 2002, p. 9.
23   For example, "Azurix Confirmed as OSBA Concession Winner," *Business News
        America*, 16 June 1999.
24   "Parliament to Probe Azurix Scandal," *The Ghanaian Times*, 20 March 2000;
        "Rocky Ride for Enron," *African Energy and Mining*, 29 March 2000.
25   Stephen Fidler, "Enron Chief Scorned Asset Division," *Financial Times*, 11
        February 2002.
26   Public Citizen, *Liquid Assets*, p. 6.

27   I reported most of this on ZNET and in *Little India* during the summer of 2000.

28   Barlow and Clarke, *Blue Gold*, p. 59.

29   Vandana Shiva, *Water Wars: Privatization, Pollution and Profit*, Boston: South End Press, 2002, p. 99.

30   The best summary that I have found is in Jim Schultz, "Bolivia's Water War Victory," *Earth Island Journal*, Autumn 2000 and, for a brief piece by the same author, "Water Fallout: Bolivians Battle Globalization," *In These Times*, 15 May 2000.

31   Gregory Palast, "Bechtel Subsidiary Drives Unrest in Bolivia," *The Observer*, 23 April 2000 and Maude Barlow, "The World Bank Must Realize that Water is a Human Right," *Globe & Mail*, 9 May 2000.

32   Barlow and Clarke, *Blue Gold*, p. 177.

33   Chris Ney, "Nor Any Drop to Drink," *Nonviolent Activist*, September-October 2000.

34   Karl Polanyi, *The Great Transformation*, Boston: Beacon Press, 1957, p. 2.

35   Ann Carrigan, "Colombia Differs with U.S. on Narco-War Tactics," Colombia Support Network, September 1998.

36   We need to recognize that FARC's history is a history of negotiation. During the reign of President Belisario Betancur (1982-86), FARC opened talks with his Peace Commission, this at a time when the army only commanded three thousand. FARC renounced violence and formed a political party, the Patriotic Union and the PU gained a substantial legislative presence in the 1986 elections. But they kept their arms. President Vigilio Barco (1986-1990) demanded that FARC lay down their arms, and when FARC refused, renewed the offensive. The story is in Alfredo Molano, "A Guerrilla Group's Long History," NACLA, September-October 2000.

37   PBS-Frontline, *Family Tree: The Salinas-Citibank Affair*, PBS, 1996-97; U.S. General Accounting Office, *Money Laundering: Raul Salinas, Citibank and Alleged Money Laundering*, Washington, DC: GAO, 2001; Andrew Wheat, "Mexico's Privatization Piñata," *Multinational Monitor*, vol. 17, no. 10, October 1996.

38   "Investors Queasy Over Mexican Scandals," *Weekly News Update on the Americas*, issue No. 232, 18 September 1994.

39   John Ward Anderson and Molly Moore, "Mexican Politician Convicted of Murder," *Washington Post*, 22 January 1999 and *Reforma*, 22 May 1996.

40   Kathleen Day, "Citibank Called Lax on Salinas Money Trail," *Washington Post*, 4 December 1998.

41   Cecilia Zarate-Laun, "The War on Drugs from the Supply Side," *Z Magazine*, July-August 1998.

42   Mark Bowden, "*Get Pablo: The Hunt for the World's Greatest Outlaw*, New York: Atlantic Monthly Press, 2001, and for a very useful review, Martha Liebrum, "Get Pablo," *Houston Chronicle*, 22 August 2001.

43   David Bushnell, *The Making of Modern Colombia: A Nation in Spite of Itself*, Berkeley: University of California Press, 1993.

44   Alexander Cockburn and Jeffery St. Clair, *Whiteout*, London: Verso, 1998.

45   Christian Parenti, *Lockdown America*, London: Verso, 1999.

46   "U.S. Troops Have No Combat Role in Colombia, Official Says," *Columbus*

Dispatch, 25 April 2002.

47   Nazih Richani, "Colombia at the Crossroads: The Future of the Peace Accords," *NACLA*, vol. XXXV, no. 4, January-February 2002. The chain of the U.S. army's War Against the Planet may run like this: Afghanistan, Iraq, and then Colombia.

48   Linda Robinson, Gordon Witkin and Richard Newman, "Is Colombia Lost to Rebels?" *U.S. News & World Report*, 11 May 1998.

49   Brent Scowcroft and Bob Graham, "Quick Aid to Colombia—For Our Sake," *Los Angeles Times*, 26 April 2000.

50   Paul Coverdell, "Starting With Colombia," *Washington Post*, 10 April 2000.

51   James Ridgeway, "Snow Job," *Village Voice*, 5 April 2000.

52   Samantha Newport and David Adams, "Ecuador reluctantly joins U.S. war on cocaine," *St. Petersburg Times*, 21 February 2001.

53   Vijay Prashad, "The U.S. Foreign Hand in the Venezuelan Coup Attempt of 2002," *People's Democracy*, 12 May 2002.

54   Ignacio Gómez, "El objectivo de los E. U. es petróleo," *El Espectador*, 8 October 2000.

55   The story is well told by Héctor Mondragón, "Plan Colombia: Throwing Gasoline on Fire," *ZNET*, translated by Jens Nielson and Justin Podur, August 2001 and there are significant details in Rene De la Pedraja, *Energy Politics in Colombia*, Boulder: Westview, 1989.

56   Human Rights Watch updated their work and produced a new report that conclusively shows this to be so. *The "Sixth Division": Military-Paramilitary Ties and U.S. Policy in Colombia*, New York: HRW, 2001.

57   Javier Giraldo, *Colombia: The Genocidal Democracy*, Monroe, ME: Common Courage Press, 1996.

58   The story broke via "BP hands tarred in pipeline dirty war," *Guardian*, 17 October 1998.

59   "New Revelations on BP Links to Colombian Violence," *Weekly News Update on the Americas*, issue No. 456, 25 October 1998.

60   T. Christian Miller, "A Colombian Village Caught in the Cross-Fire," *Los Angeles Times*, 17 March 2002.

61   Linda D. Kozaryn, "U.S. Southern Command Forges Multinational Bonds," *Defense Link*, October 1996.

62   "U.S. Pushes 'Anti-Drug' Military Aid," *Weekly News Update on Colombia*, issue No. 450, 13 September 1998.

63   Human Rights Watch, *Colombia's Killer Networks: The Military-Paramilitary Partnership and the US*, New York: HRW, 1996.

64   Diana Jean Schemo, "Congress Steps Up Aid for Colombians to Combat Drugs," *New York Times*, 1 December 1998.

65   "La agenda secreta para Colombia," *El Espectador*, 4 June 1999.

66   Molano, "The Evolution of FARC" and Ricardo Vargas Meza, "The Revolutionary Armed Forces of Colombia and the Illicit Drug Trade," The Netherlands: The Transnational Institute; Cochabamba: Accion Andina, June 1999.

67   Ricardo Vargas Meza, "The Revolutionary Armed Forces of Colombia."

68   Frank Smyth, "Colombia's Blowback," *Crime in Uniform: Corruption and*

Impunity in Latin America, Amsterdam: Transnational Institute, 1997 and Myles Frechette, "Colombia: The War That Will Not End," *When the AK-47s Fall Silent*, Stanford: Hoover Institute Press, 2000.

69   Juan O. Tamayo, "Illegal Paramilitary Groups Expand Foothold in Colombia," *Miami Herald*, 7 May 2002.

70   Thomas Friedman, "What the World Needs Now," *New York Times*, 28 March 1999.

71   I have traced the contours of the war in *War Against the Planet: The Fifth Afghan War, U.S. Imperialism and Other Assorted Fundamentalisms*, New Delhi: Leftword Books, 2002.

72   Michael R. Gordon, "Where Does Phase 2 Start? In Afghanistan," *New York Times*, 10 March 2002.

73   Ahmed Rashid, *Taliban: Militant Islam, Oil and Fundamentalism in Central Asia*, New Haven: Yale University Press, 2000, p. 46.

74   Rashid, *Taliban*, p. 166.

75   Rashid, *Taliban*, p. 166.

76   Rashid, *Taliban*, p. 179.

77   Richard Labévière, *Dollars for Terror: The United States and Islam*, New York: Algora Publishing, 2000, p. 280.

78   Michael Griffin, *Reaping the Whirlwind: The Taliban Movement in Afghanistan*, London: Pluto Press, 2001, p. 124.

79   These details are in Sitaram Yechury, "America, Oil and Afghanistan," *The Hindu*, 13 October 2001.

80   Ahmed Rashid, "Pipe Dreams," *The Herald*, October 1997.

81   Ashfak Bokhari, "The Pipeline of Greed," *Dawn*, 9 December 2001.

82   Richard Butler, "A New Oil Game, With New Winners," *New York Times*, 18 January 2002. Two weeks after 9/11, Chevron's subsidiary Tengizchevroil finished an oil pipeline from Tengiz oil field in western Kazakhstan to the Russian port of Novorossiysk on the Black Sea. This pipeline will feed Western Europe with oil from what might end up as the fifth largest oil state in the world (and, crucially, outside OPEC's ambit). The Tengiz pipeline is only one of many that sully the geopolitics of the region.

83   IPS, *Enron's Pawns*, p. 37.

84   Seymour Hersh, "The Debate Within," *New Yorker*, 11 March 2002, p. 37.

85   Françoise Chipaux, "Hamid Karzaï, un Pachtoune nommé president," *Le Monde*, 13 December 2001.

86   Marc Erikson, "Mr. Karzai goes to Washington," *Asia Times*, 29 January 2002.

87   Kim Sengupta and Andrew Gumbel, "New U.S. Envoy to Kabul for Taliban Oil Rights," *Independent*, 10 January 2002. For mystery fans, Khalilzad is married to Austrian-born writer Cheryl Benard whose novel *Moghul Buffet* (Soho Crime) may be of interest. Set in Pakistan and Afghanistan, it offers a fairly sympathetic portrait of the Taliban.

88   Joe Stephens and David B. Ottaway, "Afghan Roots Keep Adviser Firmly in the Inner Circle: Consultant's Policy Influence Goes Back to the Reagan Era," *Washington Post*, 23 November 2001.

89   Zalmay Khalilzad and Daniel Byman, "Afghanistan: The Consolidation of a Rogue State," *Washington Quarterly*, vol. 23, no. 1, p. 65 and pp. 70-71.

90   Zalmay Khalilzad, Los Angeles World Affairs Council, 9 March 2000.

91   Jonathan Steele, "Former king renounces throne to save Afghan council," *Guardian*, 11 June 2002.

Chapter 4

1   Michael Franti & Spearhead, "Rock the Nation," *Stay Human*, BooBooWax Records, 2001.

2   Richard Stevenson, "Greenspan Says Enron Cure Is in Market, Not Regulation," *New York Times*, 27 March 2002.

3   "South Korean Power Strikes End," *Deutsche Presse-Agentur*, 3 April 2002; Don Kirk, "South Korea: General Strike Averted," *New York Times*, 3 April 2002.

4   Sudha Mahalingam, "Power Reforms in Trouble," *Frontline*, 17 March 2000 and Paranjoy Guha Thakurta, "Power distribution in Delhi privatized," *India Abroad*, 14 June 2002.

5   Martin Luther King, Jr., "A Knock at Midnight," *Strength to Love*, New York: Harper and Row, 1963, excerpt in A *Testament of Hope: The Essential Writings and Speeches of Martin Luther King, Jr.*, ed. James M. Washington, New York: HarperCollins, 1991, p. 498.

6   Michael Hardt and Antonio Negri, *Empire*, Cambridge: Harvard University Press, 2000, p. xiii.

7   Hardt and Negri, *Empire*, p. 37 and p. 180.

8   Hardt and Negri, *Empire*, p. 181.

9   War Resisters League, "Where Your Income Tax Money Really Goes: The United States Federal Budget for Fiscal Year 2003," handout.

10   These comparisons are courtesy of the Center for Defense Information in Washington, DC (www.cdi.org).

11   Peter Gowan, *The Global Gamble: Washington's Faustian Bid for World Dominance*, London: Verso, 1999, pp. 39-59 and, on capital flight to the North, Mohsin S. Khan and Nadeem Ul Haque, 'Capital Flight from Developing Countries,' *Finance and Development*, vol. 24, no. 4, March 1987. I have developed the argument in *The American Scheme*, New Delhi: Three Essays Press, 2002.

12   World Bank, *Global Economic Prospects and the Developing Countries 2001*, Washington, DC: World Bank Group, 2001, Chapter One.

13   Prashad, *The American Scheme*, Chapter 3.

14   Marx, *Capital*, p. 926.

15   Hardt and Negri, *Empire*, pp. 301-303.

16   The best introduction to the Diggers remains, Christopher Hill, *The World Turned Upside Down: Radical Ideas During the English Revolution*, London: Penguin, 1972.

17   The process on the continent had an earlier history, and an earlier rebellion: for instance, in 1525 the Peasant War in Germany.

18   Emmett Grogan, *Ringolevio: A Life Played for Keeps*, New York: Citadel, 1990, pp. 300-301. I borrow most of my material and analysis from Michael William Doyle, "The Haight-Ashbury Diggers and the Cultural Politics of Utopia, 1965-1968," Ithaca, NY: Cornell University PhD, 1997.

19   "The Digger Papers," *The Realist*, August 1968.

20   Michael Hardt compares the World Social Forum meeting at Porto Alegre to the 1955 Bandung Conference and finds that the former is representative of the age of "network movements" while the latter represents an outmoded form of nationalism. Michael Hardt, "Today's Bandung?" *New Left Review*, no. 14, March/April 2002.

21   Huw Beynon and José R. Ramalho, "Democracy and the Organization of Class Struggle in Brazil," *Working Classes, Global Realities*, Edited Leo Panitch and Colin Leys, New York: Monthly Review Press and Socialist Register, 2001, p. 233 and James Petras, "The Political and Social Basis of Regional Variation in Land Occupations in Brazil," *Journal of Peasant Studies*, vol. 25, no. 4, 1998.

22   Eric Mann, "'A Race Struggle, A Class Struggle, A Women's Struggle All At Once': Organizing on the Buses of LA," *Working Classes, Global Realities*, p. 268.

23   James Petras, "The Unemployed Workers Movement in Argentina," *Monthly Review*, vol. 53, no. 8, January 2002.

24   Mariam Ching Yoon Louie, *Sweatshop Warriors: Immigrant Women Workers Take on the Global Factory*, Boston: South End Press, 2001, p. 95.

25   Libero Della Piana, "From the Cold War to the War on Crime," *Third Force*, November/December 1994, p. 8.

26   Sam Vincent Meddis and Deborah Sharp, "Prison Business is a Blockbuster," *USA Today*, 13 December 1994.

27   Prashad, *The American Scheme*, Chapter 2.

28   Robert Rockwell, "Police Brutality: More Than Just a Few Bad Apples," *Refuse and Resist*, 14 August 1997.

29   For an excellent overview of cultural conservatism in the Pakistani struggle, see Asma Jahangir and Hina Jilani, *The Hudood Ordinances: A Divine Sanction?*, Lahore: Rhotac Books, 1990.

30   RAWA, "The Criminal Taliban and Jehadis, Sworn Enemies of Human Rights," Resolution on the Occasion of International Human Rights Day, 10 December 2000.

31   For an excellent analysis, see Prabhat Patnaik, "The Assault on Reason," *Frontline*, 1-14 September 2001.

Index

About the Author

Vijay Prashad is Associate Professor and Director, International Studies at Trinity College. He is the author of two *Village Voice* books of the year: *Everybody Was Kung Fu Fighting* (Beacon, 2001) and *Karma of Brown Folk* (Minnesota, 2000). He lives in Western Mass.